'44

In Combat on the Western Front
from Normandy to the Ardennes

In Combat on the Western Front from Normandy to the Ardennes
CHARLES WHITING

CENTURY PUBLISHING
LONDON

Copyright © Charles Whiting 1984
All rights reserved
First published in Great Britain in 1984
by Century Publishing Co. Ltd,
Portland House, 12-13 Greek Street, London W1V 5LE

Whiting, Charles
   '44: in combat on the Western Front
   from Normandy to the Ardennes.
   1. World War, 1939-1945 – Campaigns – Western
   I. Title
   940.54'21   D756

   ISBN 0-7126-0148-1
   ISBN 0-7126-0149-X Pbk

Designed by Tom Deas

Maps by Frances Pitt

Photoset in North Wales by
Derek Doyle & Associates, Mold, Clwyd
Printed in Great Britain by
Butler & Tanner Ltd, Frome, Somerset

CONTENTS

PROLOGUE

General Montgomery speaking to war correspondents at his headquarters.

June, 1944. A dull, heavy mood had settled over the country. The waiting had gone on too long, both for those hundreds of thousands of young men in khaki soon to spearhead the invasion of Europe, and for the civilians who went about their normal daily business. Again there had been raids on London, the first for nearly a year or more, and there were rumours of worse things to come: strange and terrible weapons which fell suddenly and without warning out of the stratosphere; perhaps even poison gas.

The countryside of southern England basked in the hot June sun. The Channel, that all-important stretch of water which would soon be the scene of battle and carnage, perhaps disaster, was calm and glistening. Yet for soldier and civilians, the fine summer weather only heightened the feeling of emptiness, spiritual and emotional. It had all taken so long – so many weary, hard years of preparation. Would it – *could* it – succeed now?

On their black days, the soldiers were plagued by doubts. For some, years of their young lives had gone into the great venture. Now they wondered if they still had the spirit for what lay ahead. Time and time again as the day of decision drew closer, they were gripped by a terrible feeling of uncertainty.

Montgomery seemed to sense it. Travelling ceaselessly from tented camp to camp, he talked to them in their hundreds, their thousands, their hundred thousands. Seated on the grass, or standing shoulder to shoulder around his jeep, row after row of young upturned faces, British, Canadian, American, they stared up at the little man in the too-large black beret, hanging on his every word.

Everywhere he went, he made the same speech: 'No mention of England. Not a single eternal verity. No hate. No question of revenge.'[1] Courage, liberty, freedom, and

the rest of those brave words of that time were not so much as mentioned. All Monty spoke of was themselves and the enemy, waiting twenty-one miles away across the water: ' "We don't want to forget the German is a good soldier … a very good soldier indeed. But when I look around this morning and see some of the magnificent soldiers here … some of the finest soldiers I have seen in my lifetime … I have no doubt in my mind about the outcome … no doubt whatever: No doubt at all that you and I will see this thing through together." '[2] Monty's watchword was 'confidence', and he would hammer it home repeatedly: ' "We have got to go off and do a job together very soon now, you and I, and we must have confidence in one another. And now that I have seen you I have complete confidence … complete confidence …absolutely complete confidence. And you must have confidence in me." '[3]

That was the little man's speech, followed by a rousing cry of 'Three cheers for the General! Hip-hip … *hurrah!*' Sometimes he might then inspect one of the battalions present, taking his time, gazing up at each young, rigidly set, clean-shaven face, as if he were trying to etch the man's features on his memory for ever. For a fleeting moment each young man would glimpse that bronzed face with its fiercely willed mouth and those piercing, unwavering eyes. Then before he left, he might ask the battalion commander, 'What's the average age of your battalion, Colonel?'

The answer would be prompt, for all the young colonels of infantry would be well briefed: 'Twenty-five, *sir!*' they would bark, standing rigidly to attention, cane under right arm. 'Twenty-five,' Monty would muse, repeating the number, as if it were of some mystical significance, 'Twenty-five, eh? A good age …' Then he would be gone.

They were all kinds, of course, these young men in khaki who would soon go to battle: the good, the bad, peer and commoner, poor and rich, heroes and cowards. Many among them would turn out to be deserters; by Christmas, when it had all failed, a hundred thousand of them, British, Canadian and American, would be on the run from the military police on the 'other side'.

There were those among them who would one day achieve high office: a future president of the United States, a future British prime minister, a foreign secretary, as well as a future archbishop of Canterbury. They also included a clutch of future heads of the British, American and Canadian armies; writers and film directors; movie stars; a whole range of political leaders …*

But we are not concerned with the famous or the infamous, but simply with the average young man of that time: patriotic to an extent, obedient to authority (most of

* For those interested in such things: Eisenhower and Edward Heath; Lord Carrington and Dr Robert Runcie; Generals Sir John Hackett, Abrams, Westmoreland, Collins; J.D. Salinger, Kingsley Amis, Irwin Shaw, Mel Brooks, Sam Fuller, David Niven, Trevor Howard, Henry Kissinger, Francis Pym – and many more.

General Dwight D. Eisenhower and Air Chief Marshal Sir Arthur Tedder watching pre-invasion manoeuvres.

the time, at least), not demanding much, content with the meagre pleasures of military life – a woman, a packet of fags, a hot meal – and well indoctrinated by Hollywood B-movies as to the ways of the Nazi enemy and the plight of the oppressed peoples of Occupied Europe whom they would soon set free. After all, didn't their Supreme Commander General Eisenhower – 'Ike' – refer to the forthcoming campaign as a 'crusade'? Wasn't the British Second Army called 'the British *Liberation* Army?'

One day soon, they would lose their innocence, and learn that not all the oppressed peoples of Europe desired to be liberated; nor were all Germans fanatical Nazis who wanted nothing more than to die for 'Folk, Fatherland and Führer.' But that day was still to come. For the time being, these Allied soldiers could only wait 'in the wings of Europe' for the final call: the call to battle which must come soon.

Imprisoned in the sprawling army camps which

stretched right across southern England, the invasion forces had time on their hands – time to note and reflect on the little everyday details of their life: the crisp sound of hobnailed army boots on gravel; the rattle of the dixies from the cookhouses; the splash of water in the zinc bowels of the 'ablutions'; the steady tread of the sentries outside the wire … For some, these sights and sounds held poignancy; it was as if they knew that soon they might never hear or see them again.

American troops waiting for the oncoming action.

Book 1

SUMMER OF HOPE

Actors waiting in the wings of Europe,
We already watched the lights on the stage
And listened to the colossal overture begin.

Keith Douglas, RAC, Killed in Action,
Normandy, 1944

German troops parade in
front of a section of the
Atlantic Wall.

1 EVE OF INVASION

'Any way you look at it, it's not going to be any piece of cake'

American staff-sergeant, commenting on D-Day preparations.

England had been waiting, working, suffering and sometimes dying for D-Day for exactly four years. To be exact, since that June of 1940 when the beaten British Army had been chased so ignominiously out of Europe. Since that summer, Hitler had ruled unchallenged over 300 million subjects – the greatest empire the continent had ever seen.

But now the entire southern half of England from the Wash to Land's End was one great army camp, swamped with soldiers of all nationalities: British, American, Canadian, Polish, Free French, Dutch, Belgian, Czech, Danish, Norwegian. Even little Luxembourg, which before the war had fielded an army of exactly fifty men and which had been forced to dress its firemen in military uniforms in order to make up a sufficient force for a parade, had contributed a handful.

On March 10th, 1944, all movement, communication and mail had been placed under severe control. Civilian travel had come almost to a standstill. Nearly a month later, on April 6th, all military leave had been cancelled. Now anyone in khaki spotted by the 'Redcaps' outside the concentration areas was automatically assumed to be a deserter. A week later all diplomatic mail was ordered to be delayed, and every embassy in London, friendly or otherwise, was placed under surveillance. The ferry service to neutral Eire was stopped. Bit by bit the island was sealed off from the outside world. The momentous day was approaching.

In May, 1944, the roads and lanes of rural England had started to crowd with seemingly endless convoys of Sherman tanks, half-tracks, Bren-carriers, trailers, artillery prime-movers, trucks and yet more trucks, all rolling south and making the houses on both sides of the roads tremble to the roar of motors day and night.

GIs marching through Torquay.

Old ladies tied up their precious pets permanently, for fear they would be run over. Teachers gave up attempting to teach in schools near the roads; the noise was too deafening. At night, people tossed and turned in their blacked-out bedrooms, unable to sleep. Employers were forced to give their workers an extra fifteen minutes' lunchbreak so that they could dodge the one-way system the 'Yanks' had introduced into their sector of southern England. White-helmeted 'Snowdrops' (as the American MPs were called) were everywhere, carrying pistols slung low on their hips – and looking as if they might use them too.

The first wave of soldiers had been sealed in their 'cages' since April 26th, and with them, millions of civilians living within ten miles of the coast, whose homes had been declared a prohibited area. Now, soldiers guarded both the inner and outer cages, and in 'American-Occupied England', which consisted of the counties of Cornwall, Devon and Dorset, US troops checked and controlled the civilians in the outer cage just as if they were an occupying power.

Those who were children then can recall to this day seeing GIs of the two assault divisions, the 1st US Infantry and the 29th, collecting fares on the buses in Cornish and Dorset towns. Older people, many of whom were forced from their farms and properties that spring (whole villages such as Slapton, Devon, were taken over) still recollect the Yanks with considerable bitterness. But for the most part, the troops and the civilians cooped up together on the coast maintained their distance. 'Wherever we took a walk in those days,' one local remembers nearly forty years later, 'we saw GIs in camps and a big notice stating: DO NOT TALK TO THE TROOPS.'[1] It was almost as if they were condemned men and the civilians were expected to have nothing to do with them.

On June 1st, the Americans and the British started to use smoke-screens to hide this massive build-up from the enemy, and in particular to conceal from prying eyes the strange mechanical devices that were to play such a vital part in the Normandy landings. The generals were especially anxious to prevent unauthorised personnel from seeing the thousand-odd vehicles of General Sir Percy Hobart's 79th Armoured Division. Hobart's 'funnies', as they were called, were a weird collection of armoured vehicles that could swim, flail the ground in front of them to detonate mines, lay bridges, fill in huge ditches in one go, and destroy concrete pillboxes with what looked like a flying dustbin. Most deadly of all Hobart's secret weapons were the tanks which could be used to spew out that awesome, all-consuming flame – the flame-throwers. No, the enemy must learn nothing of the 'funnies', for they might save countless Allied lives when the day came.

In their Nissen hut cities and tented villages all along the coast, the 200,000 men of the initial assault force and the 2,000,000 of the follow-up counted off their last days.

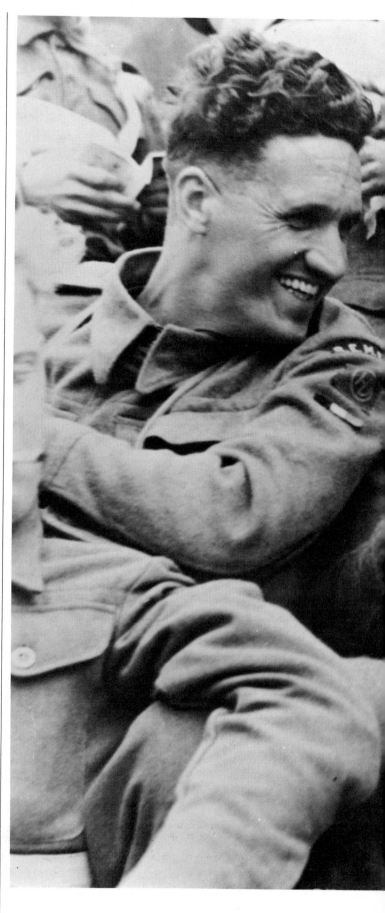

**Bound for France a few
days before the invasion.**

They read the 'Penguin wartime specials' and the US 'condensed books'; they gambled; they slept in wooden bunks, three and four beds deep; they trekked over the fields to take showers in huge screened enclosures, or to go to the latrines – 'thunderboxes' to the British, 'crappers' to the Americans and Canadians – where they would squat side by side in lines of a hundred, little khaki squares of paper which the British called 'Army Form Blank' stacked in old food cans beside them.

Mess hall queues stretched for hundreds of yards, and there were so many mouths to feed that the soldiers had to eat in three shifts. As a result, lines of hungry men stretched across the muddy fields to the big tents twenty-four hours a day, and day and night the air was heavy with the smell of frying bacon. No fewer than 54,000 soldiers were employed in servicing the British and Canadian Armies on the Hampshire and Sussex coasts alone. Four thousand five hundred new cooks had to be trained for the job, and an entire Canadian armoured division, the 5th, was temporarily employed in maintaining their installations.

The camps, or 'cages' as they were known to the troops, were all the same: a ring of barbed wire, earthen footpaths covered by duckboards, leading to tents and Nissen huts, and everywhere a proliferation of notice boards, on which were cryptic signs that made sense only to the initiated. 'Class Six', 'B-Mess', 'MI-Room', 'PX', 'Pro-Station' and the like – the shorthand of military life to which these young men had long been accustomed. But there was a difference between these cages and the camps they were used to. For once inside the cages, there was no way out. Here, the heroes of tomorrow were guarded by hard-faced, armed sentries as if they were common criminals.

An Australian war correspondent, Alan Moorehead, who was attached to the American forces, recalled the atmosphere inside the cages: '... Then you went inside and the gate closed behind you; and that, without any ceremony, was the act of renunciation. Once the gate was closed you could no longer return to the normal world outside, not even to buy a packet of cigarettes at the shop on the corner of the street, nor have a hair-cut, nor telephone your friends. You were committed irrevocably to the landing ...'[2]

Once inside the wire, the soldiers noted that civilians outside hurried by without even looking at them, almost as if they didn't exist. But soon they grew accustomed to the feeling that they were cut off from the normal, everyday world and no longer resented it. It seemed to them as if their fate had been decided long before, by some mysterious process of war. It was as if they were on a gigantic conveyor belt run by middle-aged generals far away in bright new offices in Washington or requisitioned 'olde worlde' manor houses in the Home Counties. There would sit the top brass, at long tables covered in green baize, running their fingers down endless lists of names, sending out frantic teletype messages, scuttling down corridors with those all-important buff folders clutched under their arms; until finally, at their behest, yet another khaki-clad battalion of eight hundred-odd slightly bewildered young men would drive or march into their barbed wire prison to prepare for their own particular date with destiny.

As always, the British feigned *sangfroid*. Some of their three-ton trucks were seen to bear chalked notices on the tailboard, which read: DON'T CHEER, GIRLS – WE'RE BRITISH – a dig at the Yanks, who wherever they went were warmly welcomed with cigarettes, fruit and kisses by the local girls.

As the convoys roared through Central London on their way south, tanks rolled down Whitehall itself, past the very government departments from which their orders emanated. As Captain Andrew Wilson of the 141st Regiment, Royal Armoured Corps (the Buffs), recalled, he and his fellow commanders ordered their drivers to go 'full out', hoping that the thunderous roar would shake the War Office to the foundations.[3]

That same week Lance-Corporal Wingfield, an infantryman of the Queen's Royal Regiment, paraded for the last time before his battalion proceeded southwards. Rigidly he and his platoon stood by their kits, ready for inspection. Their platoon sergeant stepped forward and announced: 'The Company Commander will now inspect you and your kit for the last time before you go overseas. He is a man of vast experience. He will ask each of you a question of vital importance to see if you are ready for battle. You must know the answer to that question. It may save your life one day.'

When the Company Commander came to Wingfield, he walked all around him, then halted. The lance-corporal stared 'frozen-faced, at his Adam's apple', waiting for that 'question of vital importance'. It was: 'How many needles in that housewife* of yours?'[4]

Captain John Foley, a regular officer of the Royal Armoured Corps, had halted his troop of Churchill tanks just outside their staging area at Lee-on-Solent. There he noticed that after the long drive south his regular drivers were weary and red-eyed. After the usual 'char and wad', he ordered the co-drivers to take over for the rest of the journey. Reluctantly his own driver handed over the control of the big tank to a new man called Hunter. Foley clambered into the turret and ordered, 'Driver, start up!' Nothing happened. Then suddenly 'a thunderous roar ripped the silence of the afternoon'. Foley ducked instinctively, wondering what had gone wrong; he hadn't seen any enemy aircraft and wasn't aware that the long-range German guns on the other side of the Channel could reach *that* far.

'Gingerly I poked my head outside again to find our precious sealing blown over half the county of Hampshire.' The harassed co-driver had pressed the wrong switch by mistake, exploding the special waterproof sealing needed to

---

* A canvas holdall containing the British soldier's sewing kit.

A Cromwell tank.

enable the tank to swim ashore safely on the other side of the Channel. Six weeks' hard work had vanished in a matter of seconds.

Thus it was that Trooper Hunter spent one of his last remaining days in England slaving over the Churchill to repair the damage. Two months later he was dead, his head blown off by an 88mm shell.[5]

At roughly the time Trooper Hunter pressed the wrong button, Lance-Corporal R.E. Wingfield's battalion arrived at 'British Occupied Aldershot,' where they were given their first French money; from here they were sent on to Eastleigh near Southampton, where they entered their cage. 'The first thing which met our eyes,' Wingfield recalled much later, 'was a large board giving details of the ever-open NAAFI* and the continuous film show. This should have put us on our guard, but our suspicions were finally confirmed when ... we marched to our quarters. There, beneath the trees, were neat two-man tents, each with two American Army cots – and sheets!'

Wingfield's mate Lofty stared at them in amazement, for in the British Army the soldier invariably slept beneath

*British equivalent to the US Post Exchange.

nothing more exotic than rough grey blankets; then he roared, 'I'll bet we're not here long. The condemned man ate a bloody hearty breakfast!'[6]

Lofty turned out to be right on two counts: they weren't destined to stay there long, and they *were* condemned men. Lance-Corporal Wingfield would manage to survive longer than most, but in eight months' time he, too, would have to pay the 'butcher's bill'.

The king came to visit them in the cages, a small, sad figure in a red cap, who stuttered painfully and looked 'like a waxworks image' as he rattled past the troops in his Bren-gun carrier.[7] To the men he appeared to be wearing cosmetics – which gave rise to comment, since only continental monarchs were supposed to rouge their faces. One colonel was heard to remark afterwards, 'The king came swannin' in, lookin' as if he'd been to Lizzy Arden's.'[7] This pronouncement was followed by incredulous guffaws.[8]

Beneath their traditional insouciance, however, the British were apprehensive. Andrew Wilson, waiting now with the rest, felt 'there was a curious uneasiness in Aldershot and Farnborough in the first, warm days of

June.' He sensed it in the Canadians too, for they 'had been waiting for action for nearly four years. They were so used to it that now they couldn't stop drinking till somebody dragged them away. For the British it was different. They were all keyed up. Everything was impending for them; and everything was withheld, like those slender nyloned legs which tapped down the Aldershot pavement.'[9]

The 'dogfaces', or the Yanks as the British invariably called them, regardless of which side of the Mason-Dixon Line they came from, were different. They were brash and bold. They didn't attempt to hide their emotions. They put an un-English zest into everything and weren't taken in by the big words and exhortations of their commanders. When Eisenhower, the supreme commander, came to talk to the 16th Infantry Regiment of the US 1st Infantry Division, the proud 'Big Red One'* stationed outside Weymouth, he told the veterans that they would soon be embarking on a 'crusade', adding: 'You establish a beachhead for us and we'll move inland and carry the ball.'

But the dogfaces weren't taken in by the pious platitudes. At the back someone called, 'You establish a beachhead for us and *we'll* move inland and carry the ball!'[10]

The same reaction greeted General George Patton, the fire-eating commander of the US Third Army, nicknamed by the Press 'Ole Blood an' Guts'. 'Yeah,' quipped the GIs cynically, '*our* blood and *his* guts!'

Some of the GIs, the unblooded ones or 'wet noses' as they were called contemptuously by the veterans, had been in England a long time. Several thousand of them had been in the UK since early 1942, when they had made an immediate impact on their 'host nation', to use the term adopted in the official handbook given to each new arrival. Jokingly the British had described them as 'over-paid, over-fed, over-sexed – and over here,' to which the GIs had replied, 'Yeah – because they [*i.e.* the British] are under-paid, under-fed, under-sexed – and under Eisenhower!'

The GIs brought with them a variety of innovations. Among them were baseball – 'a game for girls', as far as the English were concerned – 'candy bars', nylons and chewing gum; 'Any gum, chum?' soon became a national catch-phrase among small British boys. Another import, however, was racial prejudice against blacks.

In the mid-forties the US Army was still segregated, with black American soldiers drinking in different pubs, dancing in different clubs and eating at separate tables from their white comrades-in-arms. In the winter of 1944, black GIs were chased out of a British pub at Kingsclere near Newbury, whereupon the blacks fetched their rifles from camp and returned to do battle, blasting the pub and killing the owner's wife and several others. It was a tragic and ironic commentary on the great war to 'save democracy' that the

* Known thus because of their divisional patch, which featured a red '1'.

Negro troops on the march through an English town.

only battle fought on British soil during the six-year conflict was between white and black Americans. However, that pattern of hostility between black and white would soon change. During the coming battle for Europe, casualties would be so great that black Americans would find themselves fighting side by side with their white brothers at the front. The campaign would bring about the end of segregation – as far as the US Army was concerned, at least.

If the American GIs were popular with British girls, they were not particularly liked by the British people as a whole. In 1943 after the downfall of the Italian dictator Mussolini, a secret Gallup poll conducted by the British government

showed that the American allies were less well spoken of by the British man in the street than the erstwhile Italian enemy. At the root of the dislike was envy; the average Tommy received only one-fifth of the pay of the average black US soldier, and furiously resented the GIs' way with his womenfolk. The GIs were too brash, too forward, too successful. After the war, a former GI recalled that one morning after reveille his company's supply sergeant stepped forward and told the assembled men, 'We've got thirty thousand rubbers in the supply room. I want you people to do something about this!' The gleeful GIs were only too happy to oblige.[11]

Now, however, both veterans and 'wet noses' were sobered by the thought of the approaching invasion. Of the eleven American divisions in England that June, only two had been in combat previously, the 1st Infantry and the 82nd Airborne; and the 29th Infantry Division, which had been in Britain for nearly two years now and which would lead the attack with the 1st Division, had begun to have a morbid fear of casualties. Indeed, just prior to entering the cage, they had heard of another US battalion which had been surprised by German E-boats while practising a landing at Slapton Sands and had suffered severe casualties. The result had been that both Generals Eisenhower and Bradley had been forced to address the men personally in an attempt to restore their nerve. Private William Joseph Phillips of the 29th did his best to reassure his buddies: 'This outfit will never see combat,' he predicted. 'We've been in England so long that our job won't start till the war is over. They're going to have us wipe the bluebird shit off the White Cliffs of Dover!'[12] But it was no good. The 'wet noses' were scared.

As Staff-Sergeant Giles of the US 291st Combat Engineer Battalion recorded in his diary after his battalion had been alerted for combat: 'The whole outfit now has a very bad case of the invasion shakes. Very little talk about anything but assault landings, what it will be like, what the casualties will be etc. Any way you look at it, it's not going to be any piece of cake. After the alert this morning, I caught myself several times looking around and wondering for the hundredth time how the hell I got here and what the hell I'm doing here – me, Henry Giles, an old farm boy from Caldwell Ridge, Knifley, Kentucky! For the first time in years a uniform doesn't seem to fit me. A little too tight.'[13]

Even the veterans of the Big Red One were becoming uncertain. That June, while on board ship and waiting to sail, Captain John Dulligan wrote of his company, 'I love these men. They sleep all over the ship, on the decks, in, on top, and underneath the vehicles. They smoke, play cards, wrestle around and indulge in general horse-play. They gather around in groups and talk mostly about girls, home and experiences (with and without girls) … They are good soldiers, the best in the world … Before the invasion of North Africa, I was nervous and a little scared. During the Sicilian invasion I was so busy that the fear passed while I was working … This time we will hit a beach in France and from there on, only God knows the answer.'[14]

Sam Fuller, the future film producer, then a corporal with the Big Red One, had already won the Bronze Star in Sicily and would go on to win the Silver Star on D-Day; but he, too, shared Dulligan's anxieties about the future. Later he wrote: 'They [the men of the division] had had their fill of combat and they had rightfully assumed … that somebody else should carry the ball this time … They would stand no chance of walking off that beach. Their luck would not stretch that far …'[15]

They were superbly trained, of course, these Canadian, American and British young men who would make the first assault. In fact, most of them were in better physical shape than the veterans of the US 1st and 82nd Divisions and the British 50th, 51st and 7th Armoured Division, which had been brought home from Africa and Italy for the invasion. Most of the invasion force had done little else but train – in the case of the British and Canadians, for as much as four long years. No military force has ever trained as hard before or since.

For most of them it started in some remote 'boot camp' in the wilds of Canada, darkest Yorkshire or in the great sprawling plains of Texas. Here they were shorn of their hair, innoculated against all kinds of fearsome diseases, scared to death by lurid training films on the dangers of VD, told how to

keep their 'John Thomas' clean, given their first 'short-arm' inspection, taught how to keep the cadence and march, and had their civilian spirit broken in half a dozen refined and time-honoured ways.

They learnt how to scrub a floor with a toothbrush, 'spit-shine' their shoes till they gleamed like mirrors, dust the hollybushes around their huts, whitewash coal, clean latrines until, to use the words of the US drill-sergeants in their old-fashioned Regular Army hats, they shone 'as bright as a whore's belly on Christmas Eve.' Finally, having learnt how to think like soldiers and 'bullshit' their way out of every tight corner, they were trained in the arts of war. By now all trace of their previous civilian mentality was utterly erased.

Now they learned how to advance into the attack under a hail of live ammunition (probably suffering their first casualties at the hands of their own NCOs); how to run ten miles in two hours laden down with full battle kit; how to swim a hundred yards in the same gear; and how to complete the cruel assault courses at 'battle schools', training establishments devised by disciples of the Marquis de Sade. Here, soaked in sweat and sobbing for breath, they would charge at dummies with their bayonets fixed, urged on by screaming NCOs with cries of '*Get in there! Give him the point! Carve his nuts off! Rip his guts open!*' – and in some cases, have real blood thrown over them as they did so. They would sleep out in the coldest of winter nights in the wilds of Scotland, and hike through the sweltering, damp heat of a Florida summer.

And still there was more to come. For now, at spots such as Burghead in the Moray Firth or Slapton Sands, Devon, which resembled the places they would attack in France, they would be forced ashore from heaving landing craft, ashen-faced and shaking with seasickness, to take part in simulated assault landings. Mines and bombs would erupt all around them, showering them with sand; machine-guns chattered frenetically; tracer zipped back and forth with white and red urgency; mortars and artillery pounded – all in a final attempt to train them for the real-life din and chaos of war.

Their commanders went to extraordinary lengths to ensure

that their training was made as realistic as possible. For example, some four months before D-Day, twenty-nine-year-old Colonel T.B.H. Otway of the British 9th Parachute Battalion was told it would be his task to capture a key gun battery at Merville, France, during the invasion. He immediately went out with secret photographs of Merville, in search of a stretch of English countryside which resembled the land surrounding the German battery. He found a suitable spot near Newbury in Berkshire. Within two days he had it requisitioned by the War Office (which eventually had to pay £15,000 as compensation for crops destroyed). He then fenced the place in and began to build an exact replica of the Merville battery and its defences. Where the surrounding terrain didn't fit in with the photographs of Merville, the young para colonel bulldozed the fields and woods until it did. Here, in this top-secret backwater, Otway and his six-hundred-odd paras rehearsed the attack over and over again using live ammunition until they could do it in their sleep.

Yet in the final analysis, all this effort was simply training. The chief actor in the drama, the German enemy, was absent. As R.W. Thompson, the British war correspondent and former soldier, noted: during training, 'Men did not choke and drown in their own blood, gaps did not open to leave men "naked and alone", spattered with the entrails, blood and brains of their friends … Nor were the coils of wire littered with the obscene offal of war …'[16]

It was true. In the course of these long years of training, things had settled down into the routine of mock-war – a routine in which a few casualties resulted from training accidents and the occasional enemy air-raid, but which for the most part was little more dangerous than garrison duty. In the British Army, many units of wartime conscripts could hardly be distinguished from peacetime regulars. Bull reigned supreme. More attention was paid to a smart turn-out, the three-hundred-year-old British Army's ceremonial drill and 'square-bashing' than to the real shooting war, which seemed to have been relegated to some far-off future date. 'If it moves,' the Tommies quipped, 'salute it. If it doesn't, *paint it!*'

Captain Thomas Firbank, a Canadian serving with the Guards, noted that most of his fellow officers had no concept at all of the war which was being fought outside their Mess. Although he was a loyal officer and happy in the Guards, Firbank was surprised to find that the main concern of his adjutant was to ensure that the young officers had their hair cut regularly, knew the history of the regiment and learnt a short glossary of words that would help to 'set them apart from the rest of the Army'. So the wartime subalterns had to learn that London was London, and not 'Town'; that the service dress jacket was under no circumstances to be called a 'tunic', and that officers of the Brigade of Guards wore 'plain clothes' and not 'mufti'. As the adjutant explained to the bemused Canadian, 'Those fellows who live among the Wogs may wear mufti, but the Brigade has never served East of Suez.'[17] One day that particular adjutant would be in for a nasty surprise!

The US Army wasn't all that different either, in spite of the fact that it was drawn from a supposedly less class-conscious society than the British Army. The more senior US officers, in their custom-tailored uniforms, riding breeches and gleaming boots (most of them, including Generals Patton and Eisenhower, complete with mistresses), lived a social life that seemed totally divorced from the war. They went to cocktail parties with showbiz celebrities like Adèle Astaire and the Lunts, who were now flocking to London; had dinners with the aristocracy; mixed with top politicians; and if they were lucky, were presented to the King and Queen of England at 'Buck House', as they had learned to call Buckingham Palace. Very heady fare for men who only a few years previously had been obscure middle-aged colonels, contemplating a slippered retirement on a modest pension.

On April 10th, 1944, for example, Colonel Charles Codman, a wealthy Bostonian who had been a fighter pilot in World War One and now acted as a kind of social secretary for General George Patton, noted in his diary:

Jimmy Cagney, who was to give a show in the afternoon, came to lunch. Very quiet and reserved and, like Bob Hope and all the others, played straight man for the boss [*i.e.* Patton] …

In the afternoon it rained and then cleared up. Went over to Sir Robert Burrough's for tea. He has two daughters – one who hunts, one who wears a monocle – and a South African daughter-in-law. It was all … rather cosy and pleasant, particularly as none of them are too keen about anything. Even the hunting girl doesn't insist that you jump on that horse which is so quiet with the children. I brought them all back to the hall [Peover Hall, Cheshire, Patton's HQ] for dinner and for the movies – it was supposed to be one of Cagney's but turned out to be Joan Crawford – and then motored them all back again by the light of a sultry bomber moon.[18]

Commander Butcher of the US Navy, a former vice-president of CBS, fulfilled the same secretarial function for Eisenhower as Codman did for Patton. Of the atmosphere of their headquarters in London and the officers who staffed it, he wrote: 'They have sat on their fannies for so long and have never seen any action that they look like putty and seem far removed from reality. The only thing that puts them back into the war is the occasional air raid.'[19]

That spring, while attending a full-scale landing exercise carried out by the US 4th Infantry Division at Slapton Sands, Butcher was also dismayed by the high number of elderly officers in the division's higher command. 'A good many of the full colonels … give me a pain. They are fat, grey and oldish. Most of them wear the Rainbow Ribbon of the last war and are still fighting it.'[20] Nor was Butcher too impressed by the calibre of the division's younger officers. He wrote: 'I am concerned over the absence of toughness and alertness of young American officers whom I saw on this trip. They seem to regard the war as one grand manoeuvre in which they are having a happy time. Many seem as green as growing corn. How will they act in

Assault troops limbering up aboard a landing craft.

battle and how will they look in three months' time?'[21]

But now this 'happy time' was almost over. The grand manoeuvres were at an end. The time of testing was nigh, and many of those elderly colonels in their immaculate 'pinks' who had never heard a shot fired in anger since 1918 would once more be plunged into the chaos of real battle. As for those young men 'as green as growing corn', they would soon learn to fight and die. By Christmas, 1944, there would be nothing left of the division that Butcher had seen in training at Slapton Sands.

All the young men who would execute the initial assault – British, Canadian and American – belonged to proud formations whose lineage stretched back over centuries: the 8th US Infantry, formed in 1838, whose battle streamers went as far back as the Indian Wars; the 12th US Infantry, which had seen action in the Civil War; the 1st Division, which had fired the first shot of any American troops in both World Wars and had fought at Gettysburg.

They bore bold, aggressive, sometimes boastful names: the 'Screaming Eagles', the 'All-American', 'Hell's Last Issue', the 'Death and Glory Boys.' One Scottish formation purported to be of such ancient lineage that it gave itself the nickname of 'Pontius Pilate's Bodyguard!'

But in spite of their traditions and proud history, the attack formations were still composed of anxious, slightly scared young men, who spent long hours gazing out to sea and wondering glumly what lay waiting for them on the other side of the Channel. Would their training see them through? Would they even make it to the beach? And if so, would they survive long enough to get off it? As they waited, either on land or on tossing barges whose decks were awash with vomit, they must have asked themselves those questions over and over again.

An observer of the 7th Parachute Battalion of the British 1st Airborne Division, which was to drop together with the US 101st and 82nd Airborne Divisions, noted that the men's mood was 'sombre and determined', but that there was a complete absence of the joking, horseplay and high spirits usually found among parachute troops before a landing. Instead there was an atmosphere of 'quiet confidence,' mixed with 'a certain amount of honest funk.'[22]

The men of Lord Lovat's 4th Commandos, mostly veterans, unlike the 6th Airborne men, who were entering battle for the first time, were more confident. But they, too, were hardly exuberant at the thought of what lay ahead. With boots well-polished, faces clean-shaven, and looking neatly turned out for battle, they gave an impression of efficiency to their commander Brigadier Lord Lovat, who addressed them in a speech before sailing. One of his listeners recalled it as containing 'no nonsense, no cheap appeal to patriotism.'[23] But even so the mood of the men remained sombre.

Those of the men who were still on land could see storms raging in the Channel. Before them, a great armada of grey-blue ships was bobbing up and down at anchor in the heaving green water, while smoke-grey fog scudded across the sky. It was a scene that matched their mood perfectly.

On the ships themselves the atmosphere was little different. Many of the troops out in the Channel were too seasick to care what happened to them on the other side. Those on ships still in port mostly slept and ate, complaining at the greasy sausages and lukewarm tea if they were on British ships; greedily tucking into steak, peas, mashed potatoes and plentiful chocolate ice-cream if they were on American vessels.

Corporal Alexander Baron, who was going over with a composite beach company, wrote later of his British comrades: 'There was no sentimental talk, no soft singing or playing of harmonicas, no writing of farewell letters ... Three days with nothing to do but eat, sleep and gamble was an event in the lives of the men ...'[24]

Lance-Corporal Wingfield, now embarked, was also preoccupied with food. On the deck of his Royal Navy vessel, he and his mates decided to try out the new self-heating cans of soup with which they had just been issued. By pulling a string attached to the lid, one was supposed to activate a heating device running through the centre, which then began warming up the contents. Unfortunately for Wingfield and his pals, 'Half the cans immediately exploded violently, scattering burning soup all over the immaculate decks.'[25]

Next, the infantrymen turned their attention to yet another new device with which they had been issued for the great day – the 'Tommy Cooker', a small, portable, petrol-burning stove that would cause many a case of severe burns before the long campaign was over. This time, however, no one was injured by the cookers. Instead, the Royal Navy's immaculate decks were defiled once again as the tar-caulking started to melt and run, leaving behind 'a dreadful smell.'

As if that wasn't enough to ruin Wingfield's appetite, the ship's tannoy suddenly crackled into life and a voice informed the listening soldiers that Allied Intelligence had just reported on a new kind of anti-personnel mine being used by the Germans. It was called the 'S-Mine'; but the Yanks had already christened it 'the 50-50 mine'. ' "The name is derived from your chances," the announcer explained, "If you hit with the right foot, the rod flies up past your right side. If you hit it with the left, you'll be singing tenor!" '[26]

Alan Moorehead, the Australian war correspondent, was now aboard a US transport ship, where swing music blasted out 'eight or ten hours through the day' and a black GI sat in the stern 'peeling potatoes endlessly'. It was, he wrote, a time when 'one had no desire to think or write letters or engage on any distraction from the inevitable thing ahead.' The sombre mood wasn't helped by the captain, who had already made three assault landings in North Africa, Sicily and Salerno. He told the Australian, himself a veteran of war in ten countries: ' "This will be a bad one." '[27]

(Above) Members of the US Army embarking for invasion on D-Day.
(Right) German labour battalion walking past 'dragon's teeth', part of the defences of the Atlantic Wall.

But some men did write letters. Second Lieutenant George Kerchner of the ill-fated 2nd US Ranger Battalion was censoring letters on board ship just off Weymouth, when he came across one written by a Staff-Sergeant Larry Johnson, one of his section leaders. Its contents so astonished him that he sent for Johnson and told him: ' "You'd better post this yourself – after you get to France." '[28]

Johnson smirked and accepted the letter back. He had written it to a girl, asking her for a date early in June. There was nothing unusual in that, save for one thing: the girl in question lived in Paris!

As twilight faded on June 5th, 1944, the sixty pathfinders of the British 22nd Independent Parachute Company started to waddle to their six transports at Harwell Airfield in Berkshire. Each man carried some eighty-five pounds of kit, plus another sixty pounds in a kitbag strapped to their legs. They would be the first British troops to set foot on French soil, and their task would be to mark the dropping zones for their comrades of the 6th Airborne Division.

In the lead Albemarle aircraft were the ten men who were due to land first, the spearhead of the whole many-thousand-strong Allied assault force. All volunteers, they seemed to symbolise the men who made up Montgomery's army. One had been a hod-carrier before the war, another a tool-maker, yet another a bricklayer from Edinburgh. There was a kennelman from Worcester, a truck-driver from Dumfries, a 'deserter' from the Army of neutral Eire, two regular soldiers, and a Jewish refugee from Austria. They were led by a young lieutenant who had been in the chorus of a West End musical when the war had broken out five long years before. 'Three of them had fought at Dunkirk, one had fought in North Africa, but the rest were going into action for the first time.'[29]

Green as they were, these British soldiers had lived with war since their teens. They had been threatened with invasion, seen their cities bombed and shattered, lived on short rations for years – one egg a week, four ounces of meat, an orange for children under twelve – and seen their older relatives suffer and die on battlefields spread over three continents and half a decade. Unlike their American and Canadian comrades, who were also going into action for the first time, they had absorbed Britain's long-standing struggle against Germany with their mother's milk. They had grown up with war.

Their American comrades, on the other hand, were in a foreign land thousands of miles away from home, waiting to assault another foreign country in what appeared now to be a very dangerous operation. It must have crossed their minds to ask: for what? To liberate Europe? Soon they would find out just what a hollow mockery that word 'liberation' was, and would start wondering if the French would really have chosen to be 'liberated' from the Nazi yoke at such cost. But on this Monday June 5th, 1944, as the paras filed obediently into their Dakotas, such thoughts were far from their young minds. Theirs not to reason why – that could come later; for the moment, all their thoughts were concentrated on surviving what lay ahead.

All of them, British, Canadian and American, wore their faces streaked with green or black paint, and some of the men of the 'Screaming Eagles', the paras of the US 101st Division, had shaved their heads Red Indian-style, so that only a topknot of hair remained. Most were intensely possessive about the amazing variety of weapons they carried – tommy guns, carbines, trench knives, clubs, daggers and brass knuckles – not to mention lucky charms: rabbits' feet and the like. The paras were also provided with little metal toy frogs for use as a recognition signal after landing, to enable them to distinguish between friend and foe. Naturally, though, the British had to go in for something more stylish and elaborate: their Oxford and Buckinghamshire Light Infantry of the 6th Airborne Division would be rallied on landing by a traditional hunting horn!

James Byrom, a British para medic, recalled how he paraded with his comrades in front of a long line of camouflaged Dakotas. The paras, he wrote, were 'fantastically upholstered, our pockets bulging with drugs and bandages, with maps and money and escaping gadgets.'[30] Earlier they had met the RAF crew who would fly them to France, and the 'Brylcreem boys' had told them that it would be a 'piece of cake', and that there would be nothing to worry about except for a 'little flak' over the coast. Now Byrom thought the RAF types looked a little less confident, their Air Force charm a little strained.

The paras donned their Mae Wests and parachutes and tested the quick-release devices, all under the watchful, if nonchalant gaze of the RAF pilot, who made the paras feel 'self-conscious' and 'physically ill at ease'.

Finally it was midnight and they were taking off. Byrom felt 'a sudden spinal chill when the fuselage quivered under pressure of the slipstream and the power took hold of us … As the last light faded off the landscape that fell away into a misty horizon, the glow of our cigarettes grew brighter. Other aircraft in the formation were no longer visible, dipping and swaying in the wind-flukes.'[31] The 6,255 British paratroopers were on their way to France.

With Byrom and his comrades flew 13,000 Americans in 882 planes. Now the veterans of the 82nd US Airborne Division were beginning to grow nervous, recalling the confusion and heavy casualties of their drop over the coast of Sicily the year before. On that occasion they had been shot up by their own anti-aircraft guns, dropped over many square miles of enemy-held territory and in some cases virtually abandoned to their fate by nervous pilots. Some of them began to think the same thing could happen all over again.

General Matt Ridgway, their tough commander, who carried a grenade attached to his webbing and a Springfield rifle of World War One vintage, noted their nervousness as the cold blast of the pre-dawn air streamed in through the

British airborne troops ready to take off for France.

open door of the Dakota. There was a constant blundering to the 'heads', which unfortunately were too narrow to admit a para in full kit. Eventually, a crew chief appeared bearing with him a bucket, which seems to have solved the problem.

They were now over the Channel, and even at fifteen hundred feet Ridgway could tell the sea was rough; '... We passed over a small patrol craft – one of the checkpoints for our navigators – and the light it displayed for us was bobbing like a cork in a millrace.'[32] Heedless, the plane droned on, heading for the pale glow of the quarter moon now rising over France.

Far below Ridgway's Dakota, the commandos were preparing to set out for war. It was a perfect June evening, with the Isle of Wight lying 'green and friendly and tantalisingly peaceful behind the tapestry of warships'. In a line of nineteen ships, with Lord Lovat's piper playing in the bows of the leading vessel, the commando force slowly drew away from the coast and towards the gathering darkness, to cheers from all on board, troops and crews alike. Captain A.D.C. Smith, watching their departure, heard those cheers coming faintly across the water and gradually spreading to ship after ship; to him, the spectacle was 'exhilarating, glorious and heartbreaking', and he recalls: 'I never loved England so truly as at that moment.'[33] Later it was reported that the admiral in command had been so carried away by the sight that he

had tossed his gold-braided cap into the air in sheer schoolboy exuberance.

Coastguard Mr Wallace, an ex-Navy man, returned to his cottage at Worth Matravers after watching part of the thousands-strong armada depart. At the time he had felt entranced and uplifted, but he suspected deep in his heart that few of the men he had seen that night would ever return. Before he turned in that night, he said sadly to his wife: 'A lot of men are going to die tonight. We should pray for them.' Together the couple knelt down by the bed in their humble coastguard cottage and did so.[34]

There was none of the bold skirl of the pipes or the spit-and-polish of the commandos when the Americans set sail that evening, though it is recorded that several of them wore their 'Class A' uniform for the crossing, almost as if they were expecting to take part in a parade on the other side. Instead of a piper, the men of the 1st, 29th and 4th Divisions sailed to the beat of swing music and the Andrew Sisters belting out *The Boogie-Woogie Bugle Boy of Company B*.

But like the commandos, they, too, were heavily armed with weapons ranging from combat knives honed to a deadly cutting edge, to the newly-introduced bazooka. Many were also loaded down with personal possessions that would drag them down to a watery grave when they plunged into the heaving swell off Omaha Beach. Cases were recorded of men lumbering themselves with guitars and ukuleles, small suitcases and, in two instances, tennis rackets.

Ahead of them, but still at sea, thousands of their fellows, sick and freezing, had already forgotten the dangers that lay ahead; they were too seasick and miserable to care. Huddled in the great caverns of the LCTs and the cramped quarters of the LSIs, choking on the stink of diesel oil and vomit, their one thought was somehow to find an escape from their misery.

Now the Channel was packed with thousands of ships, ranging from the great US and British capital ships down to the squat little landing craft and assault boats. Here and there a man stood listlessly at the rail, watching England fall behind. But most were below, sick or alienated by the strange sensation of being suspended in time, crawling steadily forward through the grey waste between the known – which was now disappearing into the night – and the unknown of France and the awesome dangers ahead.

Now the English coast could no longer be seen, nor the silken slugs of the barrage balloons which floated overhead. The only sound was the steady throb of the ships' engines and the snarl of the Spitfires high overhead in the lowering clouds. Then even that sound was gone, and the sea of the English coast which had harboured the invasion fleet for so long was empty at last …

A Weymouth housewife recalled long afterwards:

That Tuesday morning – the 6th – I remember looking out to sea to the spot the Yanks called 'Piccadilly Corner' because it was there that the landing craft always congregated on the training exercises. And it was empty. For the first time in six months I couldn't see a ship, where there had always been scores of them. They'd gone, the Yanks, and we knew where. I thought of my friend Al who was with the US 1st Infantry Division and wondered at that moment where he was now and how he was getting on and whether I'd ever see him again. Then I was just going to turn away and get back to my shopping when I spotted one of those daft little signs that the Yanks chalked up everywhere that year. You'd find it everywhere on walls, lorries, hoardings, picture houses – everywhere! It was a drawing of a fat-nosed, stupid-looking chap peering over a wall with the words printed below, KILROY WUZ HERE. I don't know what it was supposed to mean and have never found out. But at that moment it got me. I wasn't very flighty or particularly silly in those days, but for me it seemed to say that my Al had come and gone and like the rest of the Yanks, wouldn't come back. *Kilroy wuz here*, I thought, and burst into tears …[35]

Before dawn on D-Day.

2 CURTAIN UP

'Them lucky bastards – they ain't seasick any more.'

Comment of GI during Normandy landings, on seeing corpses piled on Utah beach

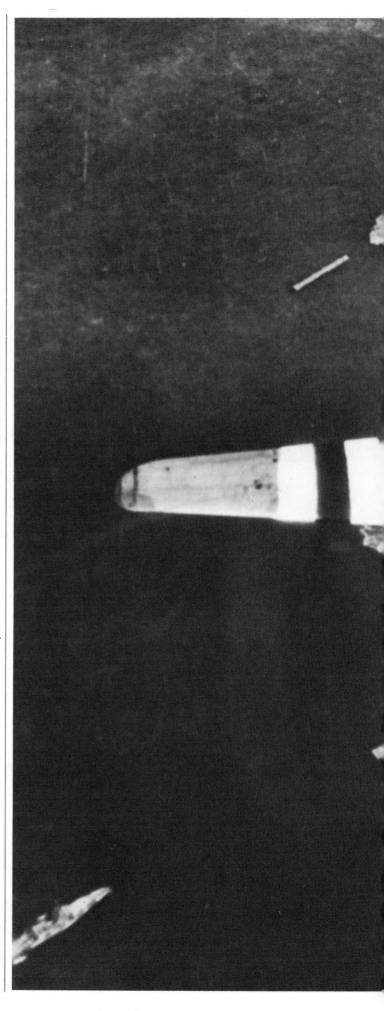

An A020 Havoc of the 9th USAF passing over Allied naval craft. The black and white stripes on the wings were on every Allied aircraft for identification.

Fantastic necklaces of white and red flak rose into the darkness. Tracer zipped through the night like lethal Morse code. Brilliant white searchlights criss-crossed the heavens. If it was all highly destructive, it was also dramatically beautiful – some even thought it noble. The greatest day in the lives of countless thousands of men had commenced. It was the early hours of Tuesday, June 6th, 1944 – D-Day.

RAF Flight Lieutenant John Macadam was flying through belt after belt of flak, sitting in the dicky seat of a glider-tug. Next to him, the pilot crouched over the controls, his face a lurid red in the glow from below. Previously he had told the glider pilot, a young sergeant, that it would be 'a piece of cake'; now he hastily reassured him over the intercom: 'Hold on, son there's a lot of stuff around here, but we'll get through it!'

'We're all right – carry on,' the glider pilot's voice crackled back.

The tug dived into a cloud to escape the flak, but the German gunners below hung on to them. Suddenly the rear gunner yelled, 'The glider's hit!'

Swiftly the pilot called, 'Glider pilot, glider pilot, are you all right?'

The RAF men tensed. There was no answer. Then suddenly an excited voice answered, 'All right, we're with you!'

Now time was running out for the British airborne men. Soon the planes would be approaching the DZs. The navigator gave the skipper the signal. 'Casting off,' called the skipper.

Macadam could just hear the glider pilot's faint, 'Thanks, skipper – and good luck!' as they lurched forward, suddenly freed of the glider's weight. As the tow-plane started to turn and head for home and bacon and eggs in the Mess, Macadam searched the sky for their

glider. But it was nowhere to be seen. The blackness below had swallowed it up.[1]

In the gliders many slept. Some smoked dolefully. A few sang the song of the glider troops, a doctored version of *Bless 'em All* with a chorus that ran: '*We're lucky fellers, we've got no propellers. So cheer up, my lads, Bless 'em all!*' One or two cracked feeble jokes, such as the comment made when an older man dropped his Sten: 'Just hark at Charlie – he's dropped his false teeth!' Some prayed, but not many. As the tugs started to cast off, there was a sudden, thrilling silence, broken only by the harsh breathing of the men and the hiss of the wind outside. Suddenly the jokes, the songs, the prayers and everything else were forgotten in the excitement of the moment.

Chester Wilmot, a BBC correspondent attached to the airborne troops, thought his glider seemed 'to stall and hover like a hawk about to strike.' Then abruptly they were 'floating in a sky of fathomless uncertainty – in suspense between peace and war. We are through the flak-belt and gliding so smoothly that the fire and turmoil of battle seem to belong to another world.'[2]

But not for long. Suddenly the young soldiers of the 6th Airborne were jerked back to reality as the pilot put the huge wood-and-canvas glider into a steep banking turn. They were going in!

'As the ground rises to meet us, the pilots catch a glimpse of the pathfinders' lights and the white dusty road and the square Norman church-tower beside the landing zone ... The soil of France rushes past beneath us and we touch-down with a jolt on a ploughed field ... It is 3.32 *a.m.* We are two minutes late. Shouts and cheers echo down the glider, and a voice from the dark interior cries out, 'This is it, chum. I told yer we wouldn't 'ave ter swim!'[3]

Now the gliders were hurtling down everywhere, skidding and sliding crazily at a hundred miles an hour, tearing across the fields of France, churning up great wakes of soil and stones behind them before coming to a bone-jarring, rending stop. Some crashed into houses. Others shed their wings like great multicoloured beetles. A few up-ended making grotesque twisted silhouettes against the ugly white, pre-dawn sky.

From them poured troops, ever more of them, forming up, ready for action; from only a few fields away they could hear the angry, surprised shouts of the Germans and the first wild bursts of Spandau fire. For Chester Wilmot and his group, the landing had gone smoothly enough, but as they marched off to battle, they all knew that it would be harder to hold the ground than it had been to take it.'[4]

Now their American comrades of the 82nd and 101st Divisions were dropping out of the sky all over Normandy. General Ridgway wrote later:

... Beside the door, a red light glowed. Four minutes. Down the line of bucket seats, the No. 4 man in the stick stood up. It was Captain Schouvaloff, brother-in-law of Fëdor Chaliapin, the opera singer. He was a get-rich-quick paratrooper, as I was, a

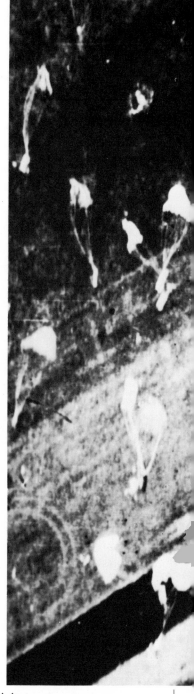

Horsa glider and abandoned parachutes litter the dropping zone north of Caen on D-Day.

man who had no formal jump training ...

A brilliant linguist, he was also something of a clown. Standing up, wearing a look of mock bewilderment on his face, he held up the hook on his static line ...

'Pray tell me,' said Schouvaloff, in his thick accent, 'what does one do with this strange device?'...

A bell rang loudly, a green light glowed. The jumpmaster, crouched in the door, went out with a yell – 'Let's go!' With a paratrooper, still laughing, breathing hard on my neck, I leaped out after him.[5]

Captain Laurence Critchell of the 501st Parachute Regiment noted as the red light glowed at the open door of his plane, that 'all semblance of formation had been lost. In the steady popping of machine gun bullets, the *wham, wham, wham*, of the 20mm tracer shells and the explosion

of the 88mm flak, the sharp arrow of the invasion seemed hopelessly blunted. But for the most part the planes blundered on. Men got sick and vomited on the floor, shrapnel tore up through the greasy pools or through the seats they had quitted.'[6]

Now the frightened paras started to jump as best they could, for the pilots had lost all control. A Sergeant Rice went out. His left arm caught in the door of the plane. 'For three seconds he hung outside the plane in the hundred mile an hour wind. When he was torn free, the metal edge of the door scraped his skin almost to the bone, taking with it his hundred and fifty dollar watch. He scarcely felt it.'

Knocked almost unconscious, Sergeant Rice floated down, the only sound the 'sharp cracking of the bullets' that struck the edge of his nylon canopy. With one arm useless, he slipped to the earth and lay still, watching tracer zip over his head in the darkness and listening to the sound of the planes, going away, 'going back to England.'[7]

As in Sicily in 1943, confusion and chaos reigned, and the 82nd Airborne suffered the same fate as before, with its troopers being spread over miles of German-held territory. Some were carried into the marshes and swamps of the area, dragged under by the weight of their equipment, never to reappear. Even chaplains were caught up in the bizarre horror. Captain Francis Sampson of the 82nd lost his Mass kit in the depths of an icy marsh. Forgetting the war in his concern for his set of precious sacraments, he dived time and time again until he was virtually exhausted. 'He got it on the fifth try.'[8] Another chaplain of the 82nd, Captain George Wood, was marching on through the night quite alone, snapping his toy signal-cricket merrily, when a weary, cynical voice nearby called out of the darkness,

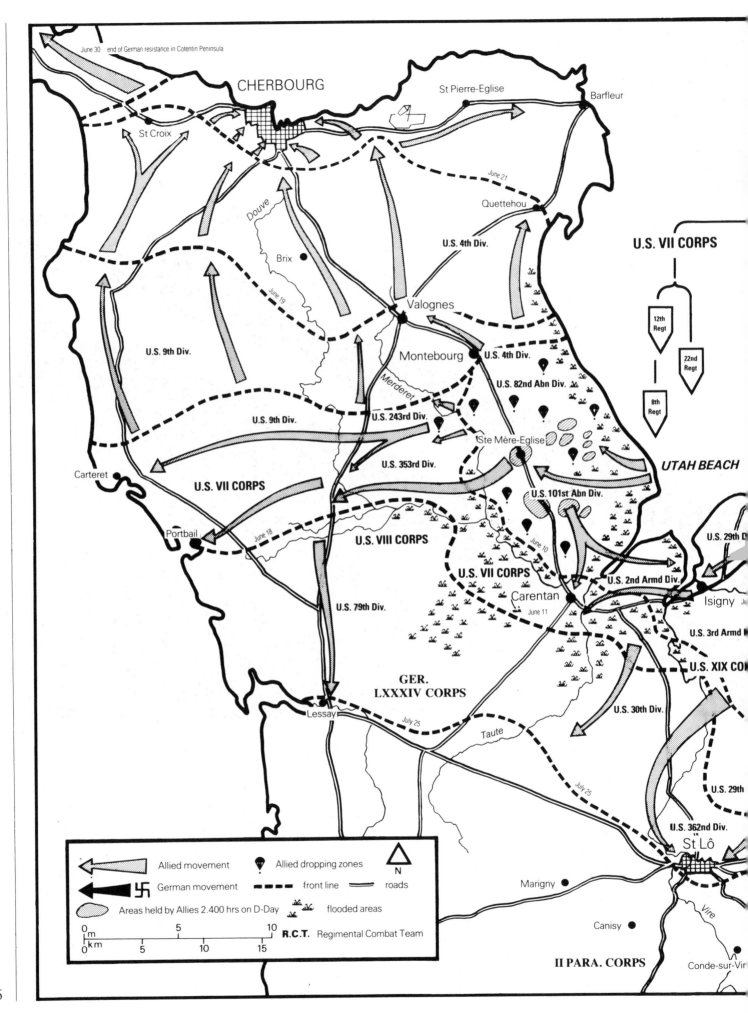

June 30 end of German resistance in Cotentin Peninsula

CHERBOURG

St Pierre-Eglise

Barfleur

St Croix

Quettehou

Douve

June 21

Brix

U.S. 4th Div.

U.S. VII CORPS

Valognes

12th Regt

22nd Regt

June 19

Montebourg

U.S. 4th Div.

8th Regt

U.S. 9th Div.

Merderet

U.S. 82nd Abn Div.

U.S. 9th Div.

U.S. 243rd Div.

Ste Mère-Eglise

UTAH BEACH

Carteret

U.S. 353rd Div.

U.S. VII CORPS

U.S. 101st Abn Div.

Portbail

June 18

U.S. VIII CORPS

U.S. 29th D

June 10

U.S. VII CORPS

U.S. 2nd Armd Div.

Isigny

U.S. 79th Div.

Carentan

June 11

U.S. 3rd Armd

U.S. XIX CO

GER. LXXXIV CORPS

U.S. 30th Div.

Lessay

July 25

Taute

July 25

U.S. 29th

U.S. 362nd Div.

St Lô

Marigny

Canisy

Vire

Conde-sur-Vir

II PARA. CORPS

Allied movement

Allied dropping zones

N

German movement

front line

roads

Areas held by Allies 2.400 hrs on D-Day

flooded areas

0 m   5   10
km
0   5   10   15

R.C.T. Regimental Combat Team

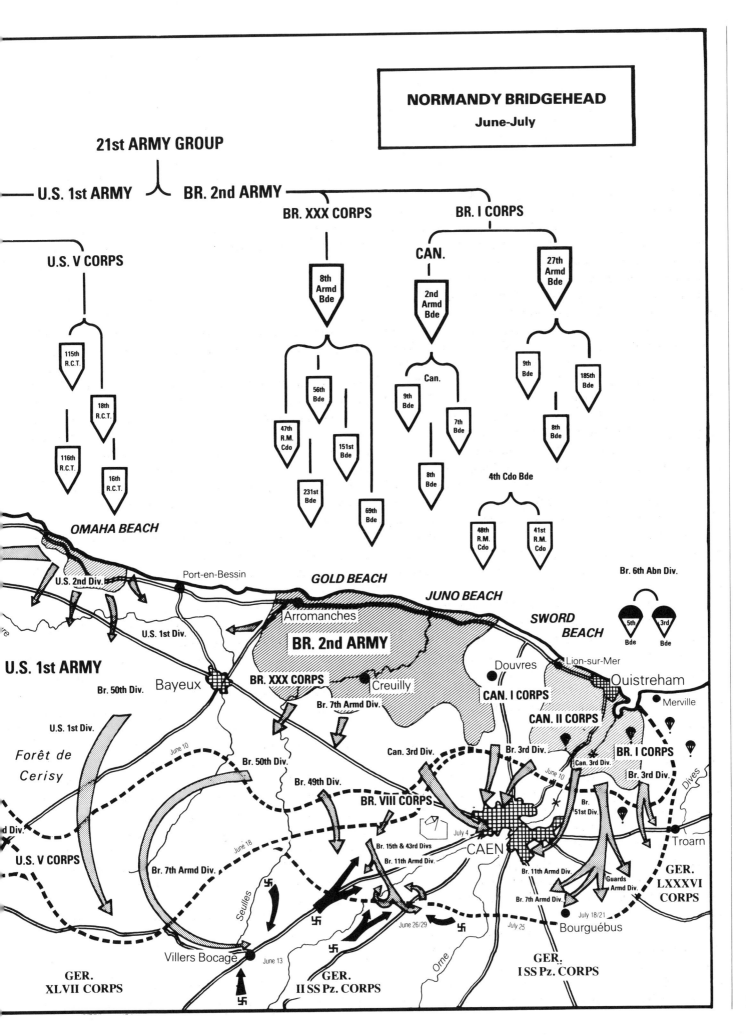

NORMANDY BRIDGEHEAD
June-July

21st ARMY GROUP

U.S. 1st ARMY

BR. 2nd ARMY

BR. XXX CORPS

BR. I CORPS

CAN.

U.S. V CORPS

8th Armd Bde

2nd Armd Bde

27th Armd Bde

115th R.C.T.

18th R.C.T.

56th Bde

Can.

9th Bde

185th Bde

116th R.C.T.

16th R.C.T.

47th R.M. Cdo

151st Bde

9th Bde

7th Bde

8th Bde

231st Bde

69th Bde

8th Bde

4th Cdo Bde

48th R.M. Cdo

41st R.M. Cdo

OMAHA BEACH

Port-en-Bessin

GOLD BEACH

JUNO BEACH

Br. 6th Abn Div.

U.S. 2nd Div.

Arromanches

SWORD BEACH

5th Bde

3rd Bde

U.S. 1st Div.

BR. 2nd ARMY

Douvres

Lion-sur-Mer

Ouistreham

U.S. 1st ARMY

Bayeux

BR. XXX CORPS

Creuilly

CAN. I CORPS

Merville

Br. 50th Div.

Br. 7th Armd Div.

CAN. II CORPS

U.S. 1st Div.

Can. 3rd Div.

Br. 3rd Div.

BR. I CORPS

Forêt de Cerisy

June 10

Br. 50th Div.

Can. 3rd Div.

Br. 3rd Div.

June 10

Dives

Br. 49th Div.

BR. VIII CORPS

Br. 51st Div.

Troarn

July 4

U.S. V CORPS

June 18

Br. 15th & 43rd Divs

CAEN

GER. LXXXVI CORPS

Br. 7th Armd Div.

Br. 11th Armd Div.

Br. 11th Armd Div.

Guards Armd Div.

Seulles

Br. 7th Armd Div.

June 26/29

Orne

July 18/21

Bourguébus

Villers Bocage

June 13

July 25

GER. I SS Pz. CORPS

GER. XLVII CORPS

GER. II SS Pz. CORPS

'For God's sake, Padre, stop that damn noise!' – and startled him out of his skin.[9]

In a way, the 101st was luckier than its running-mate the 82nd and was able to form up earlier. The 101st was scheduled to land on six DZs around the small Norman town of Ste. Mère-Eglise – the first part of France to have the dubious honour of being 'liberated' that June morning. It was an occasion few men who witnessed it would ever forget.

The first and last thing that many ill-fated 'Screaming Eagles' heard as they left their planes was the incongruous sound of the village's church bell tolling above the vicious snap-and-crackle of small-arms fire. A building in the main square had been hit by an incendiary, and the paratroopers now found themselves drifting helplessly down, not only towards the inferno itself, but towards a hail of gunfire directed at them by the local German garrison.

Lieutenant Charles Santarsiero was standing in the door of his plane as it roared over Ste. Mère-Eglise and looking down at the Place de l'Eglise, 'could see fires burning and Krauts running about. There seemed to be total confusion on the ground. All hell had broken loose. Flak and small-arms fire was coming up and those poor guys were caught right in the middle of it.'[10]

One paratrooper exploded in mid-air. His bag of grenades had been struck by a bullet. Desperately, others of his stick twisted and tugged at their shroudlines to avoid the same fate. But one by one they were picked off by the German sharpshooters below. The Germans could hardly miss, for the Americans were silhouetted a clear, sharp black against the flames from below. Man after man slumped dead in his harness, dead before he had been able to fire a single shot.

The British of the 6th Airborne Division were faring a little better, but not much, with one of their battalions, the Canadian, dropping straight into the swamps. At dawn they were only able to muster a single company. Colonel Otway's 9th did little better, losing six hundred men to the swamps and the sea. With only a hundred and fifty men left, Otway wondered whether he could now carry out the assignment for which the 9th had trained so long – the capture of the all-important German gun-battery at Merville. Just then appeared Otway's batman, Wilson, a former boxer and professional valet – excellent qualifications for a para-colonel's batman. Always the perfect servant, he produced a small flask and proffered it to Otway as if it were a decanter on a silver salver. 'Shall we take our brandy now, sir?' he asked. That seems to have decided Otway; he went on to the attack.[11]

Some had it quite easy, however. Para-medic James Byrom had landed safely, and as he was known to speak some French, was ordered by a huge paratrooper armed with a Sten gun to check out a nearby peasant's cottage: 'You speak the lingo, tosh,' the huge paratrooper said, 'all right then, you go up and knock on the door and we'll give you coverin' fire. I'll stay 'ere and my mate'll creep around the other side of the yard so's to cover you proper.'

Feeling like some pre-war English tourist on a walking tour, an embarrassed Byrom knocked on the door. It was opened immediately by a peasant woman. Politely, Byrom said: ' "*Excusez-nous, Madame. Nous sommes des parachutistes anglais faisant partie du Débarquement Allié.*" ' The reaction was immediate and surprising. Unlike one Norman woman who felt so strongly about her 'liberation' that she was discovered sniping US positions and had to be shot by American GIs, this woman made the invaders exceedingly welcome. Kisses, cognac and potent local calvados rained down on Byrom and his new-found mates. Knocking back the free booze in the warm, candle-lit farm kitchen, watched by an admiring farmer and his family, the paras were able to forget the war – for a while.[12]

Now they were almost all down, and each man was rapidly adapting to his unfamiliar, sometimes terrifying environment. Private Steele of the 82nd Airborne hung by his parachute from the church steeple at Ste. Mère-Eglise, tolling the bell involuntarily as he did so, feigning death in full view of the Germans firing down in the square. Lt. John Walas, clicking his signal-cricket, walked right into a lone German guarding a machine-gun. For a moment the two of them stared at each other in horror, then the German reacted. He fired his rifle. At that range he couldn't miss. The slug hit his hand. Next instant 'both men turned and fled.'[13] Corporal Schuyler Jackson, his outfit lost, sat with a dying US officer, talking about home and a hundred different things – anything but the battle raging all about them. After a while, Jackson offered the unknown officer some morphine. 'I've taken some already,' the officer replied. A few minutes later he died.[14]

Now everywhere the survivors of that great parachute drop waited for the dawn, and for the great seaborne follow-up force which was on its way – 176,475 soldiers and 21,651 vehicles. The paras knew that if that mighty force failed to land successfully, their own fate would be sealed; for they were far too deep inside German-held territory to fight their way out now.

Major-General Richard Gale, commander of the 6th Airborne, had the honour to be the first British general to land in Normandy, and if he was worried that day as dawn started to break, he didn't let it show. Ruddy-faced, six foot three in height, ramrod-straight with a bristling white moustache that gave him the air of a Poona colonel – which he wasn't – he rode up on a borrowed nag and was heard half-declaiming to his staff. ' "*And gentlemen in England now a-bed/Shall think themselves accurs'd they were not here.*" '[15]

That morning the corny old tag from Shakespeare seemed appropriate.

Now the invasion fleet was coming in for the landing: two British, one Canadian and two and a half American

American assault troops nearing Omaha beach.

divisions. Some of the men talked, some smoked, some still vomited into their bags of greaseproof brown paper. Overhead, great 15-inch shells roared hideously by with a sound of tearing canvas, while on the shore the pall of brown smoke was stabbed here and there by scarlet flames and the cherry-red flicker of answering enemy cannon. Spouts of angry white water vomited upwards. Machine-gun bullets ripped the length of the foreshore. Everywhere the green water was littered with débris: ration boxes, opened cans, abandoned equipment, men floating face downwards in their rubber Mae Wests, nudged back and forth by the swell.

With a lurch the first blunt-nosed landing craft hit the beaches. Soldiers sprang out, sometimes chest-deep in water, rifles held aloft. They fell and quickly rose again – not all of them, for the white tracer from the dunes beyond was already sweeping the beaches in vicious arcs – and plunged to left and right as they had been taught in those months of training, while the German machine-guns stuttered frenetically, pouring slugs at them at a tremendous rate. Panting for breath, the invaders hit the wet sand, blundering their way through the metal stakes – some with grenades attached, and known as 'Rommel's asparagus' – twisting and turning in a frenzy of anxiety, waiting for the first amphibious tanks to come waddling out of the water and clear a path through the mines ahead.

These 'DDs', or 'Donald Ducks', were ordinary Shermans with inflatable canvas screens wrapped around them; connected to their engines were two propellers which drove them through the water. Already they were floating in to shore, their commanders standing on a platform behind the turret, while the rest of the tank was under water. Some were struck by shellfire and disappeared for good, taking their crews with them, but many made it and began their climb up the beaches, shedding their 'water-wings' as they went. Closely following them were tight clutches of infantry, showered by pebbles and sand, but hanging on for grim death, knowing that this was the only way they would get through the minefields.

Alan Moorehead, watching from off-shore, noted that 'the whole scene looked at from this distance was toy-like and unreal.' Although four or five ships were already burning furiously and German shells were falling everywhere, from his relatively secure vantage-point, the operation 'lacked the element of danger or excitement, even of movement.'[16]

However, Robert Capa, *Life* photographer, already snapping his first photographs, thought differently as his landing craft struck the beach. 'The boatswain who was in an understandable hurry to get the hell out of there mistook my picture-taking for explicable hesitation and helped me to make up my mind with a well-aimed kick to the rear!'

Capa plunged into the icy water, plodded through the

shallows with bullets flying everywhere, and took shelter with a GI. From the protection of one of the steel obstacles, the soldier was firing at random into the drifting smoke. But somehow 'the sound of the rifle gave him enough courage to move forward and he left the obstacle to me. It was a foot larger now and I felt safe enough to take pictures of the other guys hiding just like me.'[17]

But there was no hiding on Omaha Beach, where the US 1st and 29th Divisions were coming in to land. There, things had gone wrong right from the start. While still in the water, the leading companies came under withering fire from the crack 352nd German Division. Almost immediately all order was lost and panic broke out. 'As the ramps are lowered, men leap into waist-deep water, slip and fall and drown; are hit and sag; wade through neck-deep runnels toward the terrible sands; shrink and cower, diving to escape the undiscriminating fire.'[18]

Now it was every man for himself. Hiding on the shingle or ducking under the waves in a vain attempt to avoid the slugs zipping everywhere, their uniforms soaked, leaderless and shaken, the men of the first wave had lost all thought of their objective. According to the divisional history, 'A' Company, 116th Infantry, had become 'inert, leaderless and almost incapable of action' within minutes of landing. 'It had become a struggle for survival and rescue.'[19] Within the first hour there were hundreds of casualties. There were now over a thousand men – infantry, engineers, seamen – on the five-mile stretch of what would later be known as 'Bloody Omaha'. Yet most of them seemed so shaken that they made no attempt to escape from that stretch of lethal sand and up the cliffs beyond.

The veterans of the Big Red One performed little better than the 'wet noses' of the 29th Division. They were held up by a line of rusting barbed wire. No one attempted to cut through it until a lieutenant of engineers and a wounded sergeant came crawling up to the bogged-down infantry. They inspected the fragile obstacle, then, standing upright, hands on hips, a contemptuous look on his face, the unknown lieutenant stared down at the cowering doughboys and barked: 'Are you going to lay there and get killed or get up and do something about it?' Nobody moved. The officer cursed, and with a last scornful look at the soldiers, he and the wounded NCO went back to the wire. Alone, and mindless of the burning white tracer whizzing over their helmeted heads, the two of them cut a path through it, then disappeared.[20]

There were other such nameless heroes on Omaha. The engineer second-lieutenant who crawled through the shingle and wet sand under fire, probing for mines with a trench knife. The infantry officer who assaulted a strong-point with grenades, then handed over his maps and compass to an NCO as he lay in the bloodstained sand, dying. The medic who rushed into the smoke, heedless of the bullets and mines, in a bid to rescue a wounded man – and died in the attempt. Yes, there were a few such men, taunting, cursing, bullying, tongue-lashing their fellows into action. But for the most part, the infantry were hopelessly

(Below) American troops met stiff opposition when landing on Omaha beach.

(Right) US Army infantry disembarking on Omaha beach on D-Day

bogged down. As the fog of war thickened over Omaha, the proud 16th Infantry, which had fought at Gettysburg, the Argonne, in North Africa, Sicily and Salerno, lay on the corpse-littered beach and let itself be wasted away.

Astonished by the strength of the German defence, some began to think the day was lost before it had even started. Technical Sergeant William McClintock came across a lone soldier who seemed quite unaware of the machine-gun fire ripping across the beach and sending up spurts of sand all around him. He sat at the water's edge throwing stones into the waves like some farmboy by his local duckpond and 'crying softly as if his heart would break.'[21]

The US 4th Infantry Division landing at Utah Beach had it better. According to one report, the troops 'yelling like Indians,' waded ashore against little opposition, their rifles held high above their heads. Such was the slowness of the German response that PFC Donald Jones, coming in in the second wave, thought it was like 'just another practice invasion', and PFC Ray Mann remembers feeling 'a little let down.'[22] But many of the young soldiers of the 'Ivy League Division' were too seasick and miserable to care either way – nor were they aware of the terrible punishment their buddies were receiving on Omaha. On board one assault boat bound for Utah, *Newsweek* correspondent Kenneth Crawford recalled seeing a young GI covered with vomit and shaking his head in disgust: ' "That guy Higgins," he said, "ain't got nothing to be proud of about inventing this goddamned boat!" '[23]

Now the German gunners were finally beginning to react, and dead bodies were piling up on Utah beach. As Colonel James Batte led his ashen-faced men through the heaped-up corpses, he heard one of his doughboys comment unfeelingly, 'Them lucky bastards – they ain't seasick no more!'[24] Captain Mabry, running behind a soldier also covered with vomit, ducked just as a mortar bomb landed on the unfortunate man. He gasped as he felt a stinging blow in the stomach, thinking he had been hit by a splinter. Instead, when he looked down, he found that he had been struck by the dead man's severed thumb.[25]

Now the German fire was intensifying. Lieutenant Francis Riley of the US Coast Guard, who had been ordered to 'disembark the troops on time regardless of casualties,' was forced to steer his vessel past sinking landing craft and drowning GIs who implored him to take them aboard. But Riley couldn't stop – only listen to the 'anguished cries for help from wounded and shocked soldiers and sailors as they pleaded with us to pull them out of the water.'[26]

But there were moments of grim humour even amidst the tragedy. As Captain Robert Cresson of the 8th Infantry started to move his men off Utah Beach, an excited GI ran up to him and gasped breathlessly, 'Sir, sir! I have two women over there!' 'Where?' Cresson snapped, surprised to find women in the middle of the battle. 'In a ditch ...' The GI pointed in the direction of a long furrow in the dunes. 'What the hell are you doing with two women in a ditch?' Cresson barked, other things on his mind. 'I don't want them to get shot,' the soldier replied, red-faced. Cresson was wondering what action to take when a sergeant with a lecherous grin on his begrimed face asked, 'How old are they?' That did it. Cresson didn't want anything of *that* kind distracting his company. Hurriedly he ordered the two terrified Frenchwomen to be led to safety.[27]

Now as the second, third and fourth waves began to disembark, the survivors of the first wave started to move off inland. Following them, Thomas Treanor of NBC noted that there were dead men along the narrow path that led up the cliffs. Suddenly a voice at his side said, 'Watch yourself, fellow, that's a mine!' The speaker was a 'soldier sprawled on the bank ... he had one foot half blown off.' Now, while he waited for the litter-bearers, he kept warning those who followed of the dangers. Treanor looked down at the man, who 'looked very tired but perfectly collected.' 'What you need is the "medics",' he said. 'Yeah,' the wounded soldier countered. 'But how're they goin' to get up here?'

Treanor saw what he meant; the single path was so clogged with men and so heavily mined as to be impassable. The engineers would have to clear it before the medics could reach the dying soldier. Treanor turned and took a 'last look at the greatest armada in history' and then

(Left) An injured American soldier has his hand bandaged by a medical orderly.
(Right) American soldiers level their machine guns to protect their buddies engaged in road building in France.

plodded on after the doughboys. Behind him, the soldier with the shattered leg slumped back into the sand, apparently resigned to his fate.[28]

In spite of the relatively light opposition on Utah, there was panic there too. But not for long, for Utah Beach was dominated by a very strong personality that day: Brigadier Theodore Roosevelt, at fifty-seven, the oldest man there and already suffering from the heart condition that would one day kill him. Roosevelt's divisional commander, General 'Tubby' Barton, had remarked just before they had sailed from Torquay that he never expected to see Roosevelt alive again. Yet here he was, stumping back and forth along the beach, map in hand – just as if 'he was looking over some real estate,' as an admiring sergeant of the 8th Infantry commented later.[29]

Suddenly the third wave of infantry came under severe German artillery fire. Eighty-eight-millimetre shells began landing everywhere. Great whirling plumes of sand shot into the sky. Acrid, choking smoke was everywhere. Fist-sized, red-hot pieces of shrapnel cut the air. Seconds later a terrified GI who had thrown away his equipment and helmet, his contorted face black with smoke, came running back, babbling incoherently. Roosevelt recognised the symptoms instantly. He had seen plenty of action in North Africa and Sicily before being relieved of his

command in the Big Red One on a charge of insubordination. He knew just how quickly panic could spread. Hurriedly the big, heavy-set general put his arm around the trembling youngster. ' "Son," he said gently, "I think we'll get you back on the boat." ' Tamely the boy allowed himself to be led away.[30]

A little later, Roosevelt, judging that the beach was now secure, turned to Colonel Eugene Caffey of the 1st Engineer Special Brigade and told him to get word to the Navy to bring in the rest of the 4th Division. Caffey nodded. Roosevelt adjusted his equipment, his heavy red face set in determination under the steel helmet. 'We're gonna to start the war from here,' he growled, and set out for the heights.[31]

As they went out at Dunkirk, so they came in now: with style, ceremony and studied nonchalance. It was a front, naturally – it always was; but the men in khaki, British and Canadian, had waited long years for this moment and they were going to make the most of it, despite the horrors that lay ahead on the smoke-shrouded beaches.

Lord Lovat's commandos went in to the wail of the pipes, played by the Laird's own piper. Major 'Banger' King of the East Yorks, who would be killed in action before the campaign was over, read the famous eve of Agincourt speech from Shakespeare's *Henry V* over the loud-hailer as his barge went in. Hunting horns sounded. Here and there a sword was waved. Naturally they sang, too: *Why are we waiting? We don't know where we're going, Roll out the barrel*, and that celebrated polka stolen from the Czechs by the Germans and from the Germans by the English in 1939, *For the gang's all here*!

This particular gang of British troops belonged, not to the Guards or any of the fashionable Home Counties regiments, but to the dour North Country battalions of the veteran 50th Division and the unfashionable county regiments of the 3rd Infantry Division – the East Yorks, the Green Howards, the South Lancs, the Hampshires and the like. Even the cavalry involved, the 13/18th Hussars, wasn't a particularly famous or fashionable regiment. But in the past they had all served their country well, and in the great blood-lettings of the First World War they had paid the butcher's bill often enough. Now, as their barges swept towards the beaches, they were prepared to do so again.

The Canadians of the 3rd Infantry Division were no different. Like the Tommies of their British namesake, 'the Iron Division' (the *British* 3rd Division), they were inexperienced in battle; but they too had waited for four long years for this moment and, like the British, they had a score of their own to settle: the bloody defeat of the

Troops waiting to go forward after landing in Normandy on D-Day.

Canadian 2nd Infantry Division at Dieppe back in 1942, which had cost the men of the Maple Leaf some six thousand dead, wounded and captured.

The Canadians' second crack at Hitler's *Festung Europa* proved no less costly. Later, a padre of the North Shore Regiment recalled: 'The beach was sprayed from all angles by the enemy machine-guns, and now their mortars and heavy guns began hitting us. Crawling along the sand, I had just reached a group of three badly wounded men when a shell landed among us, killing the others outright. As we crawled we could hear the bullets and shrapnel cutting into the sand around us ... A ramp had been placed ahead of us against the sea wall now. Over it we went ... two stretcher-bearers ahead of us stepped on a mine ... Half dazed we jumped down again behind the wall.'

A sergeant of the British Royal Engineers, whose task was to lift those mines, watched as the Canadian infantry rushed the beach along the side of the River Seulles. 'We got to the top of a rise (when) I saw my first German. He was alive, but not for long. These two Canadians behind me ... went up through this opening in the sea wall ...The Jerry came out of the emplacement with a Schmeisser. I thought, Christ! They haven't seen him ... But they just

didn't stop running. They just cracked their riflebutts down on the German and that was that!'

One of the Canadian companies in the first wave lost half its men in the first five minutes. Machine-gun fire swept their ranks, leaving the shore littered with dead and dying men in the greyish-khaki of the Canadian Army. Artillery fire began to descend on the survivors. The driver of a buttoned-down Sherman tank panicked. In an attempt to escape the murderous fire, the driver thrashed his way along a line of crouching Canadians, crushing them to a bloody pulp under the flailing tracks. Captain Daniel Flunder of the Marine commandos, who had gone in with the Canadians of the 8th Infantry Brigade, yelled at the top of his voice, 'They're my men!' But the tankmen didn't react. Enraged, Flunder beat the hatch with his swagger – to no avail. In the end he resorted to desperate measures. He pulled out a grenade and blew off the Sherman's left track. That finally put an end to the slaughter.[32]

But the Canadians weren't the only ones to be butchered. Able Seaman Ashworth of the Royal Navy was with one of the LCTs which had brought the Canadians ashore. Now he saw some Canadian infantrymen leading six German prisoners into the sand dunes. He ran towards them, hoping to get himself a German helmet as a souvenir of the great day. When he reached the dunes, the Canadians had vanished, but the Germans were still there, 'all lying crumpled up.' He turned the first man over, determined to have that helmet – and gasped with shock. The man's throat had been slit from ear to ear. It was the same with the remaining five. Young Ashworth turned away, 'as sick as a parrot', and as he recalled later, 'I didn't get my tin hat.'[33]

It was the first recorded war crime of the campaign. But it wouldn't be the last. Before the invasion of North West Europe was over, all of the Allies, British, French, American, Dutch, Poles, – and naturally the enemy, too – would be killing their prisoners in cold blood.

On the Ouistreham half of Sword beach, the bodies of the men of the 2nd East Yorkshire Regiment formed a khaki carpet from the water's edge right up to the cliffs. It was estimated that two hundred of them were killed or wounded within the first few moments of their landing on the 3rd Division's beach. 'We'd expected casualties,' one private recalled, 'but nothing like that. The lads were going down on all sides. Hardly out of the boats and they were scuppered. By hell, it was something!'[34]

Private John Mason of the 4th Commandos, who landed half an hour after the East Yorks, was shocked to find himself 'running through piles of dead infantry who had been knocked down like nine-pins.'[35] Another commando coming in with Lord Lovat's HQ at roughly the same time, recalled seeing bodies 'sprawled all over the beach, some with legs, arms and heads missing, the blood clotting the wet sand.'[36] Lance-Corporal C. Morris of the same headquarters recollected; 'Everyone was now sitting very quiet and kept looking at each other and making efforts to smile; but it was all very forced and tense, though we knew that we should be all right once we started to land and had something to occupy our minds.'[37] Corporal Fred Mears, following the East Yorks in, charged up the beach, determined to make 'Jesse Owens look like a turtle.' He, too, was shocked to see that the East Yorks had failed to spread out and had consequently been slaughtered by the hundred. But as he told himself, somewhat unfeelingly, 'they would know better the next time.'[38]

Of course, there would be no 'next time' for the young men of the East Yorks. Soon households all along the East Coast from Hull to Scarborough would be receiving the same official buff-coloured telegram from the War Office, beginning with the words, '*We regret to inform you that ...*' A little later this would be followed by a small brown parcel from OFFICER I/C RECORDS, containing a note that read: 'Late 1066,775 Pte. X, Personal Effects of, forwarded,' listing all that was left to signify the passing of yet another young Englishman: '*One leather diary dated 1944. One piece of broken shaving mirror. One comb ...*' Finally came a record of the amount of money found on the body after the looters had finished with it. '*Five French francs and 1s 1d in cash ...*'

Lieutenant Douglas Grant, who came in with the first wave that day, recalled plunging into the water among falling shells and immediately finding himself in the thick of things on the beach.

I found a disorganised group of engineers crouching in a deserted pill-box and, as I passed to see if I could not break through the wire at that point, an enemy sniper put a bullet clean through the skull of a man lying at length, and, as he imagined, in safety, on the sand. We began to run through the gap I had seen on the right. The men floundered in the loose sand under their top-heavy loads of ammunition and I ran up and down the line yelling them on with every curse I remembered ... Other troops with the stupidity of sheep, were digging in along the length of the wire; they had not sense enough to realise that the enemy would blast it as conscientiously as a drill routine. One man, sitting upright as if he was alone on the sands, clutched his knee and wept over the bloody mess ...[39]

Some British formations were lucky. They were off the beach in record time, thanks to their toughness, training and to Hobart's 'funnies', which had cleared the way for them – and which General Bradley, incidentally, had been rash enough to refuse for 'Bloody Omaha.' The Dorsets, for instance, were off and marching inland within forty minutes. The Green Howards, too, cleared the beach in less than an hour, though they had a fierce fight on their hands, for a while. One of their number, Company Sergeant-Major Stan Hollis, a tough thirty-one-year-old combat veteran went on to win the Victoria Cross for his exploits on D-Day – the only man in the whole

British stretcher bearers taking cover.

British-Canadian force to win the empire's most coveted award that day.

Most of the attack formations, however, took severe losses initially, just like the East Yorks. The 1st Hampshires, for example, were slaughtered at the water's edge. One of them, Private George Stunnel, saw men going down all about him, but spotted a Bren gun carrier, undamaged, in about three feet of water, its engine still running, and its driver 'frozen at the wheel, too terrified to drive the machine on to the shore.' Stunnel pushed the driver to one side and drove the little vehicle ashore, only to be pitched violently to the sand as a German sniper's bullet whacked into the tin of duty-free cigarettes in his blouse pocket. 'Minutes later, he discovered that he was bleeding from wounds in his back and ribs. The same bullet had passed cleanly through his body.'[40]

Company Sergeant-Major Bowers of the Hampshires, a regular like Hollis, having witnessed the slaughter of the first two companies, tried to advance with his major and a handful of survivors to attack one of the pill-boxes which were inflicting the hellish casualties. Soon, however, there were only four of them left against four German machine-guns and an 88mm cannon, and Bowers had no choice but to crawl back to report to his CO. He found him lying in the sand, badly wounded in the arm. 'What, Bowers – you still alive!' the colonel exclaimed. 'Just about, sir,' the CSM replied, and told his CO about the pill-box. The colonel absorbed the information and then, somewhat to Bower's dismay, ordered him back to the fray to knock out the German position. Bowers, however, dutifully went, and against incredible odds, eventually succeeded in taking the pill-box and putting an end to the slaughter. His reward: a nice pair of soft German jackboots in place of his own too-tight British Army ammunition boots; Bowers' feet had been killing him all morning![41]

Now, however, the survivors were beginning to clear the beaches, leaving the dead behind them. In some areas the carnage had been appalling, the casualties unimaginable, and the beaches were strewn with men of the Hampshires, the East Yorks, the South Lancs, cut down during the crazy rush up the beach, killed before they could fire a shot in anger. Now their sack-like, stiffened postures told the whole tragic story. Some sprawled extravagantly in the sand, fists clenched; some were little more than bloodstained bundles of tattered khaki, caught up in the rusting wire.

Yet in spite of the cost in human lives and misery, many *had* survived and were now pushing inland, cursing and jostling each other, faces grey with fear and fatigue as they slogged their way down the narrow, dead-straight country roads of Normandy. Those fortunate survivors would remember this June 6th to the end of their days, with pride and even with fondness. Indeed, some D-Day veterans, like D.I. Henry of New Malden, Surrey, would look back on it as 'the only worthwhile achievement' in the whole of their lives.[42]

Now 'Bloody Omaha' was the only one of the five Allied beaches not yet taken. Both assault regiments of the 1st and 29th US Divisions had suffered a thousand casualties a piece there, one-third of their effective strength. But slowly order was being restored. At first it was the nameless heroes who attempted to sort out the chaos; the private who took command of a Sherman tank while its commander skulked in fear behind a foxhole; the Sherman commander who regained his courage sufficiently to join the private in the attack; the captain, shot through the cheeks, who continued to fight and give orders to his men;

the wounded medic who scuttled from one doughboy to the next, sprinkling their wounds with sulphur powder and checking if they had taken their wound pills, before finally collapsing in the sand from loss of blood ...

But now men with names began to take charge: Captain John Finke had sprained an ankle in the landing and was reduced to limping along on a stick; but he nonetheless ordered his men into the attack, and when they refused to rise, used his stick on their backs until they did.[43] Colonel Charles Canham of the demoralised 116th Regiment of the 29th Division was shot through the wrist, but refused to be evacuated. Instead, he stayed with his badly shaken doughs until he could get them moving again.[44]

Colonel Thornton Mullins' 3rd Field Artillery Battalion had suffered complete disaster during the landing, its guns sinking beneath the waves. But Mullins was undaunted. Above the crackle of small-arms fire and the thunder of the ship's artillery, he was heard to shout: 'To hell with our artillery mission. We've got to be infantrymen now.' Twice wounded, his clothes soaked, he pushed forward to the attack, before finally a German sniper claimed him.[45]

Still the crisis wasn't over on Omaha. At noon, Major Stanley Bach, a liaison officer from the Big Red One attached to the 29th Division, scribbled a note on his pad to be despatched to the top brass who were watching the attack from the cruisers off-shore. It read: '... Beach high tide, bodies floating. Many dead Americans on beach at HWM* ...'[46] How General Omar Bradley reacted when he read those words on board *USS Augusta*, we do not know. But perhaps it crossed his mind to reflect that his soldiers had paid a high price at Bloody Omaha for his disdain for Hobart's 'funnies' and his contempt for British 'under-confidence and over-insurance.'

Undoubtedly the slaughter on Omaha would have been considerably worse had it not been for the bravery of one man. On the evening of June 5th, the night before the invasion, General 'Dutch' Cota, the big, burly assistant divisional commander of the 29th Infantry Division had told his staff, 'You're going to find confusion. The landing craft aren't going in on schedule, and people are going to be landed in the wrong places. Some won't be landed at all ... We must improvise, carry on, not lose our heads.'[47]

From the start of the landings, Cota realised that everything he had said the night before had come true. There *was* total confusion and many people *had* lost their heads – and were still losing them. Tracer was zipping everywhere, and the German mortar shells were erupting with vicious roars, sending up spurts of angry yellow flame all along the beach. But Cota was unperturbed by it all; having already decided that he would die that day, he waded into the chaos with fatalistic determination.

Ahead of him, a Ranger battalion had stalled before a fortified hill bristling with German guns. Cota immediately rallied them and urged them forward, shouting 'You men are Rangers! I know you won't let me down!' They didn't. Five hundred of them stormed the hill and took it.[48] Cota

*High Water Mark.

Moving off the beachhead.

pushed on. A sea wall barred any further progress. He ordered a machine gun to be placed on it, supervised the blowing of the barbed wire fence beyond, and then sent more troops into the attack. A first man ventured forward into the smoke billowing up from the burning grass, only to be ripped apart by a vicious burst of machine-gun fire. 'Medico, I'm hit, help me,' he screamed, as he fell writhing to the ground. He died the next instant, with the word 'Mama' on his lips. Cota himself darted forward. Nothing happened; the unseen German machine-gunner had directed his attention elsewhere. This encouraged the rest of the infantry, who moved forward and dropped into enemy-dug slit trenches. An obscene moan. Mortar bombs began to drop all around Cota and his party. Three feet away from the big general, two GIs were hit. Cota now ordered his little command to move forward once more. Obediently they did so. A German rose from a hole and threw a grenade. It exploded harmlessly. Next moment the GIs raced forward and slaughtered the lone German in his foxhole. Five Germans came forward, with hands raised. Fire rained down on them. Two of the Germans were killed there and then. The remaining three died in short order,

whether at their own gunners' hands or those of the GIs, no one knew.

'Norman Cota penetrated inland on this day, D-Day, to a point the American front-line as a whole would not reach until two days later. He would get a Silver Star and the Distinguished Service Cross from the Americans, the Distinguished Service Order, the second highest British medal, from Montgomery, and a "hell of a bawling out" too – from the army commander, Bradley – for getting too far out in front.'[49] Generals weren't supposed to risk their necks; that sort of thing could be safely left to the dog-faces.

There were now 2,500 dead, wounded and missing Americans on Bloody Omaha,* and by nightfall on June 6th, they would be joined by another 4,000 similarly dead, missing, wounded or captured Americans taking part in the invasion elsewhere, plus 3,000 British soldiers and 1,000 Canadians.

*These are estimates. In the confusion, no accurate figures were available.

But slowly the invasion forces were moving off Bloody Omaha, spurred on by men such as Colonel Charles Canham of the 116th Regiment. With a bloodstained handkerchief wrapped around his wounded hand, Canham was heard to call to his shocked, scared men, 'They're murdering us here. Let's move inland and get murdered!' One of his listeners, PFC Ferguson, looked up as Canham went by and was heard to ask: 'Who the hell is that son of a bitch?' All the same, he rose obediently with the rest and followed the slightly crazed colonel.[50]

At the other end of the beach, where the veterans of Sicily and Salerno were finally pulling themselves together, Colonel George A. Taylor of the Big Red One's 16th Infantry stomped up and down the lines of prostrate doughs, who were still hugging the embankment, disorganised, suffering casualties from mortar and artillery fire. Oblivious to the enemy fire, Taylor raged at his men over and over again, until they finally moved. ' "Two kinds of people are staying on this beach," he yelled, "the dead and those who are going to die! Now let's get the hell out of here." '[51]

3 THE END OF THE BEGINNING

'Have You Killed Your German Today?'

Slogan appearing daily on the front page of the US Army newspaper *Stars and Stripes*, during the summer of 1944

A British casualty being carried back to a regimental aid post for treatment.

Now the infantry, British, Canadian and American, plodded inland along the dusty, poplar-lined roads of Normandy, keeping to either side while the tanks and long lines of trucks laden with supplies and ammunition rattled past them to the front. Overhead, the air force provided a constant umbrella of fighters for their protection, but the sky remained empty of enemy planes.

Many of the ground troops had gone through hell on the beaches, and there was worse to come. Every day the US Army alone evacuated two thousand seriously wounded men to the UK. On one occasion General Bradley viewed the dead bodies of eleven thousand of his own men.

Dusty, weary and sodden with sweat, they marched to the sound of the guns, bent under the weight of their equipment and weapons, while the summer sun blazed down remorselessly overhead. There were thousands of such straggling columns now, looking from the air like so many giant worms. The British infantry marched with Woodbines half-smoked behind their ears and brown enamel mugs hanging from their packs, and were always ready for a 'spit-and-a-draw' and a 'brew-up'. The Americans, for their part, chewed gum mechanically, like cattle chewing the cud. After a while the men had learnt to ignore the thunder of the heavy guns or the snarl of aircraft engines – they presented no danger. But even in their weary state, they were constantly on the alert for the abrupt hiss of machine-gun fire or the harsh, dry crack of a sniper's rifle; both could mean sudden death.

All who marched through Normandy that summer – and survived – were struck by the beauty of the countryside. The grass was lush and seemed a deeper green than back in England. Everywhere the fat black-and-white Norman cows grazed lazily, undeterred by the noisy mass of men and machines pouring by, or by the dead animals which lay beside the shell-holes, their bellies swollen and their legs sticking out so that they looked like tethered barrage balloons. There were wild flowers everywhere, and those among the plodding infantrymen whose sense of beauty hadn't been altogether crushed by army life stuck yellow buttercups or white umbelliferae into the camouflage netting of their helmets as they marched ever closer to the *boom-boom* of the guns.

Sometimes, too, they sang as they went. '*Now this is number one, and I've got her on the run/Roll me over, lay me down and do it again ...*' They sang of '*Madamoiselle from Armentières who hadn't been fucked for thirty years ...*'; about the spider which approached little Miss Muffet while she was sitting on her tuffet: '*... He whipped his old bazooka out and this is what he said;/There's big balls, small balls/Balls as big as yer head;/Give 'em a twist around yer wrist and swing 'em right over yer head ...*'; and naturally that old, old song with its mocking refrain: '*What did yer join the army for? Yer must have been fuckin' well barmy ...!*' As for the veterans of the Big Red One, they sang a newer ditty about 'Dirty Gertie from Bizerte,' who 'hid a mousetrap beneath her skirtie' – with predictable results.

As far as possible the Allied soldiers fraternised with the newly 'liberated' French – especially if they were femle and pretty. By means of sign language, rude but explicit gestures made with thumb and two fingers, and the few phrases they had learnt parrot-fashion from the little book of basic French they had all been given before the invasion, they constantly tried, as the GI parlance of 1944 had it, to 'get into the pants' of the local girls.

A few were successful. In one town, men of the US 6th Armored Division were fortunate enough to find what they called a 'cat house' staffed by willing 'ladies of the night'. Eventually a corporal of the 44th Armored Infantry Battalion had to be sent to roust his comrades out of the brothel and back into the war. But his buddies were far from eager to trade sex for combat. The corporal, one Bob Brooke, was told to 'go to hell and move out without us.' His CO alerted the divisional MPs, but when the policemen knocked on the door of the brothel, they were astonished to be greeted by a 'soft voice' (according to the divisional history) and told: 'Come in quick, honey, and quietly shut the door.' The MPs were not amused. Moments later the startled doughs were being chased from beneath the sheets and back to the fighting.

For the great majority of the infantry, however, there was precious little time for such pursuits. They had to be content with fleeting and more mundane contact with the people they had come so far and paid so dearly to 'liberate'. To their surprise, they found that many of the French weren't particularly eager to be set free from the Nazi yoke. Contrary to the propaganda fed to them for years by Hollywood and the popular media back home, the French weren't all starving, nor were they all patriots burning for revenge against their German oppressors.

The Germans had, for the most part, been surprisingly '*korrekt*'. Soon indeed, French newspapers, censored as they were, would be comparing the behaviour of German troops favourably with that of the Allied soldiers – with some reason, too. In the case of Cherbourg, for example, the first big French city captured by American troops, the GIs used their weapons indiscriminately against civilians, which, according to the official report of Normandy Base Section, understandably 'created an unfavorable impression.'[1]

That was putting it mildly. By August, special military police battalions were in operation just behind the front to prevent rape, pillage and general misbehaviour directed against the French. Later, after increased incidents in September and October, Eisenhower was forced to order the execution of military personnel guilty of crimes against French civilians, and to ordain that these executions should be carried out near the scene of the crime and in the presence of the civilians concerned. According to Eisenhower's chief-of-staff Bedell Smith, discipline was so bad in the 101st and 82nd Airborne Divisions that in November the Supreme Commander was even contemplating public hangings for offenders, 'particularly in the case of rape.'[2]

Many high- and low-ranking observers of the French scene that summer noted the frosty reception accorded to the liberators. US General Leroy Lutes, after inspecting the situation in the ETO,* wrote in his diary, 'The French now grumble ... that the Americans are a more drunken and disorderly lot than the Germans and hope to see the day when they are liberated from the Americans.'[3] Lt. John Eisenhower, the supreme commander's son, newly graduated from West Point and on a tour of the front, wrote after visiting the British sector: 'The attitude of the French was sobering indeed. Instead of bursting with enthusiasm they seemed not only indifferent but sullen. There was considerable cause for wondering whether these people wished to be "liberated".'[4] And Chief of the Imperial General Staff General Sir Alan Brooke noted with displeasure, 'The French population did not seem in any way pleased to see us arrive as a victorious army to liberate France. They had been quite content as they were, and we were bringing war and desolation to their country.'[5]

Churchill, as ever, was more realistic. As he remarked after visiting Normandy: 'We are surrounded by fat cattle, lying in luscious pastures with their paws crossed!'[6]

Fat cattle indeed! Correspondent Alan Moorehead, following the troops into Bayeux, the first French city liberated by the British, asked politely for food at a local café. The repast they were served contained none of the ubiquitous rubbery powdered eggs, whalemeat or spam on offer in London's restaurants these many years. Instead, the correspondents were fed soup, omelettes, steak, vegetables and cheese, accompanied by a dry Sauterne and washed down with genuine Armagnac. Next to

*European Theater of Operations.

A flying officer buys onions from a French family.

Moorehead, a civilian with 'a round oily face' was lunching with a pretty girl. He turned to Moorehead and offered him the use of his car, which, he proudly claimed, was waiting outside with a full tank of petrol. Later, as Moorehead and his colleagues drove through the streets of Bayeux with the man and his girl, they found themselves pursued by shouts of '*Les deux. Collaborateurs!*'[7]

The infantry plodding forward under their heavy loads were only vaguely aware of these undercurrents; there were other things on their mind besides the attitude of the newly-liberated French to themselves and their former, now vanished occupiers. Lieutenant Douglas Grant, however, entering the shattered town of Troan with his company and looking for snipers, came across

a doll swinging from the iron support that had once held up a shop sign over the pavement. It was made in the form of a young girl. Her neck was in a noose and her head was realistically twisted over her left shoulder. Her draggled black hair trailed across her shut eyes, and the pallor of her waxen skin was made more livid by the dribble of crimson blood that was depicted flowing from the corners of her mouth. The body was dressed in a thin black silk dress such as a street-walker

might have worn, which, hanging in tatters down her bare legs, had been ripped and soiled. It was the image of a murdered girl … and with some diabolical power, it suggested all the muffled terror of a hunt, a capture, a rape and a slow murder.[8]

A puzzled and somewhat shaken Grant pressed on with his search for German snipers lurking in the smoking ruins of the abandoned French towns; but the image of the hanging doll haunted him. Probably it had been intended as a warning to the local girls of what would happen to them if they were found associating with their late occupiers.

For the troops now fighting their way inland, life was composed of sudden alarms and bursts of violent action, set against a background of hours of long, relentless foot-slogging. They existed in a strange limbo, a world cut off completely from civilian life, either back home or here in France.

Naturally they had their own language, unintelligible to the outsider. They spoke of 'chow' and 'sacktime'. Good guys were 'high' on their 'TO' (table of organisation). Bad

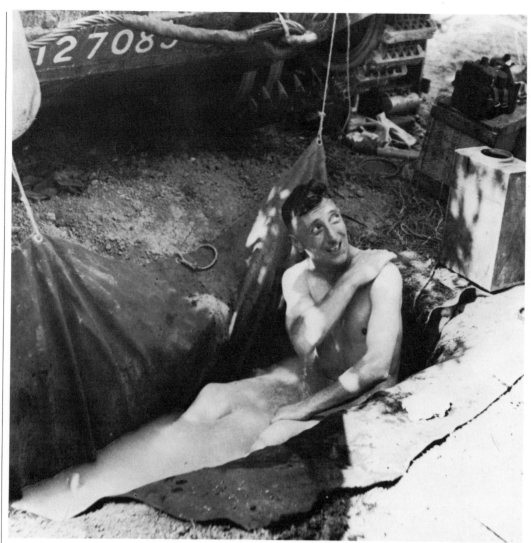

(Left) Taking a bath in a groundsheet. (Right) British troops take a rest in Douvres on their way to the front line.

guys or 'sad sacks' were told to go to the chaplain to get their 'TS slips' (tough shit slips). 'Java' was coffee; 'shit on shingle' was chipped beef on toast, and 'Hitler's secret weapon' was the sickly-sweet D-Bar, so named because of the dire effect it had on the bowels. Situations were categorised as 'SNAFU' – situation normal, all fucked up; 'TARFU' – things are really fucked up; and 'FUBAR' – fucked up beyond all recognition!

The Tommies were less inventive; but then they already had a special language dating back to the days when British regulars were accustomed to getting 'their knees brown' in the far-flung corners of empire. For them, 'dolali' was crazy, 'wallah' a man, 'bints' girls, 'doby' washing, 'bondhook' a rifle, 'gildy' quick, and 'char' was that indispensable beverage without which the average soldier couldn't or wouldn't fight – tea!

But they also invented new phrases. 'Armoured pig' was spam, 'zig-zag' was drunk and 'jig-jig' copulation. Anything stolen was described as 'liberated'. When they went to perform their natural functions in the fields and woods, they took 'a spade for a walk', because they used their entrenching tools to bury the faeces. Indeed, the long-suffering soldiers of all the Allied armies were constantly wielding their spades; they dug holes to defecate in, sleep in, eat in – and sometimes to die in.

Whenever they stayed in one spot for any length of time, they excavated regular pits for latrines, placed long poles or branches suspended between empty ammunition boxes above them, and then, in deference to the French civilians who might be offended by the sight of so many naked rumps, surrounded them with sacking screens. When they left, they filled the holes in with lime, and occasionally, with that cynical, macabre humour they all seemed to acquire after the landings, placed a rough wooden cross over the disturbed earth. More than once a Tommy or GI returning to the rear areas would be amused to find flowers placed there by a pious Norman peasant, mistaking the abandoned cesspit for the grave of an Allied soldier.

And they dug holes to cook in. Even today, forty years later, it is possible to follow their progress across France and into Belgium by the trail they left behind: shallow indentations in the earth that were once foxholes, and abandoned rusting cans with traces of olive-drab paint still clinging to them. In the forests of the Belgian Ardennes where so many thousands of men would fight and die, those rusting cans still lie concealed beneath the leaves, together with foxholes and gunpits which once formed the front-line, marking the scene of some long-forgotten, hard-fought action.

They cooked, if they were British, on 'Tommy cookers,' or

over cans filled with a mixture of soil and petrol which, when stirred to a porridge-like consistency, was supposed to give a long-lasting flame. If they were Americans, they heated the cans with the greaseproof cardboard containers in which their rations were packed.

The British ate 'Compo' (composite) rations: cans of 'M and V' (meat and vegetable) stew; 'Soya links,' triangular soya-bean sausages fried in the grease they came in; fat bacon wrapped in greaseproof paper, which could be unrolled like a sheet; and naturally, 'bully'.

Corned beef was the major component of the 'Compo ration,' together with 'Compo tea', a crude ready-mix of sugar, milk and tea. The beef could be eaten cold on 'dog biscuits', the iron-hard Compo issue biscuit (bread being rarely available); it could be fried as fritters, cooked as a hash, made into a stew with potatoes and onions 'liberated' from some unsuspecting French farmer's field, and even pulped with the 'dog biscuits' to make a kind of crude meatball. Even the available girls were categorised according to the number of tins of 'bully' it took to win their favours.

'Char' served to wash the meal down, and was particularly prized when transformed into 'sarn't-major's char' with the help of a can of evaporated milk; this was a thick, rich, creamy, dark-brown concoction in which a spoon would stand upright, and as the name suggests, it was usually reserved for senior NCOs. GS rum, issued half a mug at a time each day to the men in the line was a great comfort too. It brought tears to the soldier's eyes, and in due course removed the lining from his stomach too. Invariably, when the 'Compo' ration cases were opened, some wag would crack the same weary old joke: '*Which tin's got the cunt in?*'

American rations had been scientifically worked out by some nameless genius in Washington and were calculated to give the GI some 3,500 calories a day; but the average dogface was less than enamoured of them. A fruit bar for breakfast, washed down with a drink made from lemonade powder, followed by a Hershey bar, or worse, 'Hitler's secret weapon,' was hardly the kind of diet that prepared the soldier to give his all.

Officially, the US Army was 'dry' – unlike the British and Canadian. But no official decree could stop the doughboys from getting their hands on spirits during their progress through France. They drank everything and anything: home-brewed Norman calvados; crude, captured German *Korn*; cheap, strong *pinot*, and, where possible, high-class champagne. Everything was sold on the black market in return for 'sauce' and 'booze'; regimental insignia, Hershey bars, cans of spam and hash, even weapons. Some men spent the whole of the Normandy campaign in an alcoholic stupor.

Cattle being evacuated from the battle zone in Normandy. Note that the divisional insignia markings have been censored.

In the French town of Pontivy, for example, Combat Command 'B' of the US 6th Armored Division captured 1,000 cases of cognac and over 100,000 litres of red wine in large wooden casks, plus hundreds of other bottles of wine. The word spread through the CCB like wildfire. Corps ordered the booze to be handed back to the French, but most units managed to hang on to the precious find. One unit reckoned it 'would do our small detachment for the duration of the war.' In the event it was gone in sixty days. But there would be more, much more to come.

'*Pissed last night, pissed the night before/Gonna get drunk tonight, like we've never been drunk before,*' the Tommies sang as they marched down those roads to battle – and they meant it.

As they retreated eastwards, the Germans left behind them their suicide squads: machine-gunners, bazooka teams armed with the deadly one-shot German *Panzerfaust*, and above all, their snipers. Snipers – how they were hated by the Allied soldiers!

Tied to their trees, draped in camouflaged nets or canvas sheets the same colour as wood bark, their rations and ammunition strapped to the bough below, they would wait until some unwary Tommy or *Ami* appeared, preferably one on his own or some lone officer, still inexperienced or fool enough to display his insignia openly. Then they would level their high-velocity telescopic rifle and watch as the unwitting candidate for sudden death appeared in the centre of that circle of gleaming calibrated glass, his helmeted head neatly dissected by the cross wires. A soft crack like a dry twig snapping underfoot in a wood on a hot summer's day – and yet another invader would crumple to the ground.

The snipers inflicted some of the worst casualties. As a member of the US 30th Infantry Division's medical staff reported, in great clinical detail:

The sniper's finger presses the trigger, and the bullet passes through the helmet, scalp, skull, small blood vessels' membrane and into the soft sponginess of the brain substance in the occipital lobe of the cerebral hemisphere. Then you're either paralysed, or you're blind, or you can't smell anything, or your memory is gone, or you can't talk or you're bleeding – or you're dead.

If a medic picks you up quickly enough, there's a surgeon who can pick up the bullet, tie up the blood vessels, cover up the hole in your head with a tantalum metal plate. Then, slowly, you learn things all over again, whether it's talking, walking or smelling.

But if the bullet rips through your medulla region in the back of your head (about twice the size of your thumb), or if it tears through a big blood vessel in your brain – then you're dead, buddy![9]

The Big Red One, which had suffered so heavily on Omaha, refused on principle to take snipers prisoner when they surrendered – which in most cases they did, having taken their toll in blood. 'Could have taken four yesterday easily, but preferred to kill them,' remarked General Huebner, the 1st Infantry Division's commander, to his chief, General Hodges of the US First Army.[10]

Sergeant William McPherson, a veteran of the North African campaign fighting with the 51st Highland Division, had just seen two of his platoon shot down by snipers when the Germans came in, 'kamerading'. 'My finger itched to pull the trigger, but it would have been too much like murder. I felt I had to work off my temper somehow, though, so ... I told them I was going to murder them just as my friends had been ... To lend some truth to my story, I had them dig and they broke down. They didn't know they were digging temporary graves for British and German dead.'[11] A month later, Sergeant McPherson was shot dead while leading a patrol of the Gordon Highlanders – ironically, by a sniper!

Colonel Martin Lindsay, commanding another battalion of the Gordons, was also engaged in a running fight with the hated snipers that month. A first officer was hit, and then another. As he ran round in circles distraught with pain, he was hit again and killed. An officer and Company Sergeant-Major Muir went after the hidden Germans. The officer shot two, and Muir shot another, 'though not until he had received a nick in the neck, a bullet through his battledress blouse and a third bullet had hit his rifle.' Finally, just after a hard-pressed Colonel Lindsay had dealt with the snipers, a German mortar opened up, inflicting further casualties and bringing the total to five officers and forty-six other ranks 'for a most ineffective day's work.'[12]

Corporal Tom Galeen of Wigan described to BBC man Chester Wilmot how he went hunting for the hated snipers that month. 'We were told ... to clear the church steeple, but we couldn't get at it, so I took my PIAT* into the upstairs bedroom of the house opposite, stuck it up on the window-sill, and let fly at the tower. The bursts knocked half the top off. And later we found twelve dead Jerries up there; some had been killed by our stens and the piat had got the rest.'

Galeen's colonel, who was present, asked if the church had been badly damaged; Galeen said no: 'We just knocked the top off; we wouldn't have touched it if the snipers hadn't been there. And when I went in, sir, I did take my hat off.'[13]

And still the push went on, the infantry growing fewer and fewer, being fleshed out all the time by green replacements now swarming ashore in their thousands to fill the gaps in the ranks of the rifle regiments. Many hardly had time to nod hello to their new buddies and commanders or even to discover which formation they belonged to, before they too

*A primitive kind of British anti-tank bazooka.

became casualties.

Long afterwards, General 'Dutch' Cota, hero of 'Bloody Omaha,' stated: 'This [the replacement system] was a cruel system, probably necessitated by the nature of the war ... and I never liked it. Men had a right to go into battle as members of a trained unit, flanked by friends and associates, and, if possible, led by leaders who have trained them and whom they have come to trust. To thrust an individual, no matter how well trained as an individual he may be, into battle as a member of a strange unit is in my opinion expecting more than many men are capable of giving.'[14]

One day in the near future, General Cota would have the unique experience of being the first general officer in the United States Army since the Civil War to supervise the public execution of one such frightened replacement: a man called Eddie Slovik, who couldn't stand the strain, and deserted – and later had the doubtful honour of being the only one of his kind to be shot since 1865.

Now the strain was beginning to tell. The fatigue, the lack of sleep, the constant danger were beginning to take their toll. James Jones, a writer and ex-infantryman himself, recalls a friend who had refused to hike any more. After being court-martialled and spending thirty days in the stockade, he had still refused to march another step. In the end, to save him further problems, his CO had compromised and made him a driver. Now, even when he had to go to the latrine, a matter of perhaps fifty yards away, he would *drive* there in his jeep. As Jones commented: 'He had made his separate peace.'[15]

Others resorted to much more drastic measures to avoid combat. Some rubbed diesel into their chests in order to produce an incurable rash which would result in their being sent home. Some shot off their fingers. Some concluded mutual self-mutilation pacts, shooting off each other's toes at a distance in order to avoid the tell-tale powder burns which revealed that a wound was self-inflicted; others solved the same problem by firing at themselves through a sand-bag or a loaf of bread. Older men simply 'lost' their false teeth – for according to the 'Book', a man who couldn't eat properly couldn't fight. By the time the supreme commander came to make his first tour of inspection of the Normandy front, he was shocked to find that one hospital contained over one thousand cases of self-inflicted wounds!

The reason for the increase in cases of combat fatigue and self-inflicted wounds was, apart from natural cowardice, simple: the doughs were being kept in the line too long. In the Great War, the average infantryman could expect to be in the trenches for ten days or so before being relieved. This time, the US replacement system ensured that divisions kept going all the time, despite heavy losses, week after week, month after month, without a break for 'R & R'.* Back in Washington, far from the firing line, the

*Rest and recuperation.

57

gurus of modern psychiatry had decreed that the average infantryman could stand over two hundred days in combat before he cracked up. Few GIs ever reached that unrealistic target.

That summer, several hundred air crew of the England-based Eighth US Air Force deliberately aborted their missions over Germany and landed their Fortresses and Liberators in neutral Switzerland or Sweden, there to be interned for the rest of the war. More and more ordinary GIs, too, started to 'go over the hill,' or as the British Army had it, 'on the trot.' Voting with their feet, they simply abandoned their outfits and vanished into the surrounding foreign population. In one notorious case, a sergeant of Cota's 28th Infantry Division deserted from the line and escaped to Paris, where he bought forged papers which took him to London. There he bought a further set of forged papers which took him to his home in Chicago, where he spent the rest of the war in safety until the surrender in the summer of 1945.

Naturally, such escapades were not confined to the US Army. The British and Canadian Armies had their share of incidents, too, though their long-established 'county' regiment system, whereby men from the same area fought in the same battalion, made for more cohesion than in the US Army, which was recruited on a kind of conveyor-belt system.

In the British Army, for example, there was the case of a certain battalion of the green 49th Infantry Division. The division had spent much of its service in Iceland, hence its divisional sign depicting a polar bear. In Normandy, however, it had suffered heavy losses, and in this particular battalion only twelve officers remained after two weeks in action, the CO and every rank above that of corporal at battalion headquarters having been killed. Two companies had lost all their officers save one. Thus it was hardly surprising that the survivors acted hysterically when they came under renewed heavy shelling. Discipline had collapsed. The NCOs and officers had taken off their badges of rank. The battalion commander, a lieutenant colonel, reported to Montgomery: ' "I have twice had to stand at the end of a track and draw my revolver on retreating men ... Three days running a Major has been killed ... because I have ordered him to help me in effect stop them running during mortar concentrations." And then he said: "I refused to throw away any more good lives." '

Montgomery withdrew the battalion as unfit for battle. 'I consider,' he wrote, 'the CO displays a defeatist mentality and is not a "proper chap".'[16] Undoubtedly, that particular officer's personal file was later stamped with those ominous three letters in red ink: 'LMF' – Lack of Moral Fibre.

Others in the British Army of Liberation had their nerve broken in a different way. Captain William Douglas-Home, scion of an ancient Scottish ducal family, future playwright and brother of a Conservative Prime Minister-to-be, was serving in Normandy as a captain in the 141st Regiment, Royal Armoured Corps, which was

**Exhausted American
troops.**

(Right) A British stretcher
bearer attends to a
wounded German.
(Below) Three wounded
soldiers from Invasion
Beachheads.

At this point Waddell made the decision that would cost him his command. He let Home go.

Home himself later confessed to having a 'latent tendency to exhibitionism'. Now he allowed it full rein. In an attempt to expose the general in command of the attack, he wrote a letter to the *Maidenhead Advertiser*, explaining what had happened that day.

Scandal resulted. Waddell was dismissed from his regiment. Home was arrested, court-martialled in the Belgian city of Ghent, and subsequently sentenced to one year's hard labour. As things turned out, the world hadn't heard the last of William Douglas-Home. But it had of Colonel Waddell, who now disappeared into obscurity, leaving one of his officers, young Andrew Wilson, wondering what would become of the 141st Regiment, which 'was his handiwork' and which he had worked for nearly two years to build up.[17]

In the same week as William Douglas-Home refused to take part in the attack on Le Havre, a young American replacement for Company G, 109th Infantry Regiment, 28th Infantry Division, twenty-four-year-old Private Eddie Slovik was digging a hole with twelve other replacements outside the French town of Elbeuf, currently under attack by the 28th. The town was defended by a handful of retreating SS men and as usual, they were putting up fanatical resistance.

It was the replacements' first night under fire; but while most of the other twelve would overcome their fear and disappear into decent obscurity in due course, Slovik's first night and the events that followed it would propel the undersized soldier into the limelight and turn him into a *cause célèbre* which would occupy America for years to come. Indeed, they would even make a film about him.

With Slovik was his new-found buddy, Private Tankey, who described later what happened that night: 'We were all separate and it was dark and more shells started to come over and I really started digging like I never dug before. Shells started to drop near me, what a feeling, and I was really scared. Yes, I prayed, too, and it lifted the shelling, and I thanked God. Then the moon came out and I was laying flat on the ground in my hole, looking at the heavens with the clouds around ...'[18]

When dawn came at last, Tankey and Slovik discovered that they were the only replacements left; the rest were either dead, or had gone off in search of their company. The two young greenhorns, however, had no such desires; they had already seen enough of 'combat'. They attached themselves to – of all units – the 13th Canadian Provost Corps, a military police outfit which toured the countryside on a roving mission, nailing up notices in French detailing the provisions of Allied Martial Law.

That summer Slovik and Tankey had a fine old time, driving up and down the coast of France and Belgium, cooking for the Canadians, trading cigarettes and coffee on the black market in exchange for prize hams, and also,

equipped with the 'crocodile', a fearsome flame-throwing tank that could squirt lethal flame seventy or eighty yards. In August, Captain Home was ordered by his CO, Colonel Waddell, to co-ordinate a tank and infantry attack on the German-held port of Le Havre, which at the time was still packed with French civilians. Previously the German general in charge had asked for a truce so that the civilians could be evacuated, but this had been rejected by the British commander. As a result, if the attack went ahead, the French would be subjected to an all-out air bombardment by the Royal Air Force which would plaster Le Havre before the infantry and tanks moved in.

Home – who shortly before had written to British newspapers protesting that near Bayeux British fighters had shot up a column of German ambulances · clearly marked with the Red Cross – refused to carry out his CO's order.

Colonel Waddell, a humane man, told him to do as he was told, but still Home refused: the civilians, he insisted, had to be safely evacuated first.

The argument continued, with the colonel still showing considerable forbearance and merely remarking a little wearily to Home, 'I suppose I should have known that under the circumstances this was bound to happen.' Waddell then told Home to go to the squadron sergeant-major and arrange transport for the attack, if nothing else. But again Home declined, insisting that he would take no part in the attack at all.

apparently, obtaining willing French girls for the MPs – all with no questions asked by the Canucks and no information volunteered as to precisely how these two Yank infantrymen had come to be attached to the Canadian first Army.

But all too soon Eddie Slovik's happy time out of war came to an end. Military justice caught up with him, and eventually he faced the firing squad in the snows of the Vosges Mountains – claiming to the last that he was being done to death for no other reason than because he had 'stolen a loaf of bread'* when he was twelve.[19] Slovik learned the hard way that there was no escape from the grim reality of combat. It was kill or be killed – even for deserters.

Now the battle for Normandy was in full swing, and the enemy were fighting back desperately. The casualties in the Allied armies were mounting steadily and would continue to mount. Slovik's division, the 28th, to take but one example, would have a complete turnover of its strength by the end of the year. In some Canadian divisions, casualties were so heavy that the turnover was nearly 300 per cent.

Mostly, death came quickly. The crack of a sniper's rifle, the hiss of a high-rate machine-gun, the obscene belch of a mortar bomb, the shriek of an 88mm shell – and suddenly one more victim would be clutching a shattered limb, face ashen with shock, eyes wild and staring. '*Stretcher-bearer ... Medic ... Aidman!*' the hoarse voice would cry, and soon others would be on the scene, ripping at the tattered khaki with knives, pressing home syringes that looked like toothpaste tubes with pins at the end, sprinkling on sulphur powder and applying thick, clumsy yellow pads with their khaki-brown bandages.

Boxlike ambulances would appear, on their front a little sign that read: '*Priority One – carrying casualties.*' The wounded man would be strapped inside and off he would go, jolting across the churned-up fields, moaning at every lurch and bump, to arrive at the forward dressing stations, where harassed doctors in bloodstained overalls worked under the hissing white glare of petroleum lanterns, cutting, slicing, excising, patching, ensuring that their patients survived the next stage of their long journey.

Here, wound tags would be pinned to their uniforms, morphia dosages and other medical details pencilled on their creased foreheads, and then they would be off again, carried ever westwards in a strange white haze, their noses full of the smell of disinfectant and faeces, only dimly aware of the moans of the others packed in with them.

Later on, more senior doctors would attend to them, feeling their pulses, ripping off their clotted dressings, sniffing at the gaping wounds for the cloying stench of gangrene. A few would be given the coveted 'red disc,' which meant, for the Tommies, at least, that they had received a 'Blighty wound' and would be sent home. Soon

their relatives would be receiving a War Office telegram marked *Priority* and would no doubt worry themselves sick.

Not so the more seriously wounded. Mostly they spent the next days in a drugged sleep. Those with broken limbs were often roped up in strange postures; all were swathed in great bloodstained sticky dressings smelling of foetid broken flesh. Moaning and groaning, they would relive their battles, screaming whenever they heard the high-pitched whine of the vacuum-cleaner or floor-polisher, then slipping off into a fearful, quivering slumber once more.

US Army PFC Coffin, a fitting name for an ambulance driver, told a reporter from the US Army newspaper the *Stars and Stripes* that 'the first guy we ever hauled from the front ... had his brains wrapped in a bandage.' But after that Coffin didn't 'remember them any more. They're just a lot of faces to me,' he added, 'and some of them don't even have faces.'

Coffin claimed that he personally hated Krauts and liked

*Eddie Slovik had graduated from reformatory to prison as a young man: a fact which mitigated against him when Eisenhower considered his plea for clemency later.

(Above) SS troops on the invasion front. (Right) A German soldier lies dead beside his rifle where he fell during the German retreat in Normandy.

to hear them 'groan and whimper, because I've seen what they've done to our boys.' But he also told the reporter: 'The queerest thing in this whole ambulance job is the time you haul both Krauts and doggies in the same load, and you think that they were both shooting at each other maybe a half an hour before.'[20] His buddy PFC Muehlfelt remarked, 'There's not much you can say to the guys. You can't tell a guy who has a leg shot off that it's a rough deal. He knows it.'[21]

That summer, *Time* correspondent Mary Walsh, Hemingway's latest love, visited Normandy, where she saw her first dead American lying in a ditch. Walsh recorded that the corpses 'were beginning to give off the smell of vinegar and sugar boiling together' such as was given off when her mother had put up 'homemade dill pickles for the winter.'[22]

Later, she went on to visit an American field hospital where doctors in 'blood-spotted coats' operated constantly on seriously wounded GIs. There she saw a boy whose back was covered with shrapnel wounds, lying face down on the table. His voice hoarse with embarrassment, the boy announced to the doctor that he had to relieve himself. Mary Walsh stepped back hurriedly, but the doctor took it in his stride and told the boy: 'That's okay. Everybody does. Go ahead and crap in your pants.'[23]

Afterwards Miss Walsh visited the wards of the tent hospital, noting as she went how terribly alone the wounded and the dying seemed in their anonymity, surrounded by bottles, tubes and medical apparatus. All that linked them to the world outside was the chart above their bed, listing their name, serial number, blood type, and unit. That information represented all that was known of them. No one knew or cared 'which of the bodies had been high school captains or presidents of the local drama club, or hot men on the guitar.' Their individual identity had ceased to be of any account.[24]

American soldiers surveying dead German paratroopers.

'Sure, there were a lot of bodies we never identified. You know what a direct hit by a shell does to a guy. Or a mine,' Technical Sergeant Donald Haguall of the 48th US Quartermaster Graves Registration Company told the Press that summer.

... Or a solid hit with a grenade, even. Sometimes all we have left is a leg or a hunk of arm.

The ones who stink the worst are the guys who got internal wounds and are dead about three weeks with the blood staying inside and rotting, and when you move the body the blood comes out of the nose and mouth. Then some of them bloat up in the sun, they bloat so big that they bust their buttons and then they get blue and the skin peels. They don't all get blue, some of them get black.

But they all stink. There's only one stink and that's it. You never get used to it either ... And after a while the stink gets into your clothes and you can taste it in your mouth.

You know what I think? I think that if every civilian in the world could smell this stink, then maybe we wouldn't have any more wars ...[25]

At this stage in the campaign, those who survived and reached base hospital could at least have the benefit of a woman's care; for now, Canadian, British and American female auxiliaries were arriving on the continent in fairly large numbers to work in the various HQs, in mixed anti-aircraft units (in the case of the British),* and more importantly, in the hospitals.

The first British woman arrived in Normandy as early as D-2. She was twenty-two-year-old Corporal Lydia Alford of the WAAFs, who flew over to tend some eight wounded soldiers, mostly Canadian, who were being evacuated that same day to England. The wounded were reported to be surprised to see women so close to the front. Corporal Alford saw nothing of the fighting, but LACW Sylvia Carter, who followed her the next day, did; her Red Cross plane landed in the middle of a German barrage, and she was forced to take cover with the soldiers until it was time to load up the new casualties.[26]

In the end, many thousand British and Canadian women gained the right to wear the 'France and Germany Star' for wartime services on the continent. Although exact figures for France are not available, of those khaki-clad lady soldiers who marked so smartly off to war, singing '*She'll be wearing khaki bloomers when she comes ...*', 335 were killed, 302 wounded, 94 were reported missing and 22 taken prisoner.**

American women were not slow to follow their British sisters into the front-line, though, unlike the anti-aircraft gunners of the British ATS, they did not take an active part in fighting the enemy. Nevertheless, equipped with GI underwear of a rich, mud-brown colour, plus two girdles and three bras, the American girls came to serve and if necessary to die.

That summer, Second Lieutenant Frances Slanger, a nurse with a forward US hospital, wrote a letter to the *Stars and Stripes*, praising the bravery of her patients. She stated, 'Yes, this time, we are handing out the bouquets ... but after taking care of some of your buddies, seeing them when they are brought in bloody, dirty with earth, mud and grime, and most of them so tired ... seeing them gradually brought back to life, to consciousness and their lips separate into a grin when they first welcome you. Usually they kid, hurt as they are. It doesn't amaze us to hear one of them say, "How are ya, babe?" or "Holy Mackerel, an *American* woman!" or most indiscreetly, "How about a kiss?" '[27]

Nurse Slanger wrote her first and last letter to the

*One such unit was commanded by Lieutenant Colonel Edward Heath, one day to be Britain's Prime Minister.

**Approximately two thousand British women were killed, wounded or taken prisoner in WWII in all three services, with five girls winning the Military Medal for bravery.

Stripes by flashlight in a tent in the middle of a muddy field, 'with our GI drawers at this moment doing the dance of the pants, with the wind howling, the tent moving precariously, the rain beating down, the guns firing ... It all adds up to a feeling of uneasiness.' [28] The young American nurse had good reason to feel uneasy. Soon after she mailed her letter to the army newspaper, she was caught in a German barrage and killed – the first American woman to die in action in the ETO.

The tragic death of that young nurse serves to emphasise the fact that even in hospital, packed with the broken and shattered bodies of so many young men, the hate didn't stop.

Captain Andrew Wilson, now lying wounded in a British Army hospital, awoke one evening to find a stretcher being wheeled in and a 'horribly bandaged' German prisoner being placed in a bed at the far end of the ward. The orderlies then went out, and the new arrival lay motionless, perhaps unconscious. 'Suddenly the door swung open and Alexander, the surgeon, came racing in.' He was wearing service dress, and Wilson had the impression he might have come from a Mess dinner, but he was in a bad mood all the same. Taut with fury, he ordered the nurse to have the German taken away, and when the girl protested that the orderlies had removed the stretcher, replied: 'I don't care ... Get him out of here! I won't have Germans in my ward!' [29]

Para medic James Byrom had a similar experience that summer, when stretcher-bearers brought in a seventeen-year-old German youth, badly wounded in the back and tossing and turning in agony. His arrival coincided with 'a discussion between two doctors about the iniquity of the

Germans.' For some time they continued their conversation, deliberately ignoring the new patient, in spite of the fact that in the opinion of Byrom and the other medics, it was their 'plain duty' to attend to him. Instead, they simply went on talking and 'showed not the slightest flicker of interest.' Politely, Byrom drew their attention to the German youth's condition, but the doctor on duty still showed no concern and simply told Byrom to keep the boy quiet. Byrom did what he could and learned that the boy had been shot while trying to surrender to the paras under a white flag. Finally, the medic managed to get one of the doctors 'to stroll over' and examine the prisoner, but by that time the German's head had fallen to one side and he was dead. The doctor shrugged unfeelingly and ordered him to be taken over to Resuscitation. As they carried him over, one of the stretcher-bearers said: 'It's a bloody shame. A kid like that!'

Before laying the German youth in the makeshift mortuary with the rest of the dead, they went through his pockets and found a love letter from his girl in Mulheim. It read: 'Always thinking of you when I lie down at night. I pray, we all pray, you will come home safely.'[30]

On and on they marched, through the tumbledown grey-stone shattered villages, past the burning, dark-yellow corn, up the steep, wooded heights whose altitudes would pass into the military history books as marking the sites of terrible battles: *113* ... *115* ... *116*. There, many of them would lie buried for ever, their last resting-place marked by an upturned bayonet with a bullet-holed helmet hanging from it, or a crude cross of boughs. Written on it would be their regimental number, followed by those three fateful letters, *KIA* – killed in action.

For the survivors of those early battles, more chaos, confusion and squalor lay ahead; a terrifying, impersonal hell, where metal chased flesh, guns thumped, men shouted and yelled, smoke drifted, and all was submission to the bloody struggle which seemed to have no end save death.

Even for a veteran such as Wing-Commander L. Nickolls of the Royal Air Force, the sight of the infantry going up into battle that summer was moving. As he recalled for a BBC correspondent:

I think one of the things I shall never forget is the sight of the British infantry, plodding steadily up those dusty French roads towards the front, single file, heads bent down against the heavy weight of their kit piled on their backs, armed to the teeth; they were plodding on, slowly and doggedly to the front with the sweat running down their faces and their enamel drinking-mugs dangling at their hips; never looking back and hardly ever looking to the side – just straight in front and down a little on to the roughness of the road; while the jeeps and the lorries and the tanks and all the other traffic went crowding by, smothering them in great billows and clouds of dust which they never even deigned to notice. That was a sight that somehow caught at your heart.[31]

A group of dead German groundtroops awaiting burial at St. Mère Eglise.

4 BREAKOUT

'It's a queer sort of liberation'

Montgomery, describing damage inflicted on French towns by Allied bombardment.

American troops fighting in hedgerows. The man in the foreground is firing a rifle grenade.

'Towards the end of July,' wrote Australian correspondent Alan Moorehead, 'American and British troops were either ashore in Normandy, or about to come ashore. The bridgehead stretched like a drum. Even though a completely new system of roads and ports had been built, the traffic blocks sometimes extended for ten or fifteen miles.'[1] The build-up of men and material was such that the black drivers of the 'Red-Ball Express'* were sometimes forced to drive as much as fifty hours in a stretch to reach front-line units with vital fuel and supplies. A crisis was developing. The Allies would *have* to break out of Normandy soon.

Montgomery, still in charge of both American and British ground forces, chose to attempt to break out by what was termed the 'hinge' of the door at the French cathedral city of Caen; once open, this would allow the Americans to sweep through and out at the German-held town of St. Lô. But for the Americans to do that, they would have to break free of the Norman Bocage, an expanse of lush meadows dotted with apple orchards, from which the locals made their potent apple brandy, calvados. Each of these little rectangular meadows was surrounded by a tall, thick hedgerow, designed like those across the Channel in Kent, to keep the wind off the pastures and the plump cows which grazed on them.

These hedgerows, based on banks of earth three feet high, proved an unexpected boon to the hard-pressed German defenders. The thick bushes and stunted trees provided excellent cover, and the sunken cart tracks which ran alongside were well-suited for trenches. Almost immediately the American attackers reached them, it

*A one-way traffic supply system stretching right across France from the beaches. Trucks travelled along it day and night, and all other traffic was barred from the route.

became clear to them that in this kind of country their advantage in tanks and aircraft was virtually lost. Here it would be an infantryman's war: a slogging match, with the advantage on the German defenders' side.

The terrain allowed the German infantry to use all the skills they had learnt in three years of combat in Russia – especially since 1943, when they had been mainly on the defensive there. Their machine-guns and mortars were sited so that all the gaps in the hedgerows were covered and ranged, and they even went as far as to place ranging sticks out of sight of the attackers, so that even the rawest German recruit would know the exact distance to his target and employ his weapon accordingly. Using the system of fortified 'hedgehogs' which the Wehrmacht had employed in Russia, the defenders would cover a couple of the rectangles, usually not adjacent ones, with an easy and covered escape route already worked out, so that when they finally had to yield to the weight of the American

British infantry attacking from a concealed position near Cagny.

attack, they could fall back to the next field and begin the lethal process all over again.

To attack these hedgerows of the Bocage, the Americans developed what the German defenders called 'chessboard tactics.' They advanced over each rectangle of a hundred by a hundred and fifty yards, using mixed assault groups of engineers, tankers, gunners and infantrymen. While the artillery protected them, the engineers blew gaps in the hedges to allow the infantry to get through. The infantry, protected by tanks, pushed on and seized the field. Then the whole bloody business was repeated.

As a German officer wrote after the war: 'There was really no forward thrust, no attacking movement in these chessboard tactics; all they amounted to was the constant occupation of one small square, previously softened up by gunfire. Even more than the First World War, everything depended on the mechanics of ground fighting, on sledgehammer tactics. Equipment and sweat were more important in the long run than courage and blood.'[2]

Robin Duff of the BBC, observing the fighting in the Bocage that month, confirmed just how difficult the battle was, for, as he reported, 'In the corner of any hedge, or in any one of the incredibly leafy trees, there may be a sniper. There they sit … They chain themselves to the tree, so that they won't fall out if they are wounded and cover themselves with a sort of camouflaged apron, and then wait for men who are alone.'[3]

Another BBC correspondent, Robert Reid, noted how traffic 'both human and mechanical, began to thin out significantly' the closer he got to the Bocage fighting. As he approached the front, an officer stepped out of a hedge and cautioned him to drive his jeep slowly in case the dust drew enemy fire. A little further on he was stopped by another officer, who asked him if he could take back a couple of wounded men. 'One of them was an oficer with a shoulder wound; the other, a youngster from Pittsburg, had been hit in the leg.' They had been wounded while trying to establish a forward observation post prior to yet another attack across those naked Norman meadows. The youngster seemed to be taking it all very calmly. Reid gave him a cigarette as they rumbled slowly back down the sunken, leafy lane. The youngster took a deep, grateful drag and glancing up at the sky, said in a strange, conversational manner, 'Odd, no rain today.'[4]

For all the apparent nonchalance of that young American GI, the fighting in the Bocage was bitter and bloody. As another BBC correspondent, Robert Dunnett, explained to his listeners, the battle was being fought 'in a sort of gigantic shrubbery,' and while the tanks suddenly appeared round corners and engaged each other at point-blank range, all the infantry could do was 'watch and stalk and crouch and wait, and play hide-and-seek for their lives.'[5]

There were just three ways that the US infantry could get through the Bocage country. They could march down the roads between the hedgerows — something which was highly dangerous and not to be recommended to any soldier who valued his own skin. They could attempt to get through the gaps in the corners of the hedgerows; or they could rush the field beyond in a skirmish line. This third method, as one frustrated American infantry officer remarked, 'could have been a fair way of doing it *if* there had not been hedgerow.'[6]

As the same officer explained:

When our men appeared, laboriously working their way forward, the Germans could knock off the first one or two, cause the others to duck down behind the bank, and then call for his own mortar support. The German mortars were very, very efficient. By the time our men were ready to go after him, the German and his men and his guns had obligingly retired to the next stop. If our men had rushed him instead of ducking behind the bank, his machine-gun or machine-pistol would knock a number off. It was what you might call in baseball parlance, a fielder's choice. No man was very enthusiastic about it. But back in the dugout [*i.e.* among the staff] I have often heard the remark in tones of contempt and anger; 'Why don't they [*i.e.* the infantrymen] get up and go?'[7]

That summer, the weary, dirty, unshaven and very often frightened infantrymen lived, fought and died in those dugouts carved into the sides of the hedgerows. Charles Mercer, with an infantry company advancing on St. Lô, described the scene in one such spot, where his own exhausted doughs lay sleeping:

You could not see the sleeping men, but you could hear them. Few snored, but there was much whimpering and moaning, as in a hospital ward. Occasionally one would cry out or mumble a few incoherent words or fart loudly in his sleep. When a man parted his lips suddenly, seeking air, it sounded like a bubble popping. But the worst sound was of men grinding their teeth as they slept. You could not see them, but you could hear them and you could smell them, too. Wet clothing and sweat and the rank smell of dirty wet feet and urine and, here and there along the sunken road, the stench of human faeces. For they had fallen in here about five o'clock and they'd got out their wounded and got in ammunition and cold rations. But they weren't digging straddle trenches or doing all the folderol that the book prescribed, because they had had three days of hard fighting and they were exhausted. They pitched into the places the Germans had left and they slept, for tomorrow they had to go ahead again.[8]

Losses were high in the hedgerow fighting. The 2nd US Infantry Division which tried to take Hill 192, four miles to the east of St. Lô, lost twelve hundred men in three days at their first attempt in June. One month later they were still trying to take it. Not far off, the 29th division also became enmeshed in the tangle of the Bocage, losing all sense of direction and cohesion. In the space of two days it suffered one thousand casualties. On the same front, another US division, the 35th, fared a little better than the 2nd and 29th, but nonetheless suffered an equal number of casualties. In the end, the twelve US divisions involved paid a terrible price for their first attempt to break through the Bocage. In seventeen days they suffered no less than forty thousand casualties, the population of a good-sized town, and succeeded in advancing a meagre seven miles.

This butcher's bill was too high for the US commander, General Bradley. He tried a new approach. He flew to England to confer with the commanders of the Allied air forces. There it was agreed that the Allied bombers would turn their full weight on the German positions in the Bocage, blasting through the hedgerows and at last allowing the infantry to advance. There was, however, a catch: the bombs would be dropping only two thousand yards from the doughs' forward positions. General Vandenberg of the USAAF didn't like the idea, but he was overruled. It was ordered that a massive force of 2,246 aircraft should take part in the operation, plastering an area 7,000 yards wide and 5,000 yards deep.

The day of the great attack, July 24th, began as a fête for the top brass. General Courtney Hodges, soon to command the US First Army, plus General William Simpson, who would command the US Ninth Army, set out for the front in jeeps, accompanied by a large number of war correspondents. With them also was Lieutenant General Lesley McNair and the commander of the Mexican Air Force, who were in Europe 'touring' the war.

By noon the brass were in position. Fighter-bombers came over to mark off the killing ground with smoke flares. A little later, more dive-bombers arrived and started plastering targets only five hundred yards away from where the illustrious spectators congregated. Hodges took it all in his stride. While he waited for the heavy bombers to arrive from England, he invited his guests to coffee in a nearby peasant's cottage. But the great attack ended in failure. The two thousand-odd bombers missed their target altogether, hitting an American ammunition truck, killing seventeen GIs of the 120th Infantry Regiment, and nearly killing General McNair, who was very deaf and had been pushed into a ditch by an aide in the nick of time.

Nothing daunted, the brass tried again. On the next day, 2,400 bombers began dropping 4,000 tons of bombs and the new secret weapon, napalm. This time, the results were even more disastrous. The bombs and napalm landed right on the positions of the 120th Infantry Regiment of General Leland S. Hobbs' 30th Infantry Division.

That July day, the 30th Infantry Division suffered terrible casualties – 111 American soldiers killed outright and 500 severely wounded. Much to the embarrassment of the brass, the high-ranking General McNair was found to be among the dead. Heavy-set General Hobbs approached a begrimed Hodges, who was close to tears, and blurted out, 'We're good soldiers, Courtney, I know … but there's absolutely no excuse. No excuse at all!'[9]

Subsequently Hobbs insisted that there would be no further close-up bombing, as far as his division was

(Above) US armour advances through the Bocage.
(Below) Montgomery with General E.H. Barker, General Crerar (Canadian), US General Simpson and Air Marshal Sir Arthur Cunningham.

concerned at least; Hodges agreed. But in the event, the US Air Force would continue to bomb the 30th Division throughout the campaign. Indeed, in December, 1944, in the Belgian town of Malmédy, men of that unfortunate division would be bombed on *three* consecutive days by their own planes. No wonder the embittered GIs of the 30th Division christened their own Ninth Air Force 'the American Luftwaffe.'

While the Americans attempted to break through the Bocage at such high cost, the Canadians and British had been battering away at the 'hinge' city of Caen for over a month. They, too, had suffered greatly. The Canadians had been the first to make the attempt, launching repeated attacks and, like the unlucky 30th Division, being subjected to successive bombing raids by their own air force. Together with the Poles of the 1st Polish Armoured Division, they had suffered three hundred casualties from such 'shortfalls,' including the commander of the Canadian 3rd Division, who was wounded and had had to be evacuated. Thereafter they had been fought to a standstill by the SS defending the Caen area, suffering a further fifteen hundred casualties, one third of them killed in action. At Caen, Canada bled.

The British took up the challenge. Division after division was thrown in to the attack. The Guards went in and were repulsed after suffering severe casualties. A future Archbishop of Canterbury, Robert Runcie, then a lieutenant in the Scots Guards (and, incidentally, the first Archbishop of Canterbury to fight in battle since the Middle Ages) succeeded in knocking out a German tank, which pleased him mightily. But when he went across to view it, he 'saw four young men dead. I felt a bit sick. Well, I was sick actually.'[10]* Another young Guardee, no less a person than a cousin of the future queen and nephew to King George VI, Viscount Lascelles, one day to be the Earl of Harewood, also took part in the same battle with the Guards Armoured Division, but was less fortunate than Runcie. His tank was shot up and he was left on the battlefield, badly wounded, to be picked up by the Germans and kept prisoner in the notorious Schloss Colditz for the rest of the war.

One by one, Montgomery's inexperienced or 'green' divisions were 'blooded' at Caen. On the morning of June 26th, his 15th Scottish Infantry Division, for example, was alerted for its first battle. It was a dark morning and drizzling miserably. Porridge, soya-links and tea were served to the nervous infantrymen. 'Wads' of cheese and bully beef were handed out as 'haversack rations,' to last them through the long day to come. The men painted their faces green, checked their weapons for the last time, urinated into the hedges and ditches, and waited.

*In later years, when he was approached by anti-blood-sports campaigners and asked if he had ever killed an animal, Runcie would take the wind out of their sails by replying, 'No, I've only killed people.'[11]

76

Canadians firing a Hotchkiss gun.

At 7.30 *a.m.* precisely, 900 guns opened fire with a roar that shook the very ground. Young Lieutenant Robert Woollcombe of the King's Own Scottish Borderers described how the guns 'battered out … with loud, vicious, strangely mournful repercussions' that sent little rashes of gooseflesh running over his skin. 'One was hot and cold,' he recalled, 'and very moved.'[12]

The lead formations moved out into the dripping corn; long lines of cautious young men in khaki, well-spaced and orderly, rifles held at the port, parting the wheat like farmers setting off for a long day's harvesting. In front were the Royal Scots and the Fusiliers; behind, the King's Own Scottish Borderers. All were heading for the positions of the 12th SS, 'the Hitler Youth Division.' Of these German troops, half were teenage volunteers, so young that they weren't even allowed the usual beer rations but were given milk and sweets instead. Their veteran officers, mostly from the élite 'Adolf Hitler Bodyguard' (die Leibstandarte) joked that they were leading a 'baby division.' But as the Jocks of the 15th Scottish – many of whom were teenagers themselves – would soon discover, the defenders of Caen included some very tough babies indeed.

The Scots advanced slowly, keeping close to the creeping barrage, each man wrapped in a cocoon of his own thoughts, when out of the drifting smoke came the first bewildered blond prisoner, dressed in the baggy pants and camouflaged tunic of the SS, with the black ribbons of the Hitlerjugend around his sleeve. He was prodded to the rear at bayonet-point by a grinning undersized Jock. There was a lull in the air bursts. The smoke and mist started to lift. Sullen grey clouds rolled in. The pace quickened. Then came the order they had all been waiting for with a mixture of dread and eager anticipation: 'Rifles at the hip – *safety catches off*!' This was it!

Almost immediately the Fusiliers of that same battalion that Churchill had commanded in France in 1916 were involved in heavy fighting at close quarters for some high ground. Woollcombe's Borderers were whistled up. They charged. Now they stumbled across the first enemy dead – blond, young, suntanned, the flies already gathering around their sightless eyes and open mouths. Somehow they seemed very different from the odds and sods who made up the average British infantry platoon, usually a sergeant major's nightmare with all its different shapes and sizes of men. 'Even in death,' one observer noted, 'there was something frightening about so much fine German manhood.'[13]

One of Woollcombe's platoon shot and wounded an SS man hiding in the corn. He staggered forward, screaming with fear, blood streaming from his shoulder. Flinging himself down at the young officer's feet, he clutched Woollcombe's knees, pleading, 'Don't shoot – don't shoot! Have pity! Don't shoot!'[14]

Naive as he was, Woollcombe thought that in order to strengthen his will to fight, the SS man had been told that the British shot their prisoners. The German knew different. The Canadian 2nd and 3rd Infantry Divisions had fought a tough war against the SS; little quarter had been given. The SS had retaliated in kind. After the war, the commanding officer of the 12th SS, the youngest general in the SS known as 'Panzermeyer' (real name, Kurt Meyer), received twelve years' imprisonment for alleged war crimes against Canadian prisoners.

Now the battle for Caen grew in intensity. All day long the guns thundered. Deadly flame-thrower tanks were brought in to help the hard-pressed Fusiliers. The Germans sent the tanks of the 21st Panzer Division to help the defenders. The fighting grew ever more bitter. Casualties mounted rapidly. One company of the Fusiliers lost three-quarters of its strength and its commanding officer. The SS counter-attacked. The British went over to the defensive. And then, for Woollcombe at least, it was all over: the 15th Scottish Division had been 'blooded.'

Now the Borderers began to squelch through the mud to the rear, while the infantry of the 43rd Division came forward to take their place and enter the crucible of Caen. Woollcombe, however, found that his duties for the day were not yet over. He was ordered to collect the Borderers' dead and bury them. His Jocks had a superstitious horror of touching their own dead, so the job was left to him and a corporal who had volunteered for the task. It wasn't pleasant. He wrote:

They were deadweights, and their faces bored into you. One of them, very fair-skinned with blond hair, had a strange name ending in '-ski'. He was unblemished except for a neat red hole in the centre of the forehead. His blue eyes stared before him in sightless amazement. A trouser-button was open and his genitals showed like wax. Another was a carrier driver whose vehicle had been hit by an anti-tank shell or gone up on a mine. His arms and a leg were in rough splints and his mouth was open, dried like leather and twisted as if in a last shout. Then came the surprised platoon commander, and we covered them over with earth.[15]

A little later a fat padre turned up and tried to give Woollcombe his prayer book so that he could conduct the burial service.* Angrily Woollcombe thrust it back to him and let him get on with it. He walked over to the field littered with the bodies of the SS. Here it was his task to search the corpses for documents and identification.

'They were so unutterably dead,' he wrote afterwards. 'There was no more life in them. The mysteries of the earth were as simple as that. A surge of emotion filled you, and a conviction that life moved on elsewhere after death, and that life was the spirit. The discovery stimulated you, intoxicating, dull and heady, as we marked their graves with their upturned rifles.'[16]

But there was nothing 'intoxicating' or 'heady' about Woollcombe's appearance to the officers who met him when he returned to HQ. Someone said, 'My God! –

*Woollcombe was green, and this was his first battle. Mostly the dead were dropped in holes or slit trenches without benefit of clergy.

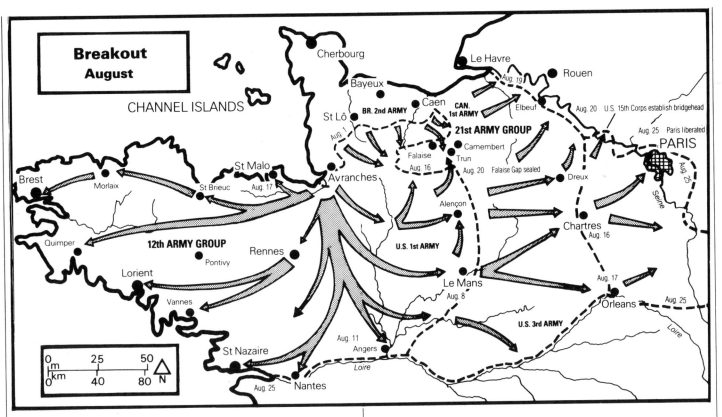

Breakout August

CHANNEL ISLANDS

Cherbourg
Le Havre
Rouen
Bayeux
Aug. 19
Caen
St Lô
BR. 2nd ARMY
CAN. 1st ARMY
Elbeuf
Aug. 20 U.S. 15th Corps establish bridgehead
Aug. 1
21st ARMY GROUP
Aug. 25 Paris liberated
St Malo
PARIS
Falaise
Camembert
Aug. 16
Trun
Avranches
Aug. 17
St Brieuc
Aug. 20 Falaise Gap sealed
Dreux
Brest
Morlaix
Aug. 25
Alençon
12th ARMY GROUP
Rennes
U.S. 1st ARMY
Chartres
Aug. 16
Quimper
Pontivy
Lorient
Aug. 17
Le Mans
Aug. 8
Orleans
Aug. 25
Vannes
U.S. 3rd ARMY
Loire
0 m 25 50
0 km 40 80 N
St Nazaire
Angers
Aug. 11
Loire
Aug. 25 Nantes

---

you're white!' and his CO handed him an extremely large mug of rum.[17]

The British 3rd Infantry Division, a veteran formation now, also fought the SS that summer in the Caen area, as Montgomery desperately attempted to force the German 'hinge.' By now the 3rd had lost almost a quarter of the strength with which it had landed on D-Day including its commander, General Rennie.

Now it grappled with the 10th SS Panzer Division guarding the flank at Caen. As always where SS troops were involved, the conflict developed into a bitter struggle. At one point, the Norfolks were counter-attacked by the SS, and in the course of the fight a Corporal Sidney Bates and his section were trapped by some sixty SS men. Bates seized a Bren-gun and charged them through a wall of lead, firing from the hip. He was felled by a vicious burst of machine-gun fire. He staggered to his feet again and pushed on. He was hit once again. Now he crawled forward, carried by that strange, crazed, intoxicating bloodlust that sometimes afflicts men on the battlefield.

The SS were shaken. Nothing seemed able to stop the lone Tommy heading towards them. They began to withdraw. Bates was hit again by a fragment from a mortar shell. He fell to the ground for good, but still continued to fire until he lapsed finally into blessed oblivion. Two days later he died from his wounds, unaware that he would be awarded his country's highest decoration for bravery, the Victoria Cross.

That same night, his brigadier, Cass, was giving out orders to the officers of his brigade when abruptly the silence was torn apart by a stray shell. It hurtled out of the night sky and exploded almost on top of the assembled officers. Nearly everyone present was wounded save Brigadier Cass. He shook himself and said in a level voice, 'Send for the second-in-command.' The battle for Caen had to go on.[18]

Now they all suffered – German, British and French. The Hitler Youth had already lost its first divisional commander, Witt, killed in action, plus most of his senior commanders and thousands of young soldiers. By now it was a shadow of its former self. But burnt out as it was, it was still fighting desperately in this, its first action. By the time the battle was over, the division would have lost exactly half its men – ten thousand in all, plus twenty-two commanders.

But the British infantry, too, were paying a bloody price for the privilege of fighting against the cream of the SS Armour, the 1st SS, the 12th and the 9th Panzer Divisions, all veterans (save for the 12th) of the year-long battles in Russia.

In the last week of that bloody June, Major Alexander Brodie arrived at the HQ of the 4th Battalion of the 51st Highland Division's Black Watch, as a reinforcement (as the British called their 'replacements'). In all, he would spend three periods of from six to eight weeks with the division throughout the campaign, during which time he would be 'wounded, not too seriously, have a good time at home as a wounded hero and return fresh to rejoin my braver and tougher friends,' as he explained much later.[19] But on first arriving, he was given a far from cordial welcome. The 4th Black Watch was a territorial battalion, in which regular officers like Brodie cut no ice at all. The colonel took him to one side and told him that he didn't like regulars either, 'but as you are here, you may stay for the time being.'[20]

A little downcast, the new major took over a company which had already suffered severe losses and had been filled out with cockneys from an English regiment. He found his surviving NCOs were 'thoroughly frightened' and confessed later that 'if I had been more experienced I would have had them posted, but I was still feeling my way, so I lacked the confidence.'[21]

On July 9th, 1944, the major's thirty-second birthday, the unwanted regular, who up to now had seen little active service, was ordered to take up his company into the attack. Knowing the shaky state of morale among his men, he ordered them out on parade and told them that in spite of what some of them might think, there was nothing heroic about the surrender of the old 51st Highland Division at St. Valéry in 1940. Then he worked round to the whole question of cowardice and surrender in battle: 'I told them that while I would not hesitate to shoot any one who ran away, I expected them to shoot me or any officer or NCO who ordered them to pack up.'[22] This fighting speech so scared the men that two stretcher-bearers who had already had a fair share of combat promptly took off and disappeared, never to be seen again.

So 'A' Company, a group of frightened misfits led by a resented officer, went into action. They took their first prisoners; they also came across wounded men from other outfits, including one Armoured Corps trooper with his knees blown off and suffering from various other wounds – indeed, the man was so badly injured that Brodie noticed his stretcher-bearer looking 'pointedly' at the major's revolver as if it would be kinder to put the poor fellow out of his misery. He and his men went on to rescue an abandoned anti-tank gun whose commanding officer had fled, leaving a corporal in charge; they saw one of their own companies coming streaming back in retreat; then finally, for Brodie, the inevitable happened.

He had just mounted an earthen embankment, when down came 'several moaning minnie bombs. A sergeant was killed outright and part of the middle joint of my right forefinger was cut off and a big piece of shrapnel went into my left thigh.'

Major Brodie's first short stay with the 51st Highland Division was over. But by the time the war was ended, he would have collected another half a dozen wounds, including one inflicted by his own side. For one day shortly before the war ended, he was sitting on the pillion of a motor bike driven by a soldier armed with a Sten-gun. Brodie had his hand on the man's shoulder just as he started up. At that moment the Sten, a notoriously unreliable and temperamental weapon, went off and the bullet went right through Brodie's arm. As he recorded wrily thirty-odd years later, 'It hurt like hell!'[23]

80 Now at last, however, the Germans were beginning to

US troops street fighting on the Cherbourg peninsula.

break. Patton had already commenced his armoured breakout into Brittany. Soon Bradley's First Army would be doing the same. Montgomery decided this was the moment to throw in his armour.

Captain John Foley of the Royal Armoured Corps had been sitting with his comrades in a French field for two weeks, waiting for the long-expected call to action, when one bright morning a four-wheeled scout car roared into the middle of the laager and skidded to a stop in a cloud of dust.

The vehicle bore the markings of the brigade HQ, and when the dusty driver stood up in the turrets, the watching tankers could see the red tabs of a staff officer on his collar. It was indeed the brigadier himself. He pushed up his goggles and beamed benevolently down at the men. 'You lucky people,' he exclaimed with delight. 'I've bought you a battle. Where's yer Commanding Officer?'[24]

For the next fortnight, Foley and his crew would hardly leave their Sherman as the great armoured battle for Normandy swept back and forth. The tankers fought, cooked, slept, drank and in many cases died in their 30-ton 400hp-engined Shermans. Each tank was crewed by five men: the commander, the gunner, the loader-wireless operator, the driver and co-driver, who also fired the Browning machine-gun. Packed inside the steel hull with these five men were a hundred rounds of ammunition; armour-piercing, high-explosive and smoke shells; cans of water and diesel; boxes containing belts of machine-gun ammunition; Compo ration boxes; Very pistols; tarpaulins; hand-grenades; battery-charging motors; Tommy cookers, and a hundred other things. The crew even found room in odd corners for photographs of loved ones and personal letters, as if this were a living room on wheels.

In the cramped interior of the tank, all communication had to take place over the intercom due to the thunderous roar of the engines and the clatter and squeak of the tracks. To add to the discomfort, the blazing sun outside turned everything to dust, which permeated every nook and cranny of the metal monsters. There were the obvious sanitation problems too. As Foley wrote later: 'Since our natural functions didn't cease just because we were living inside a round armour-plated wall with shells bursting around us from time to time, we found an unorthodox use for empty shell cases. They were just the right shape for emptying out of the turret hatch.'[25] Sometimes, when there weren't any empty shell cases available, an obliging gunner would fire off a round to make up for the lack, and any man who needed to 'take a leak' could then do so – at a cost to the taxpayer of four pounds sterling!

Of course, when more solid relief was necessary, there was nothing for it but to wait for one of the occasional shell-free spells and 'take a shovel for a walk.' One of Foley's friends was caught at just such a crucial moment by a German sniper. The German could have shot the crouching tanker in the head. Instead he drilled a neat hole in his buttocks, mercifully missing 'all the vital spots.' As

82

US Sherman tank crew.

Foley remarked later, despite propaganda edicts to the contrary, the incident showed that the German had a sense of humour, for the sniper had evidently chosen 'the larger and (he no doubt thought) funnier target …'[26]

Opportunities for humour were rare enough in this grim final slogging-match for Normandy. That month, twenty-five-year-old Lieutenant Michel Wittmann of the 12th SS Division, who had already won the Laurel Leaves to the Knight's Cross of the Iron Cross for having destroyed an astonishing total of 119 Russian tanks, was commanding his division's 1st Tiger Company.

Working his way through the Bocage in a lone Tiger, his gunner Corporal Woll, who had also won the Knight's Cross, a high honour for an enlisted man, spotted British tanks moving on a road below Wittmann's vehicle. At first his CO thought they were a 'Tommy reconnaissance unit.' Soon, however, he concluded there were just too many tanks for that. In fact, he was watching the lead brigade of the renowned 'Desert Rats,' the British 7th Armoured Division, commanded by Brigadier Hinde.

Brave as he was, Wittman hesitated as more and more tanks came rolling out of the cloud of dust below. Naturally he was aware of the superiority of the sixty-ton Tiger, but there was only one of him and scores of them. In the end Woll made up his mind for him. Pointing to the British infantry lined up on both sides of the road and making no attempt to take cover, he said bitterly: 'Look at them. They're acting as if they've won the war already.'[27] That did it. Wittmann moved into action, determined to shake the British out of their complacency: a lone Tiger pitted against an entire brigade.

The Tiger's 88mm cannon thundered. Half-track after half-track went up in flames, the infantrymen pouring out and fleeing for their lives in panic. Within five minutes the lone Tiger had knocked out twenty-five of the Desert Rats' vehicles and effectively blocked the advance of the 22nd Brigade!

Now a British Cromwell tank took up the challenge. Its solid-shot 75mm shell bounced off the Tiger's thick hide like a glowing golf ball. The Tommy didn't get a second chance. Woll swung his fearsome cannon round. The one-hundred-pounder shell slammed into the Cromwell, which reeled as if struck by a sudden tornado. Moments later it was a blazing wreck.

Brigadier Hinde, known behind his back as 'Loony Hinde' because of his fearlessness, extricated his scout car from the chaos and started to pull his brigade back, while a dozen Cromwells attempted to cover his retreat. But now four more of Wittmann's Tigers appeared and set about slaughtering the 8th Irish Hussars manning the Cromwells. They were easy meat for the 88s. Within minutes the Cromwells were either knocked out or fleeing back down the road.

The noise of the battle attracted yet more Tigers. Eight fresh ones under the command of SS Captain Moebius

appeared on the scene. Desperately Major French, commander of the brigade's anti-tank group, tried to fight them off, but his six-pounder anti-tank guns were no match for the Tigers. Fortunately a lucky shell struck Wittmann's Tiger. It rumbled to a stop, its track flopping behind it like a severed limb. Wittman knew his luck was running out. Besides, British infantry armed with Piats, their anti-tank weapon, were coming out of the village to his front. He ordered his crew to bale out, well satisfied with his day's work. For the loss of one tank, he had brought the British troops to a complete standstill. It was his last victory. Before the summer was out, he would be dead.

In the course of this protracted tank battle against the remnants of the German armour, the British and Canadians in Normandy and the Americans of Patton's Third Army in Brittany developed grimly sardonic nicknames for their own tanks, which they now discovered were inferior in many vital respects to those of the enemy. The Sherman, the standard Allied tank, became known as 'the ronson,' or, even more aptly, the 'Tommy cooker.' For already the hapless tankers had discovered that even a glancing shot off, say, the tank's rear sprocket, would turn the Sherman into a sea of flames in seconds. Furthermore, the Sherman presented too high a silhouette, was too thinly armoured, and undergunned.

The Sherman, however, was not the only deficient in the Allied armoury. There was also the 57mm anti-tank gun (six-pounder, to the British and Canadians). This was standard equipment with all Allied infantry divisions, yet its shells simply wouldn't penetrate the German armour. The British three-ton Leyland truck also fell short of requirements; by the end of the Normandy campaign, 1,500 of them were in workshops. Also found wanting were the British Sten-gun, the standard automatic; the antiquated American automatic rifle, the BAR of World War One vintage; the slow-firing British Bren-gun, which had a magazine of a mere thirty bullets – the list was endless. In every field it seemed that the Germans had the superior weapons and equipment. Even the soldiers of the world's greatest industrial nation, the United States, felt cheated now by the planners and the factories back home, which had failed to supply them adequately.

At the beginning of the invasion there had been some 80 Tigers and 250 Panther tanks, plus a larger number of German Mark III and IV tanks facing the Allied forces. But small as their numbers were against the might of the Allied armoured divisions which started pouring ashore as soon as the beachheads were secure, the reputation of the German tanks was tremendous. A veritable Tiger and Panther psychosis broke out among the Allied troops, to which was added the overwhelming fear of the German all-purpose 88mm cannon and the newish six-barrel, electrically-operated German mortar, the 'moaning minnie.'

The Tiger, which weighed anything from 58 to 70 tons,

A German Tiger tank showing added protective plates.

was armed with an 88mm cannon which was effective at 2,000 yards. At 1,000 yards, it could knock out any known Allied tank, even if the latter was in hull-down position.* On the other hand, the Sherman had to fight to within *300 yards* of the Tiger in order to make any impression at all on it, and even the largest Allied anti-tank gun, the seventeen-pounder used by the British and Canadians, hardly left a dent on the Tiger or Panther when they were in the hull-down position. Instead, the seventeen-pounder's so-called 'armour-piercing' shells merely bounced harmlessly off the German tanks' tough hides.

These deficiencies in the Allied arsenal had in fact been known to the generals ever since the campaign in North Africa in 1943. Early in 1944, too, American tank crews at Anzio had complained of the inferiority of the Sherman to the Tiger and drawn attention to the fact that the muzzle velocity** of the 57mm anti-tank gun was exactly half that of its German equivalent. At the time, C.L. Sulzberger of the *New York Times* had tried to expose the scandal. The result had been that he had been threatened with expulsion from the theatre and that General Devers, US commander in Italy, had ordered an immediate investigation – not into the substance of Sulzberger's claims, but against Sulzberger himself!

I.e. with its thick frontal armour presented to the enemy.
**The higher the speed with which a shell leaves a cannon – its muzzle velocity – the more its penetrating power.

The lower-ranking soldiers, who were at the sharp end, also complained. In August, 1944, Colonel Maurice Rose of the 2nd US Armored Division (otherwise known as 'Hell on Wheels'), who would be killed in action before the campaign was over, complained to Eisenhower about the superiority of the German armour. 'I have,' he wrote, 'personally observed on a number of occasions the projectiles fired by our 75mm and 76mm guns bouncing off the front plate of Mark V tanks at ranges of about 600 yards.'[28] In a file of attachments sent by Rose with his complaint, one of his battalion commanders, Lieutenant Colonel E.W. Blanchard, stated: 'The only Panthers I have seen not knocked out by our artillery or our air, were either abandoned by their crews or had been hit by our tanks at very close ranges ... We defeat the German tanks by our weight in sheer numbers of tanks and men.'[29] Colonel Blanchard was supported by a staff sergeant, who reported, 'I have fired at 150 yards at a Panther, 6 rounds – 4 APs and 2 HEs, without a penetration.'[30] Another tank commander said, 'Jerry armament will knock out an M4 [Sherman[as far as they can see it.'[31] Private John Danforth, who had had two Sherman tanks shot out from under him, stated, 'I think we don't have enough gun. The people who build tanks I don't think know the power of the Jerry gun. I have seen a Jerry gun fire through two buildings, penetrate an M4 tank, and go through another building!'[32]

But the brass refused to listen. Indeed, Patton cracked down relentlessly on any of his tank commanders who loaded the front of their Shermans with extra bogie wheels and spare tracks in order to provide additional frontal armour against the feared 'eighty-eight'. Hodges, too, showed great displeasure when he learned that some of his tankers were using sandbags to pad out the interiors of their tanks to protect themselves better. And when Montgomery heard from the War Office that it expected trouble in the Guards Armoured Division due to the 'inadequacy of our tanks compared with the Germans,' he wrote to Second British Army Commander, General Sir Miles Dempsey: 'At a time like this, with large forces employed and great issues at stake, we must be very careful that morale and confidence are maintained at the highest level. Alarmist reports, written by officers with no responsibility and little battle experience, could do a great deal of harm. There will therefore be no reports, except those made through the accepted channels of command.'[33]

Thus the whole problem was swept under the carpet, and until the very end of the long, bloody campaign, Allied troops continued to fight with inferior weapons, saved from disaster on the battlefield time and time again by Allied air supremacy and the sheer volume of their tanks. It was not surprising, therefore, that a single Wittmann could hold up and defeat a whole Allied brigade.

But only for a while. For now, nothing could stop the tremendous Allied armoured push eastwards. Larry Lesueur of CBS Radio was there in the last week of July as the US tankers advanced on St. Lô, and described them as 'standing high in the open hatches of their big Sherman tanks ... big husky fellows looking like professional football players in their tank helmets, a look of exultation on their dusty faces, and their huge goggles giving them a grim inhuman expression.'[34] Standing in the square of the burning township of Canisy, south of St. Lô, the American correspondent heard voices on the radio coming from the tip of the armoured spearhead: 'We're up against German anti-tank guns. Meeting intense fire on our flank,' an unknown voice reported. But the American general standing next to Lesueur refused to tolerate any hesitation. In an 'uncompromising' voice, he snapped: 'Get along there, tanks, keep pushing, keep pushing!' And the tanks duly kept pushing.[35]

At last they were through and into the burning ruins of the little Norman town, crashing through the smoking apple orchards, rumbling over the ancient grey-stone walls and slamming shell after shell into the last German strongpoints. They passed abandoned enemy tanks; stalled trucks; looted civilian cars that had run out of petrol; wrecked German field kitchens, or 'goulash-cannons'. They trundled heartlessly over the bodies that lay crumpled in the gutters like bundles of carelessly abandoned rags. St. Lô was American at last − and the door east was finally open.

That day an unknown correspondent interviewed an exhausted GI as he sat taking greedy puffs at a cigarette.

Troops advancing through the rubble of Caen.

Looking around in wonder at the smoking rubble of what had once been a prosperous, happy little French market town, the soldier exclaimed: 'Gee, we sure liberated the hell outa this place!'[36]

Caen fell too, a collection of smoking ruins by now, and over two thousand French civilians were reported to have died during the fighting. Now the Allies raced forward across the plain of Northern France, leaving Normandy to the dead, to hundreds of shattered vehicles which were already beginning to rust in the rain, and to the countless thousands of soldiers of a dozen Allied nations who now swarmed like ants around the lines of communication reaching back to the beaches. POL dumps,* COMZ supply units,** rear signals ammunitions, food, clothing, vehicle depots, ripple dipples*** – the vast, complex supply structure now extended to the most remote French hamlet. It was as if the fighting troops administering the *coup de grâce* to the tattered remnants of the German Army in France were merely a far-off minority at the tip of this tremendous supply system.

By now the panicked survivors of the German Army were virtually cut off from their homeland and trapped in a huge pocket by Montgomery's Canadians and Patton's Americans, who were now beginning to close the gap at the link-town of Falaise. A huge slaughter of the almost helpless German soldiers commenced.

The Australian Alan Moorehead was on the scene.

It begins in the back streets of St. Lambert, where the German columns first came in range of the British fire. The horses stampeded. Not half a dozen, but perhaps three hundred or more. They lashed down the fences and the hedges with their hooves, and dragged their carriages through the farmyards. Many galloped for the banks of the River Dives, and plunged headlong with all their trappings down the twelve-foot banks into the stream below, which at once turned red with blood … The drivers of the lorries panicked in the same way. As more and more shells kept ripping through the apple trees, they collided their vehicles one against another, and with such force that some of the lighter cars were telescoped with their occupants inside …

I suppose there were about a thousand German vehicles of every sort lying out in the fields behind. All these came under fire. The Germans made no attempt to man their guns. They either huddled beneath them, or ran blindly for the futile cover of the hedges.[37]

Infantryman Rex Wingfield was also on the scene as those men in dusty field-grey came shambling in with their hands raised above their heads, crying, '*Kamerad … Kamerad,*' surrendering in their thousands. He wrote: 'I never want to

(Above) US tanks pass through the town of Coutances.
(Below) German prisoners captured by the British troops in Falaise Pocket are served with tea.

*Petrol and Oil Dumps.
**US military designation for the rear area supply organisation.
***GI slang name for their replacement centres.

see men like that again.' They came in ranks six deep, crowding the narrow, shell-cratered roads. Every few yards there would be a British, Canadian, American or Polish infantryman to guard them, his rifle slung carelessly over his shoulder. But there was no fight left in these human wrecks. The Germans were past caring. All they wanted was a respite from the terrible Allied 'Jabos' (dive-bombers) which had strafed and slaughtered their packed ranks for days – that, and sleep. In a daze, they staggered into the great cages set up for them in the naked fields, bowed with fatigue, carrying nothing 'but their ragged uniforms and their weary, hopeless, battle-drugged bodies.'[38]

The numbers involved were enormous. As a BBC correspondent recorded, one staff officer complained as the survivors of fifteen German divisions went into the bag: 'I don't know what to do with them. They're just keeping coming in on us!'[39]

Moorehead noted that after the German surrender, there were vast amounts of loot for the picking. 'It is exactly like one of those crowded battle paintings of Waterloo or Borodino – except of course the wreckage is different ... There is a profusion of everything: field-glasses and typewriters, pistols and small arms by the hundred, cases of wine, truck-loads of food and medical stores, a vast mass of leather harness. Every car is full of clothing, and every officer seems to have possessed a pair of corsets to take home.'[40]

Bulldozers were used to attempt to clear the roads, which were littered with German tanks, guns, smashed-up staff cars, mobile workshops, horse-drawn carts, their skinny nags dead in the traces, all shot to pieces by Allied artillery and dive-bombers, the rocket-firing Typhoons and Thunderbolts.

As Frank Gillard of the BBC reported, viewing the carnage under a burningly hot August sun: 'Some of the most frightful slaughter of the whole of this year must have taken place up and down these roads a few days ago ...'[41]

And so it had. But the Germans were not the only ones to suffer. In the attempt to close the gap on the trapped Germans at Falaise, the Canadian 28th (British Columbia) Armoured Regiment, going into action for the first time, lost forty-seven tanks and over one hundred men on the first day alone. Of its supporting infantry, consisting of two companies of the Algonquin Regiment, fifty percent of the men were casualties on that same day.

The chase to finish off the German Army was hectic and chaotic. A tank soldier of a Canadian regiment later described their mad rush thus:

The smokescreen supposed to blind the enemy turned out to be a thick dense mist in the path of our advance, soon supplemented by the dust clouds created by the terrific bombing; the area was 'Vision Zero.' Very little could be done to keep direction, except by aiming the tank 'at the sun.' Speed, nothing but speed, and on we went, crashing through obstacles at 20 to 25mph ... very rough inside a tank going cross country ... We just barged ahead, some of the tanks appearing to be going on at crazy angles and in the confusion I didn't know who was right and who was wrong. I just kept charging 'at the sun,' blasting everything large enough to hide a field gun and taking a terrible whipping in the turret of the bucking 32-ton monster.

At Camembert, famed for its cheese, the hard-pressed German Seventh Army had set up a contact point for those soon to be trapped in the pocket. At St. Lambert-sur-Dives, codenamed by the enemy 'Erika,' what was left of Hausser's Seventh Army assembled, prior to an attempt to break out and reach Camembert. Shattered as these German formations were, their commander, one-eyed SS General Hausser (known to his men as 'Papa') knew that they outnumbered the Canadians waiting for them at St. Lambert. He therefore ordered them to hit the Canadians with all their might.

For three days the Canadians, commanded by major D.V. Currie and numbering one squadron of tanks from the 29th Armoured Regiment and three companies of infantry, held up the remnants of nearly a dozen shattered German divisions trapped on the other side of the River Dives. Then at last they were relieved, and the Germans broke through.

General von Lüttwitz, a panzer division commander, arrived at St. Lambert with his survivors at noon. He told his interrogators after the war:

... From the church in the town I directed the evacuation of my men. The crossing of the bridge over the Dives was a particularly ghastly affair. Men, horses, vehicles and other equipment that had been shot up while making the crossing had crashed from the bridge into the deep ravine of the Dives and lay there jumbled together in gruesome heaps. Throughout the whole afternoon enemy tanks tried to break through again into St. Lambert from Trun, while other tanks kept the road leading north-east from St. Lambert under constant fire. I formed separate small groups of my men, placed them under energetic officers and ordered them to march north-east. At nine in the evening of 20 August I broke out myself, but enemy infantry had by this time entered St. Lambert and the Falaise Gap was closed.[42]

Wounded yet again, 'Papa' Hausser managed to struggle out with a handful of senior officers such as the commander of the paratroops, General Meindl, and 'Panzermeyer' of the 12th SS. But for the most part the trapped Germans, including a corps commander, surrendered, and the power of the German Army in France was broken at last. The Battle for Normandy had been won by the Allies.

The cost had been high. Major Currie's gallant action at St. Lambert won him Canada's first Victoria Cross of the campaign, but that high honour could not hide the fact that Canada had paid a terrible price for this great victory. Her two infantry divisions, the 2nd and 3rd, for example, had suffered the highest casualties of any of Montgomery's formations; some 18,500 men, of whom a third had been killed in action.

All had suffered terribly. The German losses from June 6th to August 30th were 400,000 men killed, captured and wounded. The Americans suffered 124,000, the British 64,000, which, together with the Canadian losses, brought the total Allied casualties to 206,000 men since June.

On the afternoon of August 24th, 1944, General de Gaulle drove in an open car into Paris – courtesy of the British, American and Canadian Armies, who between them had lost nearly a quarter of a million men in order that he could do so. There he was cheered by the same Parisian crowds who sixteen weeks before had cheered the arch-collaborator Marshal Pétain of the Vichy Government, and who the previous June had spat upon captured American paratroopers as they were escorted through the French capital.

At the front, the weary Allied fighting soldiers slumped in their foxholes or resting in shattered French peasant cottages, knew nothing of De Gaulle's carefully engineered triumph; even if they had, it is doubtful whether they would have cared. They were exhausted, all of them. It had been a long, hard, bloody slog to get this far. Now all they wanted was rest.

Relaxing with his men of the Borderers, Lieutenant Robert Woollcombe summed up his feelings about the Battle of Normandy as follows:

The soul of Normandy hovered in the cloud of flies over the intestines of two German corpses off the high road near Beny Bocage. They had been shot into human tripe by a tank. It showed in a dirty old peasant in a broken-down cottage on the way to Estry, who bared his chest to me and revealed a Cross of Lorraine on a chain around his neck ... It was with you when marching out of the Scottish Corridor* like a man who had been condemned to the tomb and reprieved. And with the summer goes a last glimpse; that of a particular officer who once belonged to our Mess, dwelling among us like a small gale. For he was cheery and penetrating of voice to an extent that maddened, and people turned up their collars when they saw him approach, and everyone liked him. And coming from the Scottish borderland he requested when we made wills at Worthing, that if he died a clump of trees should be planted to his memory among his home hills.

When we sailed ... he was diverted to the 1st Battalion. We later heard he was found in Caen without a mark on him, quite dead from blast. Aged a rather young twenty-four ... The summer was done.[43]

*Terrain conquered by the 15th Scottish.

American troops move on towards Fontainebleau en route to Paris.

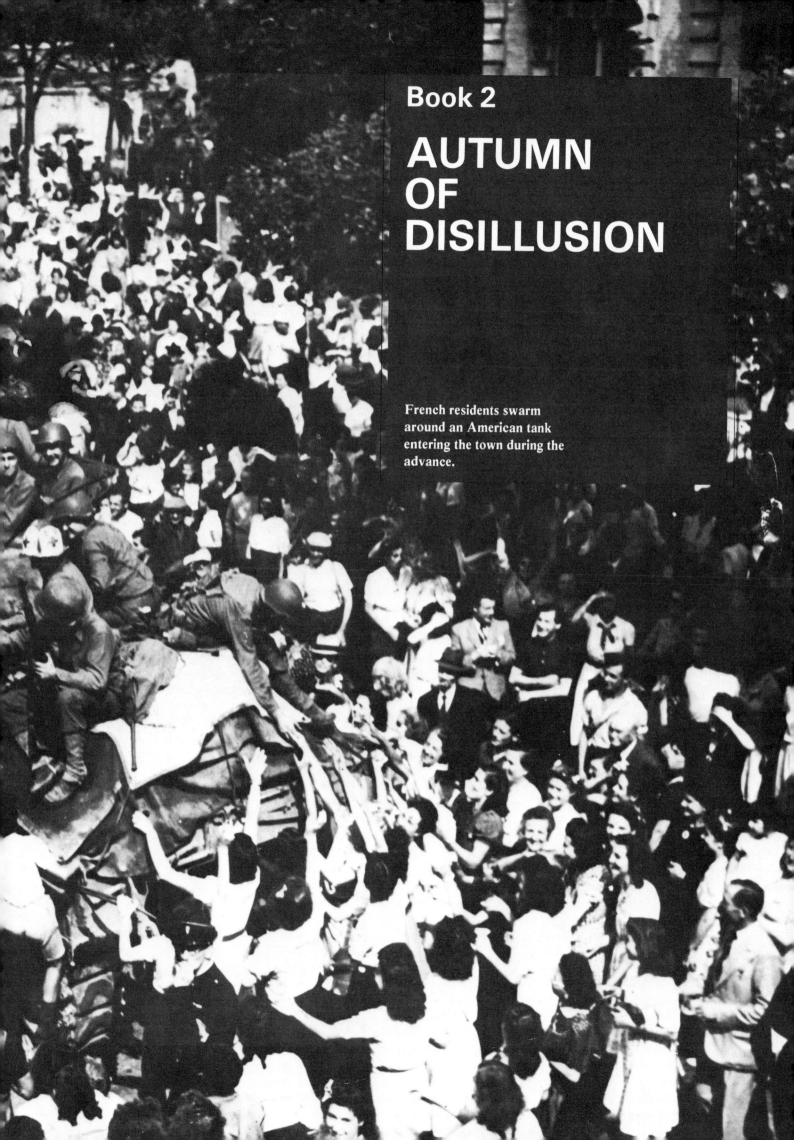

Book 2

AUTUMN OF DISILLUSION

French residents swarm around an American tank entering the town during the advance.

5 SEPTEMBER HONEYMOON

Crowds of Parisians, celebrating the entry of Allied troops into Paris, take cover as a sniper fires from the rooftops.

For the weary Allied soldiers, September '44 was the last happy time – a limbo between the horrors of the summer in Normandy and the worse horrors to come on those freezing heights which marked the frontier of Hitler's Thousand-Year Reich. It was the month of liberation and, for many, celebration.

In every town and hamlet through which the armour rattled in the great drive from France into Belgium, Luxembourg and finally Southern Holland, the natives swarmed forth, dressed in their Sunday best, giving the 'V for Victory' sign and generally according the grinning soldiers such tumultuous welcome that at times they brought the entire Allied advance to a standstill.

The happy young soldiers found themselves showered with flowers and food. Wine and beer were thrust at them. Pretty, excited girls were everywhere, jumping on board tanks and trucks and allowing themselves to be kissed and fondled by the troops – behaviour which the prudish provincial girls of the Low Countries would have considered outrageous in any other circumstances but these.

Paris was taken. The US 28th Infantry Division marched twenty-four abreast right down the Champs Elysées, with the men in the cleanest uniforms on the outside. The whole broad avenue was jammed with French people laughing, singing, cheering, crying. They threw the GIs flowers and handed them litre bottles of wine. As Private First Class Verner Odegard of the division related later: 'The first regiment never did get through. They just broke in and grabbed the guys and lifted some of them on their shoulders and carried them into cafés and bars and their homes and wouldn't let them go. I hear it was a helluva job trying to round them up later.'[1]

A bunch of GIs that day landed up in a well-known

'How ya gonna keep 'em down on the farm
Now that they've seen Gay Paree?' Popular US song of World War One

(Above) Life begins again in
Paris – a French girl with
an RAF officer.
(Above right) British armour
enter Belgium – one of the
first tanks passing through
the village of Antoinge.

Parisian establishment, Madame Hélène's, where they were
invited to take the whole place over 'gratuitement'. This
invitation was accompanied by excited female cries and the
popping of champagne corks. Later the GIs went out to
complete some other business. When they returned, they
found to their embarrassment that the French Resistance
had visited Madame Hélène's in the interim, and that all
the girls had been shaven completely bald as a punishment
for having so willingly serviced 'les Boches'. One had even
had a black swastika painted on her naked pate!

Now the British wanted their capital, too. Crossing the
border between France and Belgium, they set off hot-foot
for the Belgian city of Brussels. Tall, skinny General Brian
Horrocks, known to his troops as 'Jorrocks', was in the
lead with his XXX Corps. At the border he spotted a
Belgian boy weeping with emotion. Seeing Horrocks' red
tabs, the boy ran to him and seizing the general's hands,
cried: 'I knew you would come back!' For Horrocks it was
a particularly poignant moment. Four years before to the

day, he had been a colonel of infantry leading his stragglers out of Belgium on the road to Dunkirk, and defeat. At the time he had promised a sad-looking group of Belgian civilians, 'We'll be back.' It had been a long road, and he personally had taken many a bad knock – including a severe wound – in those long years since 1940. But he had kept his promise.[2]

Lieutenant Robert Woollcombe and his Borderers were also mobbed by the Belgian crowds that day, but having been brought up 'in the strait-jacket of an English public school' Woollcombe was embarrassed at such public displays of emotion. Indeed, seeing him surrounded by a crowd of pretty girls, one of his corporals cried joyously to the embarrassed young officer, 'Sir, don't be shy!'[3]

Deeper into Belgium they rolled, with every family en route throwing their doors open to the liberators. An Allied soldier only had to mention the words 'wash' or 'shave' and he would find himself instantly surrounded by the whole family and carried indoors shoulder-high.

Everywhere hung banners proclaiming, 'Welcome to our Liberators.' And unlike the reception the Tommies had received back in Normandy in June, this was the real thing; here in Belgium they were genuinely welcomed and liked.

The Welsh Guards and the Grenadier Guards stormed down different routes in a neck-and-neck race to reach the Belgian capital. But the King's Company of the Grenadiers, every man of them over six foot two, ran into trouble: the Germans were still making stands here and there. The Grenadiers lost twenty-two men killed and thirty-one wounded, and by the time they had got under way again, the Welsh, plus the armoured cars of the Household Cavalry, had won the race and were entering Brussels first.

There they found that printers had illegally run off thousands of Allied and Belgian flags right under the noses of the German garrison. Now the civilians waved those flags at the dusty, weary guardsmen, giving them a tremendous welcome, while the Germans were still withdrawing out of the eastern suburbs of the capital. The jubilation was such that Horrocks had to take refuge with his HQ inside the grounds of the royal palace at Laeken, the only place where he could 'get on with the war.' There the home of the Belgian Queen Mother was surrounded by high railings, which offered some protection from the milling crowds.[4]

Meanwhile, most appropriately, the Canadians raced for Dieppe, which in 1942 had been the scene of their greatest and bloodiest defeat of the war. Now they were determined to capture that coastal city which had cost so much Canadian blood. Stewart Macpherson of CBC who was with the Canadian 2nd Division which had suffered so much back in August, 1942, described their mood as they raced for the port: '... You could almost sense their desire to get as much out of their machines as possible – anything to get them into Dieppe in a hurry ... They were all there. The first troops into the town were the Essex Scottish, the Royal Hamilton Light Infantry and the Royal Regiment of Canada, and speeding up behind them were the Camerons of Winnipeg, the South Saskatchewan Light Infantry, the Fusiliers of Montreal, the Toronto Scottish, the Black Watch – all the regiments that were there on the fateful day of August 19th, 1942. But today it was their turn.'[5]

It was 'Blood and Guts' Patton's Third Army which liberated the capital of Western Europe's smallest state, Luxembourg. Its picturesque chief city, once Europe's most powerful fortress, fell without a shot being fired. Colonel Codman, Patton's aide, was thereupon given the task of escorting its exiled ruler, Prince Felix, now a brigadier in the British Army, back to his own country.

Prince Felix had been away for four years, and on the drive back he almost missed his country altogether because he mistook the Belgian frontier for that of his own state. But in the end he and Codman found their way back to the royal palace, where the Prince's only disappointment was to discover that the Germans had not stolen the heavy, old-fashioned furniture. 'Here and there,' recorded Codman, 'he raised the corner of a drop cloth to view, with a certain resignation, the ponderous furniture beneath. "I had rather hoped," he sighed, "that the boches would take all these. However, my wife will be happy and that is all that matters." '[6]

Then into Holland, with both the British and the American armies pouring into the southern half of that country. But by now the steam was going out of the great drive for the German frontier. The supplies were still being hauled all the way from the beaches, mainly by truck, and although the black drivers of the Red Ball Express, the great US trucking route east, struggled manfully, it seemed they couldn't bring up the gas to the forward troops in sufficient quantities. Besides, by now, many a load of gas had begun to disappear on the thriving European black market. In the case of the British Army, the absence of those 1,500 defective Leyland lorries had left a huge gap in the Royal Army Service Corps supply system.

Slowly but surely, the drive ground to a halt, leaving the beaten German remnants to stream back across the frontier into their homeland, that 'Heimat' they were always singing about so sentimentally. The 'Swan' as the British called it, the 'mad dash' of the Americans, was over.

That first week of September, 1944, had been roses all the way. Back home, the pundits were already predicting that the war would be over in a matter of weeks, even days. Monty had placed a bet with Ike that the Germans would surrender at the latest by Christmas. And the troops believed it. The Germans had vanished. What was to stop them from enjoying themselves? They had earned their victory and the benefits that had come with it – or so they thought.

The truth was that the good times, the days of beer, champagne, pretty girls and grateful, cheering crowds, were just about over.

So they settled down in their new surroundings – for a while. The Americans held those areas of Northern France, Belgium, Luxembourg and Holland which bordered the now silent, brooding Reich; the British and Canadians were further inland and along the Channel coast, that densely populated, flat region, interspersed with dykes and canals, where the slag heaps of the coalmines stood starkly silhouetted against the grey horizon.

It didn't take the Tommies long to get their feet under the table in their billets among the humble Flemish-speaking families of the area. After the hard slog of Normandy, they were glad of this time out of war. They needed the rest – especially the 'PBI', or 'poor bloody infantry,' whose casualties had been particularly high in Normandy. Now the gaps in their ranks were being filled – with difficulty – by eighteen- and nineteen-year-old reinforcements from England. But even they were in short supply, and in the end Montgomery was forced to break up two divisions, the battle-experienced 50th and the green 59th, to provide the riflemen the fighting divisions so desperately needed. The Canadians were in an even more difficult position, for under Canadian law only volunteers could be sent overseas – and volunteers for the infantry were in short supply.

That first week of September, when the 43rd British Infantry Division held its first medals ceremony for gallantry in action, its horsey-looking commander, Major-General Thomas, discovered that of the fifty-five officers and men scheduled to be awarded a decoration, only twenty-eight could appear on parade. The rest had been killed or severely wounded after the exploit which had originally gained them the medal. As the divisional history commented, 'The price of victory had indeed been heavy.'[7]

Now that the Tommies were resting at last, they wanted three things: 'wallop, bints and good grub' – anything rather than the canned Compo rations they had been eating for the last three months. Egg and chips, washed down with plenty of fizzy Stella Artois or Jupiter beer were

The newly liberated people of Antwerp showed their feelings towards German prisoners and Belgian collaborators by locking them in the lion's cage at the Zoo.

in great demand.

The 'bints', or girls, weren't hard to find. In the big Belgian cities such as Brussels, Louvain and Malines, there were plenty of 'cafés', many of which had been hurriedly christened 'Café Texas' or 'Café Alaska' after the Germans fled – establishments where, in the discreet backrooms away from the thick fug of the bar, under the watchful gaze of a heavy-set, peroxided Flemish blonde in black, there were obliging young and not-so-young ladies ready to slip out of what few clothes they were wearing, for a price. But not for money. Nobody as yet wanted the Belgian franc. Instead the Allied troops paid for their swift little 'jig-jig' in kind – tea, margarine, and naturally, in the case of the British soldiers, in corned beef.

One former bandsman from a Scottish pipe band who served in the field as a stretcher-bearer with the infantry, remembers going on a seventy-two-hour leave to Brussels that month with his pack filled with rations. Naturally, he made a point of wearing his kilt – a great attention-grabber which always prompted 'Ladies of the night' to pose the age-old question: what was he wearing underneath? To which, by custom and military tradition, the answer was, nothing. In one of the 'cafés' located in the grass-overgrown cobbled streets behind Brussels' Gare du Nord, the whores took it upon themselves to find out for themselves. Unfortunately, contrary to regulations, the bandsman had sewn his oiled string vest between his legs for greater warmth, which led to certain complications. At one point it seems that a Flemish 'Madame' approached him brandishing a pair of scissors and determined to cut through his vest. All in all, it was one of the most alarming moments of the war for the hapless bandsman.[8]

All sorts of sexual tastes were catered for by the willing, newly liberated ladies of the Belgian demi-monde. In Louvain that autumn, for instance, competing with British comedian George Formby of ENSA* and his ukulele, was a renowned Belgian lady entertainer of ample girth, who performed a bizarre exhibition for the 'brave Tommies.' Her turn was a little more down-to-earth than Formby's and was based on a popular BBC radio programe of 1944 called 'Penny on a Drum,' so named because the band played popular tunes when pennies were thrown on a drum. The Belgian lady had added a new element to the entertainment. In her case there was no tune; instead, when a soldier threw a five-franc piece on the drum, she squatted over it and picked it up – but without using her hands. It is recorded that once a cheeky Tommy threw her a tin of corned beef, which landed on the drum with a dull thud. Without batting an eyelid, the Belgian lady squatted down and effortlessly secreted it, to tremendous applause.

That September the scion of a famous brewing family,

*British equivalent of the American USO entertainment service.

now the CO of an anti-tank regiment, went on leave to Brussels with his second-in-command, the heir to a well-known private London merchant bank. Dismissing their driver, the two officers went off in search of a high-priced house of ill-fame. Unfortunately, the brothel they visited was bombed during the night, and the brewery heir was killed and the future merchant banker wounded. As their driver recalled many years later: 'They even had the nerve to announce in the *Times* that the poor bugger had been killed in action ... But in a way, you might say he was.'[9]

Captain Andrew Wilson, recovered from his wound, was also in Brussels at that time, determined 'to have a last look at life' before he rejoined his unit. Strolling around with a fellow officer, a Tank Corps captain, he saw that 'At every corner urchins and girls stood offering black market cigarettes. The windows of cake-shops were packed with gâteaux and pastries. In discreetly lit restaurants tail-coated waiters bent over the hors d'oeuvres trolley.'

But Wilson's friend had other things than food on his mind. He persuaded Wilson to stroll with him down the Boulevard Max, 'through a jostling flow of American and British soldiers, most of them with girls, others drunk, others just wandering, lost and amazed in the back-line Babylon.'

In a side street girls came up to them from the shadows. 'Exhibition, exhibition ...' said a little hunchback.

'Don't be had,' said the R.T.R. man. 'They kid you it's the donkey and it's only a couple of nudes.' They passed him by, looking for a bar.

It appeared as a light behind a curtain. They pushed aside the curtain and went in. Music beat down from an unseen loudspeaker, and a teen-age American had collapsed across the bar.

'Dance?' said a woman. She was large and motherly, with make-up like greasepaint. The R.T.R. man shook his head. They drank some brandy and left. Back on the corner of the Boulevard Max, a round plump figure with a blond Flemish face brushed by, and Wilson saw the R.T.R. man weakening.

The girl brushed by again.

'I'd better leave you to it,' Wilson said. 'Do you need any money?'

The R.T.R. man shook his head. The woman was coming up for the third time. 'Thanks all the same,' he said, 'Shall I see you in the morning?' he asked almost anxiously.

Next moment the Flemish girl had the R.T.R. man's arm and they vanished into the crowd.[10]

Naturally, venereal disease became a problem. 'Short arm inspections' before and after every leave were the order of the day. At such occasions, the troops would be ordered to line up and drop their trousers. Then the MO, usually with an expression of the utmost professional distaste would command the assembled soldiers to raise their shirt fronts and would then pass down the line of half-naked men, raising each soldier's 'John Thomas' delicately with his

The Liberation of Paris – French troops awaiting de Gaulle.

pencil to have a better look at it before certifying its owner fit for human consumption.

According to regulations, soldiers had to carry out certain standard prophylactic procedures before and after intercourse. The penalty for negligence in this delicate matter of personal hygiene was severe: in the British Army, thirty days in the feared 'glasshouse' ('stockade' to the American soldier), the feared military prison. VD was now classified as a 'self-inflicted wound', and victims were punished accordingly.

In the British Army, the procedure called for soldiers to sign out for 'French letters' prior to going on leave. Afterwards they attended 'Green Cross Stations,' set up in public places (there was one, for example, in the centre of Brussels' busiest thoroughfare), where their organs were

cleaned with antiseptic fluid and wrapped up in a little muslin bag for a period of several hours. The American system was little different except in nomenclature: 'rubbers' would be handed out, and afterwards the GIs reported to 'pro stations.'

Naturally, as always in such matters, the organisation broke down and many Allied soldiers returned from leave to find themselves sent to the 'pox hospital' or 'dock', suffering from 'guntac' or 'siff'. If they were particularly unlucky they would suffer from both, a condition cynically named by the Tommies 'the full house.'

The VD sufferer's plight was unenviable. He would be treated harshly by both doctors and sisters, have his rear pumped full of the new wonder-drug penicillin for forty-eight to eighty-six hours, and then be subjected to the feared 'umbrella' treatment, whereby a razor-sharp catheter was inserted into his scrotum to clear away possible lesions. Thereafter he would urinate blood and urine in six different directions for a couple of days, before being returned to the line – or, if he was unlucky and not needed, sent to the glasshouse.

That autumn, the US Army sent 606 men daily to the VD hospitals, and the figure for the British and Canadian Armies could not have been much less. By the end of the campaign it was estimated that the US Army had lost over a quarter of a million man-hours due to VD, and the VD rate was running at forty-two cases per thousand GIs. In the British Army, VD was epidemic.

But nothing, neither 'glasshouse' nor 'stockade,' could stop these young men on their hectic three-day search for pleasure. At the front, their lives were hard, brutish and often all too short; now they were out to enjoy themselves, come what may. Red Cross canteens serving beans on toast, or New England ladies dispensing coffee and donuts were no longer enough. They were looking for the 'Four Fs.' These were not to be confused with the US Army draft board's designation for a civilian unfit for the service. For the troops, the 'Four Fs' meant 'Find 'em, Feel 'em, Fuck 'em and Forget 'em!'

Pockets crammed with back pay – they hadn't had much use for money in the last three months – haversacks laden with goods to sell on the thriving black market in case they ran out of cash, the GIs descended on Gay Paree in their thousands, heading for 'Pig Alley', otherwise known as the Place Pigalle. Drunk already, or soon to be in that happy state, they were looking for one thing and one thing only.

En masse, they were a fairly unprepossessing spectacle. Their life at the front had quickly brutalised them – those who weren't brutalised already. They got drunk. They whored. They fought. They got sick to their stomachs. Their tempers were short and they were highly strung and quick to take offence.

Discipline was strict – it had to be. The MPs, in their white helmets, cross-straps and gaiters, wasted no time with trouble-makers, drunk or otherwise. A club across the back of the skull, a quick prod into the 'paddy-wagon' and then off in short order to the nearest guard-room. But the offenders rarely remained there long. Riflemen were too badly needed at the front, and besides, another taste of battle would soon take the 'piss and vinegar' out of the trouble-makers.

Most of them went back to the line of their own volition. Pockets empty, heads aching, hollow-eyed and wan, morose or blind drunk, silent or talkative, depressed or boastful, they would tumble into the waiting 'deuce and a half' (two and a half ton truck) from division, and meekly allow themselves to be driven back to the front. The war machine would swallow them up again, and it would be goodbye to the 'B-girls,' the 'canteen commandos,' the 'feather merchants' of the COMZ and the gracious ladies with their donuts and popcorn ... But not *all* went back to war. For some, wide-eyed youngsters whose first sight of a metropolis had been the day they had been shipped from New York – for some, the fleshpots of these big European cities were altogether too much of a temptation. They decided to stay behind.

Not only the Americans went over the hill, of course. In the British Second Army it was long rumoured among the rank and file that there was a 'deserters' transit camp,' run by two quartermasters from a farmhouse on the Normandy beachhead. Here, for a price, a suitable deserter would be given fake passes that would take him back to Blighty on one of the many of the empty ships plying between there and the south coast of England.

The operation had begun on a small scale, so the story

went; but soon the two quartermasters became ambitious. They turned their illegal establishment into a regular camp, collecting rations with faked requisition forms in trucks stolen from a transport dump. In the end they even invented a fake brigade's REME workshop for repair. There was no such place, of course.[11]

Naturally these deserters could only exist by theft or by dealing in stolen goods on the local black market. Those who didn't have girlfriends in the area to hide and feed them, banded together in criminal gangs, not hesitating to use their weapons if necessary.

Typical of the lengths these criminal deserters would go to was the full-scale attack they launched against the British Reinforcement Camp at Louvain. There, young British soldiers waiting to go up the line were housed three hundred to a room in an eighteenth-century cavalry barracks, with a great enamel 'piss bucket' placed outside the door at night to cater for their sanitary needs – thanks to the terrible swill they were given to eat, most of them

(Left) a new hairstyle to celebrate the Liberation of Paris. (Right) Soldiers unloading supplies.

suffered from the 'runs.'

On the same day that a dozen recaptured British deserters escaped from the guardroom by tunnelling through the floor, a second bunch of deserters, this time fully armed, broke into the quartermaster's stores. Flourishing pistols, they proceeded to loot the stores of all the thick grey Army blankets it contained, flinging them down to a waiting truck below, and were off before anyone could stop them. On the Belgian black market, the blankets would fetch 150 francs each and were highly sought-after by the poorer Belgian girls, who used them to make winter coats.

But the really big-time operators in the US Army weren't the deserters, nor even those smart young men who always prosper when an operational theatre is new and where it is easy to execute 'moonlight requisitions' – clandestine supplies of equipment and goods to fellow soldiers. The men who made the real money on the black market were those *inside* the Supply Service – the men in charge of transport battalions, railway battalions and the like, which took wares such as gas and cigarettes up to the front. As Corporal Warren Harris of a quartermaster unit then stationed in France commented bitterly after the war: 'Any guy in the quartermaster's knows when there is wholesale stealing; some of the officers in the unit are on the take too. A white rail-road unit just got carried away with the profiteering. They weren't satisfied with stealing the merchandise in the boxcars, they started stealing the whole boxcar. Finally they took a whole damn train, engine and all! It's kind of hard to explain the disappearance of a whole train. The whole damn unit was court-martialled from top to bottom.'[12]

The unit in question, the 716th US Railway Operating Battalion, had indeed, as it was reported at the mass trial of nearly three hundred men, sold millions of stolen cigarettes on the black market. In all, 182 men and 2 officers were accused of the crime, which was described by the trial judge advocate as 'treason.' Two of the offenders received fifty years' hard labour and another two forty-five years! Two weeks after their trial, another so-called 'Millionaires' Battalion' went before the judges for similar offences, but in this case reinforcements for the front were in such short supply that most of the accused were let off after volunteering for active service in the line.

In spite of the harsh penalties, the black market flourished. Indeed, by the time winter arrived, it was firmly established as an accepted part of life, and most Allied soldiers participated in it to a greater or lesser degree. That winter, the British Army's official magazine *The Soldier* printed a satirical cartoon on its back page which summed up the whole situation. It depicted an immensely fat private with a blanket trailing from beneath his bulging overcoat, looking in feigned amazement at the sergeant of the guard, who is calling him back into the barracks. The private is exclaiming, 'What *me*, Sarge?'

The message was clear. Even the Army couldn't stop the black market.

Nowhere did profiteering flourish more than in France, whence the supplies came and where there was a vast Allied supply organisation permanently stationed – this in spite of the fact that relations between the 'liberators' and the 'liberated' had reached a very low ebb.

From the very start, the French had suffered at the hands of their liberators. Tremendous destruction had been wrought in Normandy that summer. On the afternoon of D-Day, for example, 2,500 men, women and children were killed when Caen was bombed by the Allied air force. Peasants were machine-gunned in their fields by Allied fighter pilots and their farms destroyed by Allied gunfire. In a note to Chief of the Imperial General Staff Sir Alan Brooke, Montgomery wrote: '[Carentan] has been completely flattened and there is hardly a house intact; all the civilians have fled. It is a queer sort of liberation.' He also wrote cheerfully to his long-suffering Chief of Staff Freddie de Guingand at about the same time: 'Montebourg and Valognes have been "liberated" in the best 21st Army Group style, *i.e.* they are both completely destroyed!! I think Valognes probably wins; it is worse than Ypres in the last war!'[13]

Of course, for propaganda purposes the war correspondents tried to make much of the gratitude shown by the French towards the American, British and Canadian troops who had come to liberate them. The papers of that summer were full of references to little girls standing at the roadside, timidly offering handfuls of flowers to the marching troops. The reality was different, and the soldiers knew it. The French were indifferent to them. Here, unlike Belgium and Holland, invitations to get their 'feet under the table' were few and far between. Even French fighter ace Pierre Clostermann, now stationed in Normandy, noted that when French peasants came to look at his aircraft, 'they gave the impression they couldn't care less about what we were up to. Their chief worry seemed to be our landing strip encroaching on their fields.'[14] In response to this less than tumultuous welcome by the French, the fighting troops had 'liberated' their chickens and their eggs, shot their animals for food and sometimes raped their women.

Now, however, the hundreds of thousands of Allied soldiers stationed more or less permanently in France were learning just how unwelcome they were. They discovered that many French people hadn't wanted to be liberated in the first place: indeed, a hundred thousand Frenchmen were currently wearing German uniform, and, by the time the war was over, 34,000 Frenchmen would have died fighting for the SS. By a supreme irony, the last Knight's Cross won in World War Two was awarded not to a German, but to a French SS soldier fighting in the ruins of Berlin. No statistics are available later than 1943, but in that year the Paris Bureau responsible for such things reported that there were 85,000 illegitimate children in 'Occupied France' fathered on French women by German soldiers.

With Allied troops living cheek by jowl with the civilians, it was hardly surprising that ill-feeling increased even more. Staff Sergeant Giles of the Engineers, newly arrived in France, wrote to his wife to complain about the French attitude: 'The *Stars and Stripes* has had a lot of stories about how delighted the French people have been to be liberated and what a great welcome they have given us. Personally I haven't seen it. The French people I've seen around Carentan go about their affairs and don't pay any attention to us. You wouldn't think there was a war on at all the way they act. We've heard the Krauts left these people in Normandy well alone – they needed their milk and butter. So maybe being "liberated" hasn't been so wonderful for some of them.'[15]

The GIs were particularly repelled by the poor living standards in the villages and farms where they were billeted. Frequently they found that the floors of the stables were constructed in such a way that the urine from the animals drained into a tank where it was allowed to ferment. There it gave off a permanent evil odour, before finally being spread over the land together with the human manure collected from the wooden outside privies. It seemed that every farmhouse had its fragrant 'honeydew pile' of manure right outside the kitchen window, where the chickens roamed freely. More than one GI was heard to comment on the thrifty French peasant's apparent obsession with faeces, human and otherwise: 'Jesus Christ, here they crap on their own cabbages!'

The casual French toilet habits shocked and alienated even the toughest GIs. In the States, 'the land of the round doorknob,' as the GIs called it affectionately, the business of 'going to the bathroom' meant exactly that. Not so in France. Here, it seemed, men urinated shamelessly wherever they happened to be standing, even if there were women present.

More than one red-faced GI, filled to bursting with weak French beer, found himself urinating against the

French civilians enjoying American troop rations.

tar-painted walls of a pissoir under the bored gaze of French housewives busy peeling their potatoes and preparing their meals. As Sergeant Giles observed: 'People who build pissoirs in the open streets are people I don't even pretend to understand. What really gets you is to see a man walk into one of those things, not even a door on them, and cut loose with women passing right besides him ... I've always read the French are the most cultivated people in the world. A pissoir cultivated? Not in my book!'[16]

Hardly surprisingly, these young Americans, ordinary men of no great education, suddenly uprooted and thrust into a strange environment, were full of prejudice against the French. The 'Frogs' ate snails and 'stinking, runny cheese'. They ate mushrooms and weeds such as the dandelion, or *pisse-en-lit*; they had never heard of good old American hamburgers. They situated their 'cathouses' right next to the churches, which everyone attended very sanctimoniously every Sunday – including the whores. The 'Frogs' didn't work like good Americans did; they took a couple of hours off for lunch and washed it all down with a good deal of 'dago red'. They didn't even know what iced tea was! There were other culture-shocks in store for the GIs. The 'Frog' women didn't shave their legs, let alone their armpits. Girdles were unheard of outside of 'Gay Paree'. Most of them didn't even have toothbrushes. In summer, the country women didn't even wear drawers ...

And so it went on, this litany of disapproval and downright dislike from the boys of the 'ZI.'* Their mission was to liberate the French, but ironically, by the time the campaign in Europe was over, they had come to realise that they had more in common with their enemies, the Germans: thrifty people like themselves, who were clean and industrious and lived in houses with proper plumbing and steam-heat. As Staff Sergeant Giles summed it up that summer, 'Everything in France seems to be stone or brick and so old. Seems they're a hundred years behind in their ways, too.'[17]

In the middle, standing between the white American and the French civilians that summer, were the so-called 'invisible soldiers' who made up the largest contingent of US servicemen in France. These were the black Americans who ran the Red Ball Express, manned the quartermaster depots, filled the graves registration details and acted as gunners in the rear-line anti-aircraft detachments guarding the ports and beachheads. These black servicemen lived in a strange limbo between their white comrades of the US

*Zone of the Interior, in military parlance, *i.e.* the USA

Army, many of them 'crackers' who looked down on them as second-class citizens, and the white French civilians, who, not having come into contact with blacks before, didn't really know what to make of them.

Black Americans hadn't welcomed the USA's entry into World War Two with any great enthusiasm; it simply didn't seem to them to be 'their' war. It was reported that a black sharecropper told his plantation owner at the time of Pearl Harbour: 'By the way, Captain, I hear the Japs done declared war on you white folks.'[18] Another black student in the South spoke up for many when he declared, 'The Army jim crows us. The Navy lets us serve only as messmen. The Red Cross refuses our blood … Lynchings continue. We are disenfranchised, jim crowed and spat upon. What more could Hitler do than that?' Indeed, a poll of black people after Pearl Harbour revealed that eighteen per cent of them believed they would be treated better under Japanese rule than in white America![19]

Due to public pressure from both black and white organisations, large numbers of young black men were drafted into the armed forces and sent south for training. Here the northerners among them were shocked to discover that they were treated as third-class citizens in a segregated US Army and were regarded as lower than animals by the white civilians. Often they trained with wooden bullets, were forced to sit apart from their white comrades on buses, and were turned away from bars and restaurants. As many of them commented after the war, in the South, even German POWs were treated better than native black Americans wearing the uniform of their country. One remarked bitterly, after being refused service in a restaurant, 'If we were *untermenschen* in Germany, they would break our bones. As "colored" men in Salina, they only break our hearts.'[20]

Those black servicemen who were shipped to England for the invasion found that although they were objects of wonder and curiosity to the British civilians, most of whom hadn't seen black men before, they were treated for the most part without prejudice. In England they could even dance with a white woman. But their white fellow-Americans had brought their prejudices with them. More than once when a white soldier from the South discovered that a black American had drunk out of a glass before him in a pub, he would break the glass on the bar and fling a shilling at the barmaid to pay for the damage. At dances, whites tossed the blacks out, refusing to breathe the same air as 'those animals.' In Manchester, the sight of a black sailor kissing a white girl caused a race riot, and the city had to be declared out of bounds to all Americans for two weeks afterwards.

More horrifying incidents took place. A female reporter spending a holiday in Weymouth attended a US Army dance there and late that night heard some 'dreadful screaming.' Next day she found out that 'a black soldier had been castrated by his white comrades for dancing with a white girl all the evening. This was an almost all-Southern outfit, the 1st Division, and offending GIs

(Above) 'Red Ball' Express speeds delivery of supplies to US forces. (Below) Black US soldiers unloading supplies from the 'Red Ball' Express.

were merely transferred round to different outfits, the officer being a "southern gentleman" himself.'[21] A few days later the same woman reported that when climbing down from the pier for a swim, she found herself treading 'on a black man with a knife in his back.' He had, it seemed, been guilty of a similar 'crime.'[22]

The blacks, enraged by such incidents, sometimes fought back, and often with the help of British soldiers. One episode at Wrexham, when British commandos pitched in on the side of their black comrades, became known locally as 'the Battle of Mount Street.' In May, 1944, the *Daily Mirror* collected thirty thousand signatures to save the life of a black GI who had been sentenced to death by Eisenhower for allegedly raping a white woman in a village near Bath. He was freed that June.

In France, the black servicemen found that white American prejudice still pursued them. Admittedly, black Americans had got off to a bad start. Exactly three days after the D-Day landings, two black soldiers had been arrested by the MPs and charged with the rape and murder of a French woman. And by August, Normandy Base Section was reporting to Eisenhower at Supreme Headquarters that 'unfortunately most of these undisciplined acts [rape, murder, looting *etc.*] were caused by colored troops.'[23] To set against this, however, black gunners had performed well at the long siege of Brest on

the Brittany coast, and the brass often quoted approvingly the case of the black gun-layer who reportedly cried after every shell fired, 'Ramcke,* count yo' men!' But no matter how bravely they fought, black Americans in France felt they could never escape the prejudice against them: prejudice that, under American influence, was now beginning to rub off on the French.

This was hardly surprising when Eisenhower talked about his kitchen staff as 'my darkies' and Patton routinely referred to black soldiers as 'niggers'. Patton did, however, take a less condescending view when he welcomed one of the four all-black fighting units, the 716th Tank Battalion,** into his command. He told them: 'Men, you are the first Negro tankers ever to fight in the American army. I would never have asked for you if you were not good. I have nothing but the best in my army. I don't care what color you are as long as you go up there and kill those Kraut sons-of-bitches. Everyone has their eyes on you and are expecting great things from you. Most of all your race is looking forward to your success. Don't let them down and damn you, don't let me down!' Patton ended his little pep talk to the amazed black tankers with his usual string of profanities. 'They say it is patriotic to die

*The fanatical German paratroop general in command at Brest.
**In the ETO there were two black tank battalions and two artillery, commanded mostly by white officers.

for your country. Well, let's see how many patriots we can make out of those German motherfuckers! There is one thing you men will be able to say when you go home. You may all thank God that thirty years from now when you are sitting with your grandson upon your knee and he asks, "Grandfather, what did you do in World War II?" you won't have to say, "I shovelled shit in Mississippi!" '[24]

The typical attitude of the brass to black servicemen was exemplified by General Hughes of Eisenhower's staff, who, when he went to present a medal to Corporal Bradley, a black driver with the Red Ball Express, was told by the corporal in charge that it was the first time the men had lined up – for an identity parade after a rape. Hughes had chuckled, perhaps not realising the full implication of the statement.[25]

Ingrained Southern prejudice was further fuelled by the fact that there were so few blacks serving in combat units. As a result of this, white front-line troops saw their black comrades as sitting out the war in France, safely distanced from the shooting. The reason was that senior American officers didn't trust black Americans as combat soldiers, in spite of the fact that blacks had been fighting in the ranks of the Armies of the Republic since the days of Old Salem Poor, who had fought heroically at Bunker Hill during the War of Independence.

The US brass had some grounds for their lack of confidence in black troops. Experiences with black combat troops in Italy and the Pacific had been unfortunate, and the commander of the US Fifth Army in that theatre, General Mark Clark, went so far as to describe his 92nd black Infantry Division as the worst he had. Later, in 1945, that particular division would crumple twice under enemy attacks and create anxiety along the whole Allied line.

Nor did the brass trust the blacks with the highly complex equipment of a combat outfit. White officers felt they were too poorly educated to take satisfactory care of trucks, tanks and other vehicles, and reported that they drove them without sufficient oil, or too long in low gears, and burned out the motors.

Nobody would deny that black educational standards at this time were low. Sixty-seven percent of all black enlisted men from the South had less than a high school education. But how could it be otherwise in a part of the country that was too prejudiced to spend more than a pittance on black education?

So, for the time being, the black soldier in the rear echelons continued to carry out his humble, mundane tasks, the only danger he faced being the occasional wrath of his white comrades on leave from the front. Black Sergeant Chester Jones, for example, took off a few hours from his job with the Red Ball Express to visit Paris with a buddy. They landed in a brothel and Jones' buddy was inside and upstairs before I could blink an eye.' Suddenly two drunken white infantrymen also on leave staggered into the place and, seeing the black men talking to white French women, immediately pulled their pistols on the

Perimeter defence.

blacks. One of the whites stumbled over to Jones and snarled: 'You black sons-of-bitches don't sit with white women at home and I'll be damned if you do it here when I'm around!'

Jones got the message. He took off, 'expecting a bullet any minute,' and reported the incident to the rest of his group, who were still with their trucks. They then returned in a fighting mood, armed with carbines, and 'stomped' the two whites, knocking one of them clean across the room. The truckers tossed them out into the street after mopping them up. They didn't return with reinforcements '... If there is a humorous side to this incident, my friend joined us downstairs eventually, totally unaware that anything out of the ordinary had transpired.'[26]

Incidents such as this drove some blacks to extreme measures. After being beaten up by white GIs soon after arriving in France, Master Sergeant Floyd Jones of the black 578th Field Artillery Battalion never went on leave without being armed to the teeth. He related later: 'I was always accompanied by a .45, a knife, comparable to a Bowie knife, and a couple of live grenades. I wasn't wearing that arsenal for fun. No bunch of white GIs were going to beat the shit out of me again ... When I went on furlough I looked like an infantryman heading for the front line. Whenever I saw a bunch of white GIs heading my way, I just unbuttoned my coat and as the saying goes, "let it all hang out." Believe me, they walked on by ...'[27]

But things were about to change for black American soldiers serving in France, in a small way, at least. Soon it was decided by their commander, General Lee, that due to a shortage of riflemen at the front, blacks would be accepted as combat infantrymen together with their white comrades. 'It is planned to assign you,' he said 'without regard to color or race to the units where assistance is most needed ... for your comrades at the front are anxious to share the glory of victory with you. Your relatives and friends everywhere have been urging that you be granted this privilege. The Supreme Commander, your Commanding General and other veteran officers who have served with you are confident that many of you will take advantage of this opportunity and carry on in keeping with the glorious record of colored troops in former wars.'[28]

Surprisingly enough, in view of the blatant hypocrisy of the appeal and the poor treatment most black men had received during their service in the armed forces, something like 2,500 blacks volunteered. In one black engineer battalion stationed in France, 171 out of 186 men volunteered to fight as infantrymen, with four first sergeants accepting a reduction in rank to that of private in order to do so (naturally, the white infantrymen weren't going to have black men commanding them). In another COMZ unit, a laundry company, 100 out of 260 chose to fight; as one of them told a reporter from the *Stars and Stripes:* 'We're all in this thing together now, white and Negro Americans in the same companies. And that's how it should be. That's why I volunteered. Most Negro troops are in the service outfits. We've been giving a lot of sweat.

Montgomery visiting the Albert Canal area of the battle front, where he met some of his Armoured Commanders.

Now I think we'll mix some blood with it.'[29]

And so they would, in due course. But so would *all* of the Allied combat troops in Europe. For the honeymoon was over. Now the battle would commence again and not cease for many months to come. The troops had seen the last of 'Gay Paree,' many of them. There would be no victory for Christmas, or for long after that. Instead there would be battle and more battle. In the end, of the two million young men, black and white, who saw action in the months to come, some 700,000-odd would be killed or wounded in combat.

For the men on the ground, it started on the morning of Saturday, September 16th, 1944. At ten-thirty officers of all General Horrocks' XXX Corps divisions started to assemble in the cinema opposite the railway station in the ugly Belgian mining town of Bourg Leopold, only recently liberated from the Germans. The cinema, which had once shown the films of Jean Gabin and Arletty to its shabby miner audiences, was as ugly as the town itself, but the assembled officers were too excited to pay much heed to their surroundings. Their was an air of expectancy, an instinctive feeling among those present that a major offensive was about to be launched.

By eleven o'clock the place was packed, and heavily armed British MPs took up their positions at all entrances and exits. Now the cinema was sealed off from the outside world. One minute later, right on cue, the corps commander entered, tall, lean, ascetic-looking, striding down the aisle with a quip and a jest for his more senior commanders as he went: 'Hello, Errol, what's this I hear about a mobile cocktail bar?' ... 'Hello, von Thoma,* how's the Wicked Wyvern?' ... 'Hello Jo, how's Stonk Hall?** I'm not coming to visit you again after the way I was treated last time. Do you always live in a barrage?' And so on, until he finally mounted the little stage.

There he took a pointer from the waiting staff officers, who pulled back a black curtain to reveal an enormous sketch map of Holland between its frontier with Belgium and the Zuider Zee. Three great arrows decorated it, forming a triple-pronged fork. Tapes, red and purple, encircled three Dutch cities – Grave, Nijmegen and Arnhem. At the time, the names were virtually unknown to the assembled officers. But those who survived what was to come would remember them as if they had been carved on their hearts as Queen Mary once said 'Calais' had been on hers.

' "This is a tale you will tell your grandchildren," began the Corps Commander, then, his sense of humour getting the better of him, added as an aside, "and mighty bored they will be!" '[30] Patiently General Horrocks waited till the laughter had died down and then he commenced his briefing.

*General Thomas of the 43rd (Wyvern) Division.
**'Stonk' is the soldier's term for a mortar barrage.

6 DISASTER AT ARNHEM

'Christ – of course we would have done it again!'

British soldier, quoted after failure of Operation Market Garden

On Sunday morning, September 17th, 1944, the ill-fated Operation Market Garden, the 'lightning stroke' with which Montgomery hoped to end the war in 1944, was launched. With an ear-splitting roar, vast wedges of aircraft rose from their airfields in the British Midlands and started to head south. Cattle panicked in the fields; traffic ground to a halt as drivers stopped their cars to look up; civilians disturbed over breakfast while perusing the 'Sundays', stared out of the window in amazement at the huge armada flying by in the sunny September Sky. In a poorer suburb of London, a Salvation Army band fell silent, overwhelmed by the thunder of so many planes – all save the drummer, who beat out the 'V for Victory' motto on his big bass drum.[1]

From their bases around Grantham in Lincolnshire, the planes carrying the British 1st Airborne Division and the US 82nd Airborne flew south to join their comrades of the US 101st Airborne, and then swept on to form up over the Channel. From there onwards they flew in three mighty columns, some ten miles broad and at least a hundred miles long, the most formidable airborne force since D-Day. The great adventure, designed to open Holland to the advancing Allied armies and from there to deal a death-blow to Germany's industrial heartland, had commenced.

As the sound of aircraft engines died away, the civilians returned to their Sunday papers, wondering perhaps for a while what the airborne armada signified before becoming immersed again in the stories with which the papers regaled them this Sunday morning. The *News of the World*, for example, informed its readers that 'Hitler's batman' had just been captured in the Belgian town of Ghent. Here he had told his interrogators that the Führer 'alternates between kindness and brutality and is very

The first two gliders to touch down, showing where wing tips interlocked. In the foreground are members of the Artillery Regiment.

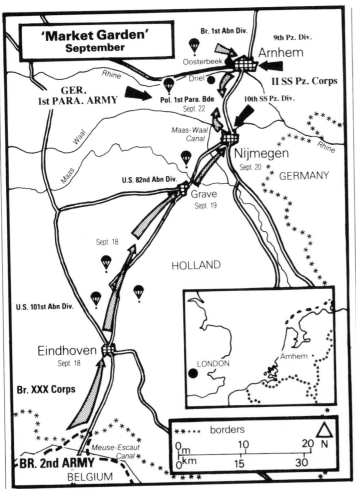

nervous ... and he is not averse to blondes. One of them is a typist who visits him in a special car.' The *Empire News*, now alas defunct, carried the epoch-making news that Monty's pullover, 'lost in the withdrawal of 1940,' had just been returned to him at the Belgian town of Louvain and that he was 'wearing it again.' The more highbrow *Observer* warned that 'returning evacuees' had been hit by the 'new flying bombs.' 'Motor shares', its financial editor noted, had fallen. All in all, it seemed to be a Sunday not unlike many other Sundays in this long, dreary war.

In fact, this was perhaps the most momentous Sunday of the whole conflict. For today, the now Field Marshal Bernard Law Montgomery planned to capture key bridges across the Waal, the Maas and the Rhine, and thus allow the Allied forces to cross into the Reich. In order to do this, his paras, British, Canadian and American, would be dropped behind German lines and would seize and hold the bridges until Horrocks' XXX Corps linked up with them; then the whole of Dempsey's Second Army, plus the newly created US Ninth Army under General Simpson, would follow up and crash straight across the border into Germany. Thence they would smash through Germany's industrial region, the Ruhr, and head straight for Berlin. Within days the war might be over, and the 'boys' would be home for Christmas. That, at any rate, was the plan.

Now the airborne armada started to cross the enemy-held coast. Flak opened up on them immediately. The dive-bombers and fighters went into action. Swooping down at four hundred miles an hour, they plastered the German flak positions with rockets and bombs. Majestically, the transports, tugs and gliders sailed on into Belgium.

Now the planes of the US 101st Airborne passed over Horrocks' waiting XXX Corps. Below them stretched mile after mile of stalled armour and infantry, ready to set off on the great link-up once the bridges had been secured. The paras craned their necks to get a better view, and were suitably impressed. The Limeys had a lot of muscle down there. To their front, orange smoke-flares exploded and began to burn. It was the signal. They were crossing the British front-line.

More flak opened up. White tracer curved upwards, gathering speed by the second. Brown puffballs rocked the planes violently as shells exploded around them. Here and there a transport was struck. A few streamed down to the ground in flames, scattering white, blossoming parachutes in their smoking wakes. Still the pilots held their tight formations. The DZ wasn't far off now, and even pilots who had been severely wounded managed to hold on. Second Lieutenant Herbert Shulman was one. 'I'm gonna drop these troops right on the DZ!' he cried, his face contorted with pain, as smoke and flame streamed from his stricken plane. He did just that. Moments after the last 'Screaming Eagle' had shouted his *Geronimo*!* and leapt out into nothing, Shulman's plane fell out of the burning sky and slammed into the ground, a mass of flames.[2]

But even in the midst of horror there were moments of grim humour. As the paras in one transport plane lined up to jump, a flak shell ripped a great hole in the seat just vacated by a 'Screaming Eagle.' Turning to his buddies, he shouted disgustedly, '*Now*, they give us a latrine!'[3] Another paratrooper, Private Robert Boyce, was poised at the door of his plane, ready to jump, when he saw some Dutch civilians standing three hundred feet below, giving the planes the 'V for Victory' sign. Spontaneously he quipped to his friends, 'They're giving us two to one we don't make it!' Then he jumped with the rest.[4]

In spite of the fact that one in four of their transports were hit and damaged, the men of the 101st made what was considered a perfect jump, and within the hour were moving off to seize their objectives, the bridges and river crossing for a stretch of fifteen miles immediately to the front of Horrocks' XXX Corps.

Ahead of them, and south of the British 1st Airborne Division which would land last at Arnhem, the men of General 'Gentleman Jim' Gavin's 82nd Airborne Division also ran into flak. Mindful of the night-horrors of their jump into Normandy the previous June, the veterans came down with guns blazing. Captain Briand Beaudin pumped slug after slug from his Colt .45 as he came floating straight for a German flak battery. First Lieutenant James Coyle did the same, hitting the deck just a few yards away from a young German soldier. He snapped up his weapon, ready to fire again, but the boy had thrown away his rifle and helmet already and was running for his life. 'He was

114

*War cry of the 101st, after the legendary Indian chief

Paratroop drop.

only a kid,' Coyle recalled years later, 'about eighteen years old. I couldn't shoot an unarmed man. The last I saw of the boy, he was running for the German border.'[5]

While the men of the 101st Division successfully captured the bridge across the River Maas at Grave and began to advance on the railway bridge across the Maas-Waal Canal, the 82nd started to assemble in force. This time the 82nd were attempting something new – the landing of a whole battalion of field artillery at the same time as the first wave came down. Understandably they were taking no chances.

In the event, the operation went smoothly, except when the commander of the 376th Parachute Field Artillery, Colonel Griffiths, broke his ankle during the drop. Undeterred, Griffiths ordered himself to be placed in a wheelbarrow found by one of his gunners and was trundled thus from gun to gun until he was satisfied they were all correctly positioned. That done, he allowed himself to be wheeled to 'Gentleman Jim' and reported, sitting upright in his barrow, 'Guns in position, sir, and ready to fire on call!'[6]

Now the second wave of gliders came drifting in, carrying supplies and support troops. So far the flight had been successful, but at this point things began to go wrong. Soon after his glider was released, co-pilot Captain Anthony Jedrziewski saw to his horror that he was heading straight for Germany 'on a one-glider invasion.'[7] The same thing happened to Captain James Connelly's Waco glider, only in this case, things were worse: the pilot had been killed by flak. Connelly, who had never flown a glider before, had to take over the controls and somehow managed to bring the Waco down inside the Reich. Together with one survivor, he managed to find his way back to the battle soon to commence.

Now the gliders of the Airborne Corps HQ came swooping in under the command of that elegant guardee, General Browning, husband of the popular novelist of the time, Daphne du Maurier. All landed safely. To everyone's surprise, Browning, as immaculate and ramrod-stiff as ever, left the glider, gazed at the littered DZ and exclaimed to Colonel George S. Chatterton, 'My God, we're here, George!' Next instant, the normally super-correct general doubled across the fields to the trees beyond, which marked the frontier with Germany. There, while his staff watched open-mouthed, he ripped open his flies and urinated. Returning to his astonished command, he explained: 'I wanted to be the first officer to pee in Germany.'[8]

Horrocks had been watching the great airborne operation from the roof of a factory near the Meuse*-Escaut Canal since eleven o'clock that Sunday morning. The sight of the air armada had been comforting, but he was 'under no illusion that this was going to be an easy battle.' Another

*The French-English form of 'Meuse' becomes 'Maas' in German and Dutch.

thing worried the corps commander, too; the fact that this was Sunday. Horrocks wasn't a particularly religious man, but in all his long military career, embracing two world wars and a revolution, no assault launched by him on a Sunday 'had ever been completely successful.'[9]

Yet everything for XXX Corps started 'swimmingly,' in the words of the guards who would spearhead the link-up with the paratroopers. At the point, Captain Mick O'Cock of the Irish Guards radioed back the message: 'Advance going well. Leading squadron has got through.'[10]

Hardly had his words been received at Horrocks's HQ when German guns on both sides of the single road leading north to the paras opened up with a roar. White, glowing armour-piercing shells hurtled towards the Irishmen's tanks. Within two minutes the first three tanks of the leading squadron and six of the follow-up were out of action – 'brewed up', to use the tankers' phrase: sprawled across the narrow, elevated Dutch road, blazing furiously, or lying with their tracks shot off, crippled and unable to move. 'We had just crossed the border when we were ambushed,' Lieutenant Cyril Russell recalled. 'Suddenly the tanks in front either slewed across the road or burned where they stood. The awful realisation dawned on me that the next one to go was the one I was sitting on.'[11]

Lance-Corporal James Doggart didn't even have time to come to that fearsome conclusion. 'I don't remember seeing or hearing the explosion … I was suddenly flat on my back in a ditch with the tank leaning over me. I had a Bren-gun across my chest and next to me was a young lad with his arm nearly severed. Nearby another of our men was dead.'[12]

At the rear of that tank column, Lieutenant Barry Quinan had the horrifying experience of seeing tank after tank of his trapped squadron being hit, with the fire coming ever closer to his own vehicle. He saw one tank commander 'trying to shield his face from a sheet of flame that engulfed the whole machine.'[13] Then it was his turn. Out on the high single road, with German paratroopers dug in on both sides, the tankers were sitting ducks. Horrocks' great drive to link up with the embattled paratroopers attacking the bridges had run into trouble right from the start.

But it wasn't only the Germans who slowed down XXX Corps' drive north. The bad habits which the British Army had picked up in the course of their four-year wait to return to the continent, plus the traditional British attitude to work, also didn't help. Lieutenant John Gorman, who had just won the military Cross for bravery in action, noted that on the first night of the push, instead of pressing on to rescue their comrades, the big Guardsmen bedded down as soon as it got dark. At this stage, the initial opposition on both sides of the road had been overcome, and it wouldn't have been too dangerous to carry on. But instead the Guards stuck to the routine of their training schemes in the UK. As Gorman noted, 'Habit seemed to

A group of British paratroopers in Arnhem.

dictate that one slept at night and worked by day.'[14]

It was the same with Captain John Foley's squadron. While British paratroopers had begun to fight for their lives at Arnhem, his men settled down for the night, to be regaled by their kind Dutch hosts with food and tea. Next morning, the thoughts of Foley's men were still on tea; it turned out that the tea served them by their Dutch hostess was the last in Eindhoven – the Dutch woman 'had sworn she would keep it for when the English came, because the English so love tea.'[15]

It seemed as if in the middle of what was to be one of the campaign's most desperate struggles, the British 'teabreak' mentality still prevailed.

While the advance continued along that forty-yard-wide corridor northwards, the paras of the two American divisions slogged it out with the enemy, well aware of the desperate situation of their British comrades further on at Arnhem. At Best, several score of them were killed in close combat, including Lieutenant-Colonel Robert Cole, who had previously won America's highest award for bravery, the Congressional Medal of Honor. In the same fight, Private Joe E. Mann was badly wounded in both arms and had to have both limbs strapped to his sides by the medics. It was in this almost helpless position that he saw a German stick grenade come sailing through the air to land among his buddies. Unable to free his arms, Mann manoeuvred himself on top of it and shielded his comrades from the blast. As his company commander, Lieutenant Edward Wierzbowski, bent over his shattered body, Mann spoke only once. He croaked, 'My back's gone.' Then he was dead. That day, another winner of the Congressional Medal of Honor died on the battlefield.[16]

But in spite of the American paratroopers' desperate attempts to break through to Arnhem, the operation was already beginning to turn very sour. At Eindhoven, war correspondent Alan Moorehead searched for hours in the darkness for a bed for the night. Already the Dutch civilians had decided which way the wind was blowing and had fled their homes. The result was that the poorer Dutch houses were already packed with refugees. Furthermore, the Dutch civilians wanted nothing more to do with their liberators, not with the Germans just up the road. At one point, Moorehead and the other correspondents called at a great castle untouched by the war and inhabited solely by an elderly aristocratic lady and her maid. 'No,' the lady of the house replied severely to their request for accommodation, 'you cannot stay here. You have not the right.' Finally they found lodgings in a roadside café, but were awakened in the middle of the night by a Dutch resistance man who reported that German tanks were coming down the road. Moorehead no longer cared. 'We were too tired ... The relief of Arnhem seemed hopeless, we had lost our kit, we were cut off and consequently our messages were not getting through. We were cold, wet and dirty ... It was one of those recurring moments in the war when one says: 'This is enough. I will not put up with anything any longer.'[17]

The Americans, despite the success of their part of the operation, were also becoming pessimistic about the future of the great push. Although they and the Guards had fought well together on several occasions, the paras didn't think the Englishmen were pushing hard enough. Colonel Tucker of the 504th US Regimental Combat Team, well up in front, fumed at the slowness of his British comrades: 'We had killed ourselves crossing the Waal [in one battalion alone there had been 134 killed, wounded or reported missing] to grab the north end of the bridge. We just stood there, seething, as the British settled in for the night, failing to take advantage of the situation. We couldn't understand it. It simply wasn't the way we did things in the American Army – especially if it had been our guys hanging on by their fingernails 11 miles away. We'd have been going, rolling without stop. That's what Georgie Patton would have done whether it was daylight or dark

... They were fighting the war by the book. They had "harboured" for the night. As usual they stopped for tea ...'[18]

Colonel Tucker's bitter mood wasn't improved by the fact that from his command post he could see that only three British tanks had come to assist him and his hard-pressed paras. These were manned by Grenadier Guardsmen under the command of Captain Lord Carrington, one day to be his country's Foreign Secretary. 'All night long,' Colonel Tucker recorded later, '(he) kept calling for more security. I asked him what it was he feared since there was a whole American battalion 1,000 yards to his front. He said he wanted people dug in around his tanks – that we didn't have. I knew we had to get well out, then clean up the areas in back of us.'[19]

Tucker's disenchantment with the British Army was symptomatic. That third week of September 1944, the American Army seemed to go sour on Montgomery and the British. Nothing of any great significance marked the change. But thereafter not a single American general save Eisenhower had a good word to say for the British Army and the British soldier. In practice, if not in theory, the real, *effective* military alliance between the Americans and the British was about over.

Meanwhile in Arnhem, the beleaguered paras were fighting for their lives. For the British 1st Airborne Division, which had landed outside the key town of Arnhem, things had gone badly from the start. Cut off from his division, the commanding general, General Robert Urquhart, had been forced to go into hiding for the first 36 hours of the operation in order to avoid being captured by the enemy. Thereupon two of his brigadiers had begun to feud over who should take command, and the row had quickly developed into an open slanging-match. Finally, the attempt of three battalions to link up with their comrades of Colonel John Frost's 2nd Parachute Battalion, which had captured the key Arnhem road bridge on the first day, had failed, and the battalions had suffered severe casualties, including two commanding officers. The retreat into what was to become the 'cauldron' had commenced.

Regimental Sergeant Major 'Chalky' White, a bantam-sized regular, already wounded, struggled to bring some order to the withdrawal of one of those battalions, the 10th, but found the going tough. In spite of all the later propaganda to the contrary, his men were badly undertrained. Individually they may have been brave and bold, but they certainly weren't an élite formation; indeed, in its last ten months in England, the battalion hadn't once trained together in its full strength. Now this lack of training was beginning to tell.

As 'Chalky' White attempted to set up a skirmish line so that other paras pinned down by German machine-gun fire could withdraw, he discovered to his dismay that the officers of the 10th were shouting at each other in obvious confusion. His moustache bristling angrily, he raced over to them and cried, 'Will you stop that shouting, gentlemen,

A patrol of British paratroopers searching a ruined house in Oosterbeek.

please![20] His CO, Lieutenant Colonel Ken Smyth, appeared from the centre of the confused throng, his face flushed angrily, and bellowed, 'Don't you bloody well shout at me like that, Sergeant Major!' It was an all-too-typical incident as they retreated to the place where they would make their final, bloody stand.

General Urquhart, now at his HQ in the Hartenstein Hotel, the centre of the 'cauldron,' was aware that things were not as they should be. Sitting at his desk, he was alarmed by a cry from outside: 'The Germans are coming!' He flung a look out of the window. Small groups of young soldiers were running from their slit-trenches in panic, among them a tall young officer. Swiftly he called his Chief of Staff, Colonel Charles Mackenzie, and together they confronted the panic-stricken soldiers. At first they attempted to get them to go back to their positions with words. When words failed, they were forced to use threats of physical violence. Eventually the message got through, and reluctantly the men returned to their posts. Later, however, when Mackenzie inspected the perimeter defences, he found a slit-trench and its Bren-gun abandoned once more. Afraid that the rot was already beginning to set in, he informed Urquhart, who told his senior commanders that they would have to take the most severe measures to halt the growing uneasiness and edginess among the men.[21]

There were heroes, however, many of them in the ranks of the 1st Airborne. Some were recognised later and rewarded, others were fated to suffer and die without their heroism ever receiving recognition save from those who fought beside them. One such was Captain L.E. Queripel. During the retreat of the 10th Parachute Battalion, already broken up into tattered little groups of survivors, Queripel, a burly, dark-haired officer from the German-occupied Channel Islands, already wounded in the face, found himself in a ditch with a handful of men, with the SS only yards away. Twice he picked up German stick grenades, 'potato mashers,' and heaved them back at the Germans. Piling up the last of their grenades in front of him on the edge of the ditch, he ordered his men to make a run for it. As they pelted for the rear, he fired his last magazine at the Germans and then crouched there with the grenades to wait for the SS. No one ever saw him alive again. He won his country's highest award for gallantry, the Victoria Cross.[22]

An aptly-named Major Robert Cain of the 2nd South Staffordshires won the same award for his bravery during that terrible week in the cauldron. More than once he tackled German tanks with his primitive anti-tank weapon, the Piat. Once he was temporarily blinded, his face lacerated by shell splinters, and had to be dragged off to the regimental aid post, yelling, swearing, and sobbing, but half an hour later he was his old self once more and back in action. Of the five men who won the Victoria Cross that week at Arnhem, Major Cain was the only one who survived to receive it from his king. The rest were all decorated posthumously.

But they weren't all heroes at Arnhem. Many were still in their teens and had never been under fire; it was hardly surprising they lost their nerve. Glider pilot Louis Hagen, a German Jew who exactly ten years before in 1934 had spent his days cleaning out the slop-bins in a concentration camp located near the German town of Torgau, had just returned from a patrol and was ordered to report on it to General Urquhart at the Hartenstein Hotel. There, lurking in the cellars, he found men of all ranks and regiments hiding out. 'They looked like people who had been seasick for days … Nothing in the world could coax them up. Down there they vegetated, ate, slept and relieved themselves in a world where only their fear was reality.' Some he recognised. 'There was Sergeant A, quite a close friend of mine back at the station. He was a good-looking chap of twenty-eight, always neatly turned out, a good pilot.' Hagen tried to persuade his friend to leave the cellar for his own good, 'because he was obviously going through hell.' But he refused, and finally Hagen left him to the twilight world of the cellar and the not-too-tender mercies of RSM Lord, who proposed to use force to turf out the 'dodgers.'[23]

In the cellars of the gardener's house nearby, Hagen found another comrade, a man for whom he had little affection: 'Staff Sergeant G, the tough guy of our flight … always getting into scraps with the chaps of other units … and calling me 'la-di-da' and 'Miss Hagen' because I wore pyjamas and did not swear. He used to brag about what he would do once he met the Germans. He would take the first German child by the legs and tear it in two … as the only good German was a dead German. There was no sense in reminding him of this because, now that he was so consumed by fear, he was only pathetic.'[24]

The hotel headquarters were now under almost permanent, pulverising bombardment by the German guns, and the effect on the men was appalling. One barricaded himself in a shed and refused to come out. Periodically he would shout 'Come on, you bastards' and empty a magazine of his Sten-gun all around the shed. No one dared approach the place, until finally there was a long silence. His comrades broke down the door and found the man lying inside, dead.[25] Another wandered around all night, his eyes glittering crazily, shaking the exhausted men in the slit-trenches and asking them, 'Have you got faith?'[26]

A medic, 'Taffy' Brace, came across another paratrooper softly singing 'The White Cliffs of Dover.' Brace nodded his approval of the man's fine voice and his calm under the circumstances, for Brace was a Welshman and knew a fine voice when he heard one. To his surprise, the singing soldier suddenly grabbed him violently by the throat and hissed, 'I'll kill you. What do you know about Dover?'[27]

By now, the bombardment was so intense and unremitting that many men broke down altogether; for them, madness was their only refuge from the horror and carnage. Surrounded on all sides, pounded by gunfire day and night, despairing of ever being reached by Horrocks'

German prisoners captured in the suburbs of Arnhem.

XXX Corps, the men in the cauldron were down to the last of their food, water and ammunition. In Urquhart's HQ, Sergeant Major Lord distributed boiled sweets as if they were precious gems, two per person. Water had to be either drained from the radiators of wrecked vehicles or fetched from the nearby well, which involved a mad dash under fire across a carpet of dead bodies; the water, when finally hauled up, was stained pink with blood. Down in the cellars, wounded men were packed like sardines; bandages had run out, and there was now morphia only for the most serious cases.

Yet in spite of the unbearable personal stress and the desperate plight of the wounded and shell-shocked, Louis Hagen recalled an extraordinary civility among the men: 'The life we led at Arnhem was nearer to an animal existence than anything we could have conceived, and yet the more savage the fighting got, the more civilised the men seemed to become ... There was such gentleness and friendship among them as would have made any of them almost uncomfortable back on the station. Although they were fighting like tigers and in that fight had to be completely ruthless, there was no tough behaviour and coarseness of speech. It was almost uncanny.'[28]

And there were plenty of stalwarts left who fought on and on, even though they knew their position was hopeless. Major Dickie Lonsdale was one. Swathed in dirty, bloody bandages and standing in the pulpit of the shell-shattered church at Lower Oosterbeek, Lonsdale delivered a rousing address to his tattered band of survivors: 'We fought the Germans in North Africa, Sicily and Italy. They weren't good enough for us then. They're bloody well not good enough for us now!'[29]

On the morning of September 20th, 1944, seven miles away from the cauldron, Captain Eric Mackay of the Sappers crawled from man to man, handing each of his dirty, battered engineers two 'bennies', or benzedrine pills. For forty-eight hours the men of his squadron, plus those of Major Gough's Reconnaissance Squadron and Colonel Frost's 2nd Parachute Battalion, had been holding the bridge across the Rhine against elements of two German SS panzer divisions, the 9th and 10th, and before them they had another long day. The 'bennies' were Mackay's last, but he knew his men needed them desperately. Most of them had had no sleep for 72 hours, no food for 24 and no water for 12. In spite of the dangers of the 'pep pills,' which made some argumentative, gave others double vision, and could cause wounded men to hallucinate, Mackay knew they needed the 'bennies' if they were to keep going. They had to hold their positions in the wrecked houses guarding the northern end of the bridge if there was to be any chance of a link-up with Montgomery's Second Army.

This morning, Mackay was horrified by the appearance of his survivors. 'The men were exhausted and filthy and I was sick to the stomach every time I looked at them,' he wrote later. 'Haggard, with bloodshot and red-rimmed eyes, almost everyone had some sort of dirty field-dressing and blood was everywhere.' Indeed, as some wounded were carried down into the cellar, he noted that 'on each landing blood had formed into pools and ran in small rivulets down the stairs.'[30]

But now, as the new dawn approached and the sky turned a dull grey, the first German Tigers once more started lumbering forward, with SS infantry crouched in tight bunches behind them. At point-blank range the enemy tanks started to pound the paras' positions with their huge 88mm cannon. Building after building went up in flames or crashed to the ground, but against impossible odds the sappers, the infantry, the reconnaissance troopers all fought back, and by the end of the morning forced the Germans to withdraw, leaving more field-grey shapes crumpled awkwardly on the bridge as they went.

It was a last and hollow victory. Now those among the 700 men on the bridge who were still on their feet knew they hadn't a chance of being relieved, either by the Second Army or by their comrades trapped in the cauldron. Yet still they refused to withdraw. As Colonel Frost, the burly, moustached paratrooper whose career had begun in the Red Devils back in 1940 told Major Gough of the Recce, whose first taste of action this was, he didn't see how he could 'fight on out to the last minute, then go, and have our wounded [there were 300 seriously wounded men in the

The bridge at Arnhem after the attack.

cellars] roasted.'[31]

Around noon, Frost himself was seriously wounded and had to be carried down to the cellar by his batman. Father Egan, a Catholic priest, saw him brought in and thought he looked 'dead-tired and dejected.'[32] Others were shocked to see that their CO had been badly wounded, since he had been the heart of the defence of the vital bridge. One of his subalterns, John Blunt, said. 'We subalterns had always considered him irrepressible. It hurt to see him carried in like that. He had never given in to anything.'[33]

Lying on a stretcher nearby, Private James Sims, a nineteen-year-old wounded in the leg, heard someone call out to Frost anxiously across the crowded cellar: 'Sir, can we still hold out?'[34]

The inevitable end for the defenders of the bridge came that afternoon. By now the Tigers were firing at the shattered buildings from a range of only 70 yards. All of the houses were now wrecked and burning fiercely, offering practically no cover. Germans were slipping in behind the survivors' positions, and Arnhem itself was firmly in their hands. Now the paras started to pull back, desperately trying to find other positions.

Private Cardale, a former theology student whose piety had earned him a great deal of coarse joking at the hands of his tough comrades in the 2nd, 'mouse-holed' with the rest, dodging from one blazing house to the next. Here, among the smoking brick rubble, he came across a dying comrade, a man who had often pulled his leg in the past. Now the dying man's eyes flickered open, and he asked, 'Are the medics on their way?' 'Yes, they're not far behind,' Cardale lied, and passed on.[35] Suddenly ahead of

him a soldier fell, caught by a sudden burst of German machine-gun fire as he doubled across a battle-littered street. SS men in camouflaged tunics appeared from all sides, carrying sub-machine-guns. The fight went out of the survivors. They dropped their weapons and surrendered. Just before they were marched away between two light tanks, Cardale recalls, 'We flung away our helmets and put on our red berets* – our last act of holding our heads high.'[36]

A comrade of his, Private 'Paddy' Tucker from Ulster, and the rest of his machine-gun section had no choice but to abandon the house where they were sheltering. It was falling down about their heads, and the upper storey was well ablaze. 'Outside and dig in the garden!'; barked an NCO. At this point a young signaller remembered an old Dutch lady who had been trapped with them throughout the fighting. 'What about the woman?' he cried. 'Stop here, I'll get her!' their captain yelled, and ignoring the hail of white tracer, he dashed forward. Almost immediately he was hit. With a yelp of pain he dropped to one knee, but finally managed to get up again and hobble into the house. Moments later he reappeared, his tunic smouldering. 'She's dead,' he reported laconically. 'Now get yer heads down and when the house cools off, nip back in again before the Jerries.'[37]

As things turned out, they never had time to 'nip back'. For it was at this point that Major Gough, now the senior British officer, asked for a truce in which to evacuate the wounded, including Colonel Frost. The Germans agreed, but came too close for Major Gough's liking. He told them to stand back. Above the crackle of small arms fire from elsewhere, the Germans explained that they could not move the wounded unless they used the British jeeps.

Reluctantly Gough waved them closer. Glumly Frost, lying on a stretcher, removed his badges of rank and said to Major Douglas Crawley, who was lying wounded next to him: 'Well, Doug, we didn't get away with it this time, did we?' Painfully Crawley shook his head. 'No, sir, but we gave them a damn good run for their money.'[38]

For the men who remained, it was now a case of either surrender or escape. 'It was a terrible moment,' Private Tucker remembered many years later. 'We knew now there was no hope. But there was no panic. As the order came "move back to the school," the lads fell back in single file with the houses burning all around them as if they didn't want to leave the bridge.'[39]

Having carried a useless field telephone ever since the battle had started, Tucker finally flung it away and tried to make a break for it on his own. As he groped his way out of the terrible lunar landscape, he remembered the optimistic briefing he had been given back in England: 'You'll be on the bridge exactly twenty-four hours,' the

officer had told them. 'Then the Second Army will link up with us. From Arnhem,' he had added smilingly, 'we'll turn left for the advance on Amsterdam.' How absurdly simple it had all seemed![40]

Now those who hadn't already surrendered were scattered everywhere among the blazing ruins. Major Gough had to order one badly wounded RASC officer, David Clark, to surrender. Clark obstinately refused. 'You're a strong chap,' he told Gough. 'You could carry me piggy-back.'[41]

Now the Germans came in, throwing stick grenades. Gough dived under a pile of firewood and tried to hide himself there. Hardly daring to breathe, he heard the crunch of jackboots all around him on the broken glass and rubble. Suddenly someone tugged at his telltale protruding boot. He felt himself being dragged out, and had to laugh when he saw the 'impossibly young faces' staring down at him in amazement.

He was taken before an SS major, who saluted him with a 'Heil Hitler' and remarked, 'I understand you are in command. I wish to congratulate you and your men. You are gallant soldiers. I fought at Stalingrad and it is obvious that you British have a great deal of experience in street fighting.'

The middle-aged major stared back at the German. 'No,' he said, 'this is our first effort. We'll be much better next time.'[42]

Meanwhile, Captain Eric Mackay was also trying to escape, this time by shamming dead. A German soldier ran past his sprawled body and routinely kicked him in the ribs to check if he was really dead. Mackay accepted the blow without a murmur. The German ran on. But the next SS soldier wasn't so trusting: he thrust his bayonet into the 'dead' Sapper. Mackay came back to life with an angry yell of protest. Next moment he was surrounded, and rough hands were slapping him back against the nearest wall. 'The situation was so funny that I laughed,' Mackay recalled later. As the Germans stared at him, Mackay tossed his empty Colt.45 contemptuously over the garden wall, 'so they couldn't get it as a souvenir.'[43]

Private Tucker and a certain Sergeant Cloves were hiding from the Germans behind a pile of bricks and rubble. Exhausted as he was, Cloves immediately fell asleep and began to snore loudly. Angrily Tucker clapped his hand over the NCO's mouth and hissed, 'Can't you bloody well pick a better place for a kip!'[44]

Later, the two of them split up and Tucker got hopelessly lost, before finally ending up in a church with three para officers and a private. 'There's a Jerry with a machine-pistol covering the exit,' one of them hissed. One of the officers crawled forward and drew a bead on the German, but when he tried to fire, the hammer clicked and nothing happened. His Colt, like Tucker's, was 'on the blink.' Next, the private volunteered to draw the German's fire. He dashed forward, but he was too tired and slow and was cut down by a burst of machine-gun fire. Tucker and an officer hauled him back in. 'I'm getting bloody cold,' he

*The paras of the 1st Airborne were extremely proud of their red headgear; it was deemed a great honour to be able to wear the red beret.

124

British troops sheltering.

gasped. Then his head lolled to one side. He was dead.

Tucker was pushing on again, alone, when he saw a group of men wearing red berets. He stumbled towards them, thinking he had found the rest of the division at last. Too late he saw that they were prisoners, covered by a German machine-gun posted at each end of the alley. The SS frisked him. One of them gave Tucker a peppermint drop. Finding that he spoke some English, a still-defiant Tucker told him: 'The Russians'll give you lot some stick for the way you've treated them after the war.' The young German was unmoved. 'We treat them the way you treat the Irish,' he retorted. Tucker grinned. 'Is that so?' he said. 'Well, listen, I'm Irish – so what do you say to that?' But the SS man didn't believe him.[45]

Later, as Tucker was transported to the cage in a truck packed with Red Devils, Major Hibbert and Major Mumford of the 1st Airborne rushed their guards and made an escape bid. The SS were furious, and one of them, a young soldier, retaliated by firing pointblank into the truck. In the resulting massacre, eight men were killed outright, including the soldier-writer Anthony Cotterill. Shortly afterwards, the survivors were hauled down from the bullet-riddled truck. Tucker and a pal, 'Soapy' Hudson, attempted to help a badly wounded para, but he refused, insisting that he could manage alone. He staggered to his feet, the back of his head looking, according to Tucker, as if 'somebody had thrown a handful of strawberry jam at it', but immediately collapsed, his most precious possession, a looted tin of tomatoes, rolling from his smock.

Next, Tucker and a fellow-Irishman, Private Fitzpatrick, found themselves being lined up against the nearest wall with the rest. At twenty-three, Tucker had seen more

(Above left) Dead SS man on Nijmegen bridge.
(Above) Men of the Second Airborne moving forward into Arnhem.

action than most, but in all his six years of fighting since Palestine in '38, he had never dreamed that it would end like this. It seemed the SS were planning to shoot them down in cold blood.

In the nick of time, however, the Red Devils were saved by Major Gough, who via a German interpreter explained to the young SS men: 'These are British soldiers, not Russians.'[46] Thanks to their timely intervention, Tucker and his comrades were led away, leaving the dead to stiffen on the pavement behind them.

Lying on another pavement, waiting to have his wounds treated, Private James Sims was also in German hands now. He recalled how quiet and withdrawn his wounded comrades seemed. 'The thought that we had fought for nothing was a natural one,' he wrote later, 'but I couldn't

help but think about the main army, so strong, and yet unable to make those last few miles to us. The hardest thing to bear was the feeling that we had just been written off.'[47]

At 5.00 on the afternoon of Saturday, September 20th, Polish paratroopers headed for the drop zone at Driel, outside Arnhem, in a desperate attempt to link up with and relieve what was left of the 1st Airborne inside the cauldron. The landing was a disaster. The Poles drifted helplessly down into a merciless hail of German anti-aircraft fire and were shot to pieces. Only 200 of the men in the grey berets ever reached the British. Yet still Horrocks, whose tanks were now a mere four hundred yards distant from the beleaguered paras, was determined not to abandon the men who had fought so long and hard to hold the Arnhem bridgehead. He therefore ordered Lieutenant Colonel Gerald Tilly's men of the 4th Dorsets, belonging to the 43rd Infantry Division, to make a final attempt to cross the river and relieve Urquhart and his men.

Tilly, understandably, was less than delighted by the assignment and feared that his men were going to be sacrificed for nothing, like the Poles. But the thirty-four-year-old colonel was a good soldier; orders were orders. He personally selected the men who would go, walking from soldier to soldier, tapping them on the shoulder and saying, 'You go ... you stay behind.' He still hadn't told his battalion exactly what was in store, but he knew he had to 'pick the veterans who were absolutely sure – essential – leaving the others behind.'[48] Eventually, having made his selection, he called over his second-in-command, Major James Grafton, and told him: 'Someone other than me has to know the real purpose of the crossing ... I'm afraid we're being chucked away.'[49]

After three hours' wait in a cold drizzle, the heavily-laden infantry began to cross the river, with Tilly himself in the first wave. In spite of a heavy barrage put down by the whole of the 43rd's artillery, the Germans were alert and waiting and immediately swept the water with tracer. Boat after boat sank. Men went overboard, never to reappear. The night air was rent with screams and agonised cries for help as the merciless German fire tore the first wave apart. In the end, of the 420 officers and men who had made the assault, only 290 reached the other side. As he disembarked. Colonel Tilly was met by grenades trundling down towards him like bowling balls. 'Get them with the bayonet!' he yelled above the racket, and dashed forward, whereupon he and those of his men who were still able to follow him were swallowed up by the thick murk of war. That was the last ever seen of him until after the war. Only a handful of Dorsets ever managed to link up with the Red Devils; their sacrifice, just as Tilly had feared, turned out to be in vain.[50]

By now Urquhart knew that there was no alternative: the survivors of the cauldron would have to pull back and Arnhem would have to be abandoned. Like good British soldiers, many of them shaved in preparation for the great withdrawal. Private Robert Downing, one of the survivors of the ill-fated 10th parachute Battalion, was told by a sergeant, 'There's an old razor over there. You get yourself a dry shave. Hurry up. We're crossing the river and by God we're going back looking like British soldiers.'[51]

And so, after nine days of hell, they started to leave their positions. For many, this was the most bitter moment of all; yet even as they withdrew, they maintained their defiant attitude. One of them, Sergeant Stanley Sullivan, summed up their mood when he scrawled on the blackboard of the little school which had been his post, 'We'll Be Back!!!'[52]

They would, indeed, come back. But it would take

Devastation caused by enemy shell and mortar fire.

another seven bitter months and many hundreds of thousands of lives, both military and civilian, before they did so. The great adventure which some had hoped would end the war so swiftly, had ended in failure.

Those who survived the river crossing under sporadic German fire struggled into the collecting posts set up by XXX Corps that night, dressed in all kinds of cast-offs. One even wore a pair of old-fashioned ladies' bloomers! Some were stark naked.

A few collapsed, but many came back soldiers to the bitter end. Colonel Payton-Reid of the 7th King's Own Scottish Borderers, one of the few battalion commanders to survive, brought his men out washed and clean-shaven and marched them four miles to Driel, where they were given their first hot meal for a week. As he sat there, the colonel recalled 'all the acts of heroism and unselfishness I had seen. I felt … what a proud and privileged thing it is to be a soldier.'[53] Major Geoffrey Powell of the 156th Parachute Battalion, hardly able to believe he had come through it all alive, formed up his fifteen survivors in columns of three. Finally, reaching the reception centre, he dismissed his handful of tattered survivors for all the world as if they were back on the parade ground in England. '156th Battalion – halt! Right turn! Fall out!' Standing there in the grey drizzle, Powell watched them head for shelter. 'It was all over,' he thought, 'but by God we had come out as we had gone in. Proud.'[54]

However, some of the survivors were received coldly, even harshly by their comrades. Urquhart himself had to wait for some time before Browning was roused from his sleep to receive him, and when the Guardee finally appeared, he looked to Urquhart, 'as if he had just come off parade instead of his bed in the middle of a battle.'[55] Later that day, another of the 'blood-bathed heroes of Arnhem,' as Churchill would later call them, failed to salute when Browning's jeep passed, escorted by five bodyguards carrying tommy-guns. The jeep squealed to a stop and an elegant aide raced over to the dazed soldier who had still not recovered from his ordeal. He asked the para why he had failed to salute the general. The man replied, 'I haven't seen a general for a long time, sir, and I wasn't looking.' The elegant aide raced back to Browning to report this and then raced back to the waiting para with the words: 'General Browning says you are not allowed to wear your red beret for the next fourteen days.' With that, the jeep set off again, complete with escort, leaving the para to wonder whether the brass really had any idea what they had been through on the other side of the river.[56]

Captain Eric Mackay, who had manged to escape from the Germans although he had been wounded in the attempt, waited all day for the survivors of his squadron to come in. While he did so, he examined the faces of men from other outfits. 'They all looked unbelievably drawn and tired. Here and there you could pick out a veteran – a face with an unmistakable, "I don't give a damn" look, as if he could never be beaten.'[57]

As the hours passed and still none of his men turned up, Mackay grew more and more angry. 'I hated everyone. I hated whoever was responsible for this and I hated the army for its indecision and I thought of the waste of life and of a fine division dumped down the drain. And for what?'[58] In the end, Mackay discovered that there had been only four other survivors from his 200-strong squadron.

The men of the 1st Airborne Division had come a long way for their date with death. Some of them had been mere schoolboys and apprentices when a certain Lieutenant, acting Captain Frost, had carried out the first real para attack on *Festung Europa* at the Bruneval radar station. Others had been ordinary infantrymen at the time, slaughtering their forerunners, the German paras, at Crete. but together they had sweated in the desert, fought in Sicily, whored in Italy, gone 'Yank-bashing' in the pubs of Grantham, and covered mile after mile of the dripping moors of North Yorkshire in 'the airborne gallop'. Prior to D-Day, the division had been so eager for action that it had rebelled on discovering that it would not be taking part in the landings. Now it was destroyed. Of the senior officers, only General Urquhart and Brigadier Hicks escaped. Both other brigadiers were either captured or missing. Three battalion commanders were killed in action; four were wounded and taken prisoner; another was wounded and on the run from the Germans. Twenty-five medical officers stayed behind to tend the wounded, including the most senior doctors of the division. Only two of the fifteen padres returned across the river. The 1st, 2nd, 3rd, 10th and 11th Parachute Battalions ceased to exist. Of the 156th, the Borderers, the KOSB and the South Staffs, only a quarter of their original number survived. Of the 8,905 officers and men of the British 1st Airborne Division who had flown into Holland so confidently on Sunday, September 17th, plus the 1,100 glider pilots who had taken them in, only 2,163, with the addition of 160 Poles and 75 Dorsets, returned. The butcher's bill had been appallingly high.

Following the withdrawal, Warrant Officer John Sharp of Frost's 2nd Battalion waited all that long day for survivors of his outfit to come in, asking other men time and time again where they might be. Eventually he found that exactly 17 men out of the 600-odd who had defended the bridge at Arnhem had returned. As the hard-boiled sergeant major remembered long afterwards, 'I don't think I was the only one there that day with tears in my eyes …'[59] But nearly forty years later, Private Paddy Tucker, who survived his wound and eight months in a German POW cage, could look up from his hospital bed with a trace of that old 'bash-on airborne spirit' and declare, when asked if he would again embark on the disastrous adventure of that September: 'Christ, of course, we would have done it again!'[60]

Allied dead after the attack on Arnhem.

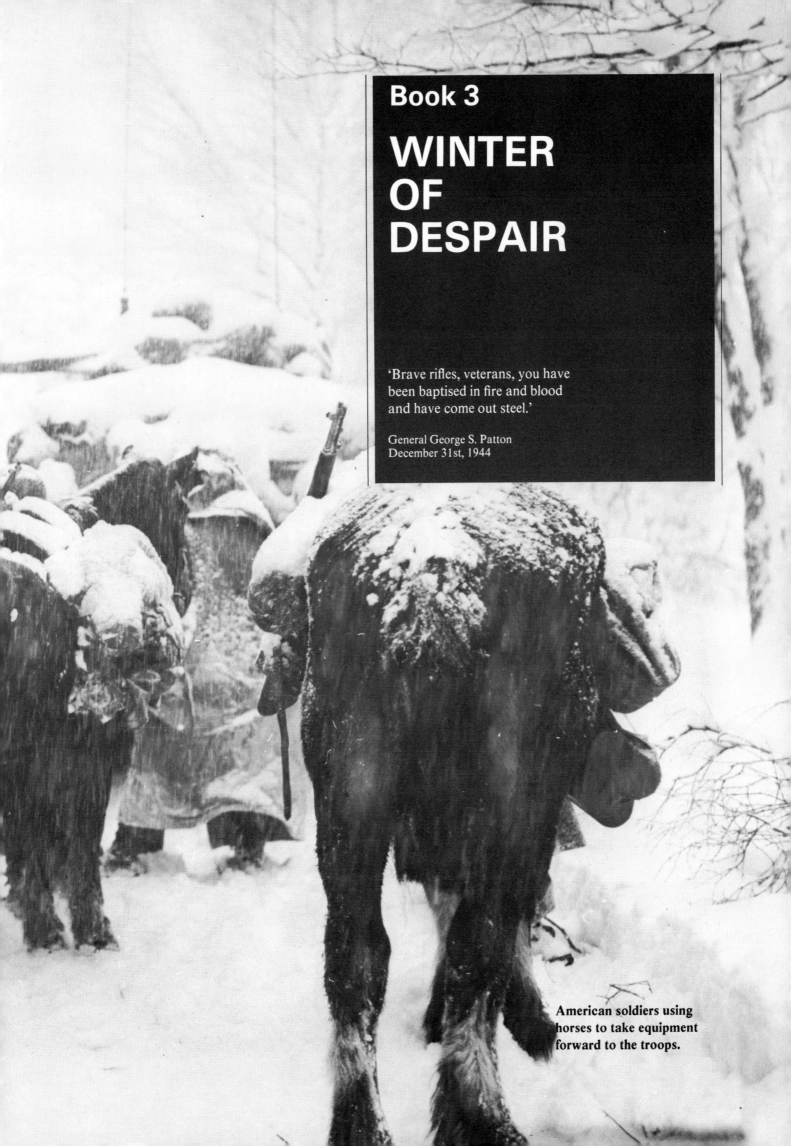

Book 3

WINTER OF DESPAIR

'Brave rifles, veterans, you have been baptised in fire and blood and have come out steel.'

General George S. Patton
December 31st, 1944

American soldiers using horses to take equipment forward to the troops.

US prisoners.

7 INTO THE BAG

'For you the war is over ...'

Standard formula used by German interrogators to greet newly captured Allied soldiers

In St. Elisabeth's Hospital at Arnhem, now run by the SS, Lieutenant Peter Stainforth of the 1st Airborne, who had been badly wounded in the chest, heard the first walking wounded from his old division come marching into captivity. 'I felt a shiver of excitement run down my spine. I have never been so proud. They came in and the rest of us were horror-stricken. Every man had a week's growth of beard. Their battledress was torn and stained, and filthy, blood-soaked bandages poked out from all of them. The most compelling thing was their eyes – red-rimmed, deep-sunk, peering out from drawn, mud-caked faces made haggard by lack of sleep and yet they walked in undefeated. They looked fierce enough to take over the place right then and there!'[1]

Now defeated British paras started to march into captivity in ever-increasing numbers, to become for the rest of the war 'Kriegies' – their own term, loosely derived from the German for prisoner of war: *Kriegsgefangener.*

During the nine-day battle of Arnhem, the Allied Airborne Corps had suffered a total of around 17,000 casualties. Following it, some 6,000 British paratroopers, 1,500 of them wounded, together with about 1,000 American paras from the 101st and 82nd Divisions went 'into the bag.'

Corporal Tom Hoge, a correspondent with the *Stars and Stripes* had been unfortunate enough to parachute straight into German hands. Immediately he found himself before a German major who spoke flawless English. After offering him an American cigarette, the German began his interrogation: 'Well, you must have a lot of news for me ... As a correspondent you must have picked up a lot of interesting information about this ambitious airborne operation that has failed so unfortunately and completely.' Hoge denied this. The major expressed himself 'disappointed' and told him, 'All we are asking of you is information we already know. In the past two days we have questioned several hundred airborne men, including a number of officers. They were very reasonable. They realised that they had been sacrificed by your High Command on an impossible mission and so they weren't at all hesitant in telling us all we asked.'

Hoge, however, stood firm, whereupon the major changed his tactics from 'sweet' to 'sour', as was customary on such occasions. 'You say you are an army correspondent,' he said. 'We have no proof of that. You have no papers to show it. All we know is that you were found wandering around behind our lines with no gun and low civilian shoes on. You could be a saboteur. Perhaps we had better turn you over to the Gestapo. They are quite good at questioning one of your kind.'

This none-too-subtle threat made Hoge sweat, but he still remained steadfast, and in the end the major gave up on him. 'You will be transported to a prison camp tonight … For you the war is over.'[2]

It was a phrase still ringing in the ears of many thousands of Allied prisoners as they were escorted to Germany and assigned to the various POW cages for Allied prisoners. These camps … 'Oflags' for the officers, 'Stalags' for the enlisted men – ran the length of central Germany from north to south and now contained 180,000 British and 30,000 American prisoners, some of whom had been POWs for years.

One such veteran, Sergeant John Dominy of the RAF, who had been a Kriegie since 1940, was there to witness the scene as the first paras from Arnhem marched into the Stalag at Fallingbostel in Northern Germany that autumn. By means of a secret radio, code-named the 'canary' for security reasons, the prisoners already knew of the 1st Airborne's epic stand, and the whole camp turned out to watch the Red Devils enter.

'They were marched along the road past our camp by RSM Lord,' wrote Dominy. 'He had the swagger of a Guardsman on parade. They were carrying their wounded and their guards, a shambling, dishevelled lot, just about keeping pace with the steady Praetorian tread of the finest soldiers in the world. We came instinctively to attention and Bill Lord, noticing our two medical officers standing with us, gave his party "Eyes right!" and snapped them a salute which would not have been out of place at Pirbright or Caterham.* This was the sort of show England really could put on. None of us would have missed seeing it.'[3]

By the time the camp was finally liberated by the 8th Hussars seven months later, Regimental Sergeant Major Lord had taken almost complete charge of the 4,256 British and 2,428 American prisoners there, 1,000 of whom were in hospital suffering from wounds and malnutrition. His own clerks ran the offices, and there were even paratroopers on guard at the gate to the camp, looking spick and span in white gaiters and belts and highly polished boots.

*The Guards' training depot.

Other Arnhem veterans didn't arrive until later, for the wounded were forced to travel by slow goods train, packed in by the score with scant food and water and no medical aid. For Private James Sims, the wounded nineteen-year-old para, the nightmare journey lasted four days, in which he was packed in a cattle truck with men dying all around him. The elderly German guards refused to remove the dead until they reached their destination, since they had signed for a certain number and wanted the tally to be correct when they arrived at Fallingbostel.

At the station the bodies were finally off-loaded and stacked on the platform in heaps like so many logs, while the wounded, including Sims, who had been shot in the leg, were hauled out and ordered to make a gruelling one-mile climb up to the camp. As they set off, a German soldier on leave took pity on the pathetic wrecks. Sidling up to them, obviously afraid of being seen, and without saying a word, he passed out all his remaining cigarettes to the British paras.

Sims was placed with the other wounded in the camp's lazarette, and spent his first night in the POW cage lying awake, listening as his comrades tossed and turned, reliving the horrors of battle in their dreams. As he recorded later: 'It was like watching a movie over and over again. I began to wonder if some men would ever get over it.'[4]

For most of the veteran Kriegies, the first year of captivity had been the worst. It had all seemed so pointless. As one recorded: 'It was open-ended. I mean, we could have been there for ten years as far as we knew – there was no end. The Russians were 1,500 miles away and although no one ever admitted that we could have lost the war, there seemed no means that we could have won it, so we could just have been stuck there forever,'[5]

One officer who had been captured in 1940 while serving with the 51st Highland Division, related afterwards: 'I can remember that in about November 1940 I had a bottom bunk. I had one blanket and I remember there was snow on the ground and when the snow was carried in on the boots into the barrack room, the whole floor was covered with water. And I lay on this bottom bunk so cold and so hungry that I prayed that when I went to sleep that night I shouldn't wake up. That's how despondent I was.'[6]

Food naturally was a major preoccupation of new and old Kriegies alike. They were supposed to receive the rations of non-working German civilians, i.e. 1,900 calories a day; in fact, 1,500 was nearer the mark. As a result, most of the young men lost at least 40 pounds in captivity, and in some camps even more. In one much-publicised case, US prisoner of war Private Joseph Demier was found to weigh only 70 pounds on liberation, and it took him all of three months in a stateside hospital before he regained his original 120 pounds.

That September, Sims, the new boy at Fallingbostel,

American and British airmen having liberated a prisoner of war camp in Stalag V11.

made a note of a typical day's fare: 'Breakfast – a cup of acorn coffee. Dinner – half a pint of watery soup and three small potatoes. Tea – a cup of rose-leaf tea, one slice of sour black bread, a minute portion of margarine and a spoonful of ersatz jam, complete with wooden pips.'[7]

Food even replaced sex as the major subject of day-dream and fantasy (most of the prisoners who had been inside the 'bag' for any length of time became temporarily impotent anyway). At the Allied POW Camp at Sagan, US Lieutenant Larry Phelan, a former advertising copywriter, summed it all up in a poem which he dedicated to his wife ('the loveliest girl in the world – who won't like it a bit'). It ran:

> I dream as only captive men can dream
> Of life as lived in days that went before,
> Of scrambled eggs and shortcakes thick with cream,
> And onion soup and lobster Thermidor,
> Of roasted beef and chops and T-bone steaks,
> And turkey breasts and golden leg or wing,
> Of sausage, maple syrup, buckwheat cakes,
> And chicken broiled or fried à la King.
> I dwell on rolls or buns for days and days,
> Hot corn bread, biscuits, Philadelphia scrapple,
> Asparagus in cream or hollandaise,
> And deep-dish pies – mince, huckleberry, apple.
> I long for buttered creamy oyster stew;
> And now and then my pet, I long for you.[8]

The doggerel wasn't calculated to endear a man to his beloved, but far away in remote Poland, it kept those half-starved American Kriegies agog with salivating, lip-licking excitement.

Further south in Hammelberg POW camp, captive American officers were equally concerned with diet, one of the main topics of conversation being whether the green maggots which floated on their thin midday soup should be eaten or not. The matter remained unresolved until the Battle of the Bulge, when Colonel Joe Matthews of the ill-fated 106th US Infantry Division was captured and sent to the camp. Matthews, a former agricultural chemist, decreed that the maggots were a 'valuable source of natural protein' and should be eaten. Thereafter 'Green Hornet soup,' as it was called, was consumed with gusto, maggots and all.[9]

Corporal Tom Hoge, now incarcerated in Limburg Stalag, a notorious hell-hole which had served the same function in World War One and which was packed with Kriegies of all nationalities, found that there, too, food was the men's primary concern. After a rollcall lasting an hour and a half, carried out under the command of a 'sadistic Prussian colonel who bore an insane hatred of every nation allied against the Reich,' the men were given for breakfast 'a piece of black bread two inches thick, a dab of evil-looking brown syrup called treacle and a cup of flax tea.'[10] Dinner wasn't much better: 'A lump of lard (in lieu of margarine) and a small bowl of watery soup usually

Germans provided for 22,000 Russian POWs at a camp in Hemer. They are seen here preparing food out in the open.

138

made from the nauseous-tasting tops of sugar beets. Supper consisted of the same soup warmed over, or on special occasions, three cold boiled potatoes. The craving for meat (horse meat once a week on Sundays was their only ration of meat) was acute. We have more than once seen several men taking turns gnawing on the shin bone of a horse found in the bottom of the soup pail.'[11]

Once the new prisoners-of-war were 'registered' with the Swiss Red Cross, their protecting authority, they could expect to receive Red Cross parcels. These did much to relieve the drab monotony of life behind barbed wire, although Kriegies were often disappointed to find that most of the goodies contained in the parcels needed cooking – and firewood was at a premium. Already most of the wooden planks supporting the double and triple bunks had vanished for fuel. Moreover, the Germans in the quartermaster's store routinely pierced all cans to prevent the Kriegies stockpiling food in readiness for a possible escape. Thus, treacle and jam became mixed up with tinned herrings and corned beef. Truly as the old British Army marching song had it, 'There was jam, jam, mixed up with the ham in the quartermaster's store.' As winter approached and the colder weather set in, this unholy mixture froze, congealing into a solid, iron-hard mass. 'However,' as Private Sims remembers, 'we were so hungry that we would eat the frozen concoction as though it was a block of toffee.'[12]

The effect on the men's digestive system can easily be imagined. In Hoge's camp, the Red Cross parcels were torn open straight away by the new inmates, who then had to eat the contents in one go to prevent them being spoiled. As a result, 'many of the men became gravely ill after eating such rich food and (were) sent to a lice-ridden barracks the Germans called their dispensary. Later we heard one man had died of acute indigestion.'[13]

However, in comparison with the Russians, most of the prisoners from the Western Front agreed that they were well treated. When Private Kelly, a medic serving with the 1st Airborne, was taken to Stalag 4B at Muhlberg, he found 20,000 prisoners of all nationalities, ranging from American to Greek. But of all the prisoners, the Russians were undoubtedly treated the worst by the camp guards, who beat them, kept them half-starved and generally treated them like animals. 'When food was thrown over their barbed wire they fought for it like wild beasts. I saw some cheese thrown over once and when the scrum was over their faces were smothered with cheese, in their hair and eyes. They just wiped it off their faces and stuffed it into their mouths.'[14] At the time, Kelly was sympathetic, but after the several years as a prisoner of the Russians in the post-war cages of the Soviet Gulag, he understandably lost some of his fellow-feeling.

For Corporal Tom Hoge, life in a German prison camp could best be measured in degrees of starvation: 'Following Hitler's favourite method of using varying levels of persecution for various occupied countries, the Germans have a different policy for the PWs of each nation. At the bottom of the list is the Russians whose treatment is barbarous.'[15]

He went on: 'Sad as the Americans' lot was, that of the Russians was far worse. Standing in the bread line each morning we saw companies of ragged, unkempt Red Army prisoners, many too ill to more than hobble, herded toward town on a work detail. Any man who didn't walk fast enough received a gun butt across the back of his head. And if he still didn't move, he was usually thrown to the ground by one of the powerful German police dogs who roamed the camp and held by the throat while a guard clubbed him into insensibility.'[16]

Several incidents were reported in which Russian prisoners kidnapped the guard dogs at night and ate every single piece of them, leaving the pelt spread out for the amazed guards to find on the following morning.

One evening, one of Hoge's friends was eating his bread ration when he was called over to the barbed wire which separated the Russian and American cages by a Russian POW, who offered him a cigarette in exchange for a piece of bread. The American broke off a chunk and was handing it to the Russian when a guard saw what was going on. Without challenging, he fired three shots into the Russian's back. The latter's clothes caught in the barbed wire and he hung there limply, twitching occasionally, until he died. Several hours later, two Russians were ordered out to 'cut the body down and remove it.'[17]

Father Francis Sampson, a paratroop padre at Neubrandenburg Oflag, some hundred miles north of Berlin, told appalling stories of conditions in the camp. His first meal as a prisoner consisted of cabbage soup with worms floating in it, and another new arrival was forced to drink out of his shoe because he didn't have a bowl. In the camp's lazarette, the medics had hardly any supplies at all, and conditions were so desperate that one Polish doctor had to amputate both legs of a young GI using toilet-paper compresses and newspaper bandages in a vain attempt to stop the bleeding.

Once again, however, it was the thousands of Russian POWs in the camp who were treated the worst. Sampson recalled a conversation he had with one guard, nicknamed by the Kriegies, 'Little Adolf', which vividly illustrated the brutal attitude of the camp authorities towards the Russian prisoners. The German guard told Sampson, 'Those Russians are not human. Do you know that when a man dies in there they keep him for days?' Sampson insisted that this was only in order that they could continue to draw the dead man's rations, but Little Adolf refused to listen. 'Your own Dr. Hawes has examined those bodies and verified cannibalism,' he persisted.

Sampson had indeed already spoken to Hawes about Russian cannibalism, but he couldn't altogether blame the Russians. After seven weeks of being hungry himself, he knew that 'there was little a starving man wouldn't do to remain alive.'

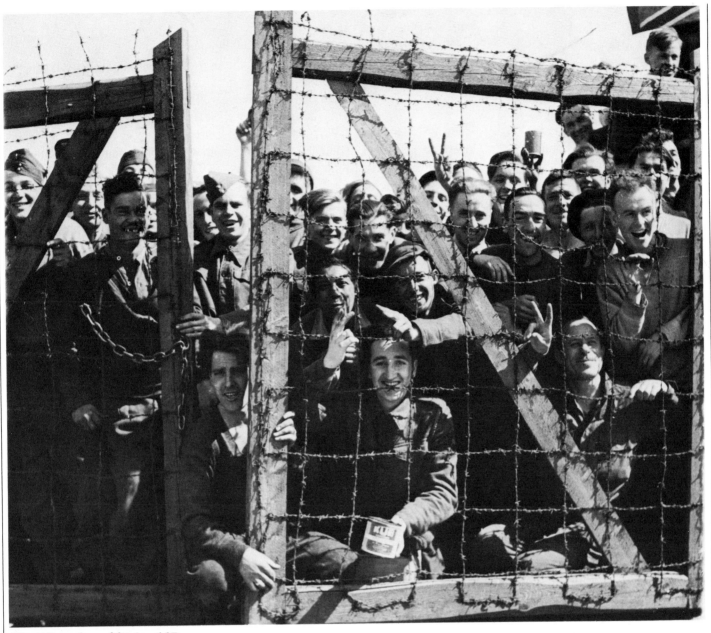

The Liberation of Stalag 11B.

Accompanied by the guard, Sampson visited the Russian compound and was appalled by what he saw there. Dying Russians lay everywhere, packed in their huts so tightly that in their death frenzies their stick-like limbs intertwined. With eyes that were devoid of all hope, they stared up at the priest as he walked by. 'See,' said Little Adolf, 'they are only animals.'

At this point, the guard walked off, leaving Sampson with a French priest who was doing his best to tend the dying prisoners and who told Sampson that the Germans were about to send another consignment of Russian bodies to the graveyard, adding, with horror, that not all the Russians were dead yet.

Hearing this, Sampson decided he had to intervene.

Hurrying out, he was just in time to see that the French priest had been right: a large horse-drawn wagon was heading for the cemetery, piled high with bodies, some of which were still showing faint signs of life. He sped to the main gate, hoping to stop it, but only found more brutality. A Russian prisoner was being searched by a German sentry. The German ordered the Russian to undo his trousers, and a loaf of bread fell out. The German picked it up; the Russian crazed with hunger, snatched it back. The guard jabbed him with his bayonet, yet still the Russian refused to surrender the bread. Thereupon the guard smashed the Russian to the ground with his rifle butt and started to kick and pound him.

Father Sampson pleaded with the German to stop, and

141

finally the Russian was dragged away to the guard-room, battered and bloody, but still clutching his precious loaf. Not for the first time Sampson found himself asking which were the 'animals', the Russians or their barbarous captors.[18]

After the protracted battle for Germany's frontier and the West Wall,* British, Canadian and American prisoners started to stream into the cages in their thousands, there to experience all the hardship, boredom and uncertainty of the Stalags and Oflags: the hour-long freezing rollcalls; the icy huts; the evil-smelling latrine buckets – 'thundermugs,' as the British called them; the lack of women. Crowded together in one grey, miserable herd, the POWs had little else to do but brood on the past, the unfairness of their capture and the uncertain future that lay ahead.

Living at such close quarters, the Kriegies found that minor habits could become major sources of irritation. There was one case of a Kriegie who took to scratching his back with his fork at meal-times and so maddened his fellow-POWs that he had to be moved to another hut for his own safety. Depressed by their imprisonment, the men would watch enviously as beetles or mice scuttled in and out of the camp at will, free to come and go as they pleased.

Some, of course, settled down to serious study and gained qualifications by correspondence course which they hoped to use later in civilian life – always assuming there *would* be a civilian future for them. Many took up languages, German being particularly vital for those who planned to escape, though British figures showed that only two percent ever made the attempt.

Theatricals were one way of relieving the boredom and were particularly popular in camps with a nucleus of veteran Kriegies. At Stalag Luft III at Sagan, Poland, commanded by US Brigadier General Arthur Vanaman, the camp's highest-ranking US prisoner of war, there was even a traditional American 'Little Theater' with seats made from Canadian Red Cross boxes. Admission was one coal briquet to heat the place, and footlights and reflectors were constructed from large British biscuit tins. 'The women's parts were of course played – with no reluctance – by men.'[19]

Here, as in other camps, female impersonators often became identified with their roles and continued to play them 'off stage.' Naturally they were the object of wistful attention among men starved of female companionship for so long. One ex-Kriegie reported that in his camp, where most had been behind the wire since 1940, regular 'tea-dances' were held after the men returned from working outside. 'We'd get a quick wash and a shave, those who were that way inclined put on "powder" – flour or chalk – and then we were off dancing cheek to cheek, as if we were back at Palais or Mecca in blighty.'[20] Surprisingly, however, there was very little evidence of homosexuality in the camps, and several Kriegies with years behind the wire reported later that they never came across a single case in all their time in captivity.

What sexual emotion the Kriegies still possessed was for the most part invested in wives and girlfriends back home. But many relationships didn't survive the long separation, and the result would be a letter from home in which the unfortunate Kriegie learned that his woman had 'found someone else.' One man whose wife sent him a letter of that kind recalled later, 'I have no recollections after that for days. I was like a zombie.'[21]

The Americans called these letters 'Dear Johns,' the British 'Mespots,' the name being derived from the pre-war five-year 'unaccompanied' tour of Mesopotamia which wrecked the marriages of so many British soldiers. Such 'Mespots' were often posted in groups on the camp noticeboards so that those who read them realised that they weren't alone in their misfortune. It was a sound piece of human psychology, but it didn't work all the time. Now and again a crazed man would rush the wire, courting death at the hands of the sentry manning the machine-gun in the stork-legged guard tower.

In the end, the Kriegies adapted or cracked. They learned how to keep a crease in their trousers when no irons were available by soaping along the inside of the crease and sleeping on the garment. They learned how to make a razor blade last for months on end by sharpening it on the inside of a jam jar. They learned how to make lights from string wicks and boot polish. They learned how to keep their bunks free from lice by placing each leg of the wooden bed in little boot polish tins filled with spirits. They learned many things they had never dreamed of before – and above all, they learned the value of freedom. As one of them expressed it forty years later, 'You don't know the value of freedom because you've never lost it. But those of us who've lost freedom ... we know what freedom means. It's wonderful to be able to get up, and I can walk outside this house, whereas for five years I was totally enclosed.'[22]

In the opinion of their British allies, the Americans adapted poorly to this sudden loss of freedom. Even the Germans remarked upon the inability of their captives to discipline and organise themselves behind the wire. Camp Commandant General von Goeckel who ran Hammelberg Oflag (where Stalin's son Josef had killed himself in 1942 by approaching the wire and forcing a guard to shoot him, and which now housed Lieutenant Colonel John Knight Waters, Patton's son-in-law), felt that his American prisoners let themselves go completely. They took no heed of their senior US officer, Colonel Cavender, neither saluting him nor taking orders from him. They didn't wash or shave. Some of them even had to be forced out of the huts to relieve themselves. In Goeckel's opinion, they were like 'silly high school kids, who would never have been promoted to officer rank in the German army.'[23] It was a view shared by many, including Private Sims, who thought that the American NCOs seemed 'quite incapable of exercising any discipline in conditions in which discipline

*Called by the Allies the 'Siegfried Line'

Waffen SS troops.

was essential to survival.'[24]

In an official German survey of American POWs in late 1944, a German officer interrogator wrote: 'Some of the American prisoners made a curious impression. They were uncommunicative and complained of the personal risk to which each participant in the European war was subjected … The impression they made on us was that they were fighting not because of convictions but for the money they got out of it, carrying out orders in sober and businesslike manner.'

Surprisingly enough, many enlisted men, British, American and Canadian, spent a great deal of time outside the camps, often as long as a week at a stretch. These were the men sent out in 'Arbeitskommandos' or working parties, to clear up the damage caused by the 'Brylcreem boys' of the RAF and USAAF.* Naturally, they also took every opportunity to enjoy the favours of sex-starved Fräuleins whose menfolk were away at the front, the 'romance' often being helped on its way by the goodies the POWs brought with them from their Red Cross parcels.

One corporal, a former infantryman who had lost a foot at Crete and had been a Kriegie since 1941, was often on working parties in bomb-damaged Munich. There, he and the rest of the Kommando were quartered at night in a school, under the guard of a group of old men who were easily bribed with coffee and cigarettes. 'Every night during the blackout we'd sneak out,' he remembered gleefully

*A term coined by the footsoldiers, who envied the fliers their fancy uniforms and egg-and-bacon breakfasts.

many years later, 'and into town. We had stuff the Jerries hadn't seen for years – Swiss milk chocolate and what they called "real bean coffee." The Fräuleins were very obliging as a result. I swear that if old Patton's Yanks hadn't come along in the end and liberated Moosberg that April, I'd have shagged myself to death!'[25]

A handful fell genuinely in love with German girls and 'deserted' from their particular POW camp in order to live with them. However, terrible punishments were meted out by the State to any German woman found to have had dealings with the enemy, and already the Germans had publicly executed one Polish prisoner of war for having an affair with a German woman. There was no reason to suppose that British or American POWs would be dealt with any differently.

Sergeant Al Brenner, a POW since 1943, was assigned to a working party when he became involved with a woman whose husband had been killed in Russia for 'Folk, Fatherland and Führer,' as the Nazi slogan had it. Brenner took the plunge. He deserted to the woman's farm and lived with her until April 1945, when the farm was finally captured by the British. Asked if he wished to be repatriated, Brenner's laconic answer was, 'Hell, no – why?'[26]

Naturally, some of the Kriegies went over to the enemy, and in many cases the women they encountered while out on working parties were their downfall. Often they turned these prisoners, some of whom had fought bravely for their countries, into stool-pigeons, renegades and outright traitors who bore arms for the Nazi cause.

The 'British Legion of St. George' was created by John Amery, the profligate son of an ex-British Cabinet Minister, who was hanged by the British authorities after the war. This organisation finally became a part of the Armed SS, and some of its members, though not many, actually did fight for the Germans. A few joined for ideological reasons, having been members of the British Union of Fascists, the Blackshirts, before the war. One such, a forty-year-old RAF officer, declared contemptuously after being sentenced to ten years' hard labour: 'This shows just how rotten this democratic country is! The Germans would have had the honesty to shoot me!'[27] Most, however, joined either because they had been threatened with punishment for consorting with German women, or because they had been promised the favours of a woman if they did so.

The case of John White was typical. White, a British infantryman assigned to an Arbeitskommando, was working alone in a sawmill, when one day the young daughter of the miller put her arms around him and drew him close. White claims he tried to resist, but in the end, as he confessed at his trial at the Old Bailey, 'I gave in to her.' Soon after, two middle-aged civilians wearing felt hats and ankle-length leather coats came to fetch him with the usual, 'Kommen Sie mit!' White had been on the 'outside' long enough to recognise them as Gestapo men. The policemen told the frightened young Englishman that if he didn't co-operate, he would be shot. He co-operated – and the Waffen SS gained another recruit.[28]

Corporal John Galaher needed less persuasion. As the resident camp stool-pigeon, he had already spied on his fellow-Canadians in return for money and visits to the local whores. Readily enough he joined the 'British Free Corps,' as it was now known, for more of the same.[29]

Some traitors also joined other SS units and in some cases took an active part in the fighting. Obersturmbannführer Gerd Brenner of the élite Adolf Hitler Bodyguard recalls two Englishmen, a London bus driver and mechanic in peacetime, who were captured in Greece by his unit and fought with the SS throughout the campaign in Russia. However, when they were finally sent on leave in 1944, they were stopped by an officious border official who told Brenner that he couldn't 'allow Englishmen to fight in a division which bore the Führer's name.' Sadly they parted, and the Englishmen went back behind the wire.[30]

Nor was it only Englishmen and Canadians who volunteered for the Waffen SS. New Zealanders, Australians, South Africans and Americans also joined up. Even today, the US Army refuses to put a figure on the number of American renegades, nor were any traitors prosecuted after the war by US courts. But individual cases were reported. One such case was that of Lieutenant Tyndall of the USAAF. Born in Texas of an English father and French mother, Tyndall joined the British Free Corps and worked in the US POW camps disseminating Nazi propaganda. Finally he became dissatisfied with his inactive life, volunteered for active service with the SS in the East, and was never heard of again.

Large numbers of possible recruits for the Free Corps were sent to special camps, to be worked upon by the Germans. Six thousand Boer prisoners were collected at Luckenwalde, many of them from the ill-fated 2nd South Africa Division which had surrendered at Tobruk. These were thought by SS General Berger, in charge of recruitment for the SS, to have special potential as recruits.

So too were the Irish. Nearly a thousand Irishmen were gathered at Luckenwalde, drawn from the Irish Republic, the United Kingdom, the Commonwealth and the United States. There they were harangued by a Swiss SS colonel,* a stage-Irishman named McGinty who had been in Germany since 1918, and several IRA officers, who made repeated appeals to the men's latent Irish nationalism, all of which fell on deaf ears. In the end, the Irishmen were sent back to their original camps. In World War Two there would be no 'Wild Geese'** from Ireland fighting on the enemy side.

Eventually some fifty Englishmen were recruited into the British Free Corps and this new unit was paraded from city to city as a propaganda device, spending its free time

---

*Although Switzerland was supposedly neutral, one well-known Swiss firm supplied its coffee products and chocolate to both the German *and* American armies.
**Name given to the Irish Brigade recruited by the Germans in WWI.

144

An Indian serving in the German army.

whoring and drinking, until finally as the Red Army broke into Germany, they were alerted for active service at the front. Without exception they took to their beds – and that was the end of the British SS.

One sizeable collection of traitors (or patriots, depending on your viewpoint) that *was* recruited from Allied POW camps in Germany that year was the so-called 'Indian Legion', which consisted of over 3,000 Indians, Sikhs and Moslems. Under the command of a German colonel, they fought against the British, Canadians and Americans in France and later in Holland – though it has to be admitted, not very effectively. Although most of them surrendered in the end, they were never brought to trial for fear of provoking further unrest in British India. The imprisonment of Sikhs and Moslems who had fought for the Japanese in Burma had already brought about widespread disturbances and in 1946 caused a mutiny in the Indian Navy.

As the autumn of 1944 gave way to a grim winter, things began to move again in the grey, humdrum lives of the Kriegies. In camps close to the Reich's borders on East and West, 'latrine-o-grams', or rumours, started to circulate. It seemed that for some reason or other, the camps were going to be evacuated. Some prisoners concluded that the Russians or the Western Allies were getting too close. Others thought of worse possibilities. Perhaps Hitler was going to use them as hostages in order to prevent the further massive bombing of German cities by the Allies. Perhaps he would order them to be executed in progressively larger numbers until the Allies' hand was forced. Hadn't he ordered the chaining of Kriegies back in 1942 as a reprisal for the Canadian handcuffing of German prisoners at Dieppe?

Some POWs decided to get out while the going was good. At Stalag IID at Stargard in Pomeria there was a mass escape of 1,500 Canadians. The facts are vague, but it is thought that there were a considerable number of deaths. Other POWs, too scared to break out, thought they would be liquidated by the Germans come what may. Some of them had been barbarously treated and were convinced that Hitler would never let them live to tell the tale. Like those US and British prisoners of the Japanese who had seen germ warfare experiments carried out on living victims, these Kriegies knew too much.*

London and Washington were also concerned over the fate of the Kriegies. The British government had had various communcations link-ups with the camps since mid-1940 and were now surprisingly well-informed about conditions there. In some cases, private codes were used, known only to the individual prisoner and his loved ones in the UK; in others, codes were agreed upon with certain individuals before they were even taken prisoner. The philosophy was simple. London reasoned that the POWs

*Approximately 27 percent of Allied prisoners in Japanese hands died. Some 4 percent in German hands suffered the same fate.

Dutch SS men before their departure for the Eastern front.

could provide them with valuable information right from the heart of the Reich.

Many camps were linked with London by clandestine radios, such as the one at the Heydekrug RAF camp. This had been made by Kriegies from an old French mess-tin, tin-foil, altar candles and stolen wire, plus valves, also stolen. 'Perhaps the home-made earphones were one of the most interesting pieces of equipment,' recalled one of the NCOs imprisoned there, Sergeant John Dominy. 'The magnets were made by crushing razor blades and annealing them into a core, which was then wrapped in wire from an electric shaver. Diaphragms came from the ubiquitous thin seals on tinned cigarettes and the whole earphone was placed in a plastic tooth-powder container with a hole cut in the lid. The phones were then stuck in a scrum cap and you were in business.'[31]

Thus informed of the Kriegies' plight, London and Washington now pondered what should be done if the POWs were ever used by Hitler in some form of gigantic blackmail. There was talk of landing paratroops near the twenty-odd Allied POW camps; of smuggling weapons

through to the Kriegies via the Red Cross,* of threatening reprisals against the half a million-odd Germans in Allied captivity.

While London and Washington discussed, wise SBOs and SAOs (Senior British Officers and Senior American Officers) and the so-called 'trusted men' or 'Vertrauensmänner,' as the senior representatives of the enlisted men were called, made their own preparations. Food was hoarded, special clothes and packs readied. In the East, men made little sledges, and prepared the escape kits which they had sewn into their clothes in Europe.

At the US camp at Sagan, Poland, an American Kreigie noted in his diary: 'Our barracks looks like a gathering of the Ladies' Aid Sewing Circle.' There, ragged, skinny Kriegies sat cross-legged on their creaking bunks, cutting glove patterns from the bottoms of greatcoats. Others sewed scarves into balaclava helmets, or improvised trousers out of stolen potato sacks. They were not going to be caught out.[32]

*Some Kriegies had already managed to arm themselves by buying machine-guns from the camp guards on the black market.

That winter, Brigadier General Arthur Vanaman called his Americans together and told them solemnly: 'Our best chance of survival is to stand together as one team, ready to face whatever may come. God is our only hope and we must trust Him.'[33] At Ziegenham in the south of Germany, not a hundred miles from Patton's Third Army fighting in Northern France, more optimistic Kriegies asked: 'Is it going to be Parcels, Patton or Peace?'[34]

It was going to be neither – not in this year of Our Lord 1944, at least.

And so the Kriegies waited apprehensively, while the wind howled outside their huts and the first snow of the winter fell in a solid white sheet. Many felt a strange excitement, a compound of fear and anticipation. Others experienced a feeling of peace and calm. After the long, dreary months, perhaps even years of captivity, it seemed that something was going to happen at last. But what?

No one knew. And as the first winter snow piled up higher and higher in Poland and in that remote, densely-wooded border area of the Eifel between Germany and Belgium-Luxembourg, tension grew and grew.

8 BLACK CHRISTMAS

'Aw, nuts!'

Response of Brigadier General McAuliffe to German offer of surrender at Bastogne

At the beginning of that winter, Captain Erich Huett, a tall, blond-haired German officer, was wounded near the Lorraine town of Metz and captured by the French Maquis. Fortunately for him, he was rescued from the bloodthirsty partisans by a French doctor and handed over to the men of Patton's Third Army, for Captain Huett was an SS officer, a member of the 17th Panzer Grenadier Division, 'Goetz von Berlichingen,' and the Maquis usually made short work of SS officers.

Huett, however, was not unduly concerned. Although the SS division's title derived from the name of a famous medieval German robber-knight, it was also a well-known German euphemism for 'kiss my arse.'* Like his comrades, Huett displayed that particular devil-may-care attitude to perfection.

On his second day in the US hospital where his wounded leg was being treated, Huett was ordered to fill out the usual Swiss Red Cross form to notify his relatives that he had been captured. True to the divisional motto, he immediately filled in the details, using his Waffen SS rank designation of Hauptsturmführer. The fact that the hospital now housed an SS officer caused a minor sensation. The American nurses who tended the German officers were shocked and excited. One even simpered, 'You're pretty nice – for an SS officer!' Thereafter, as Erich Huett recalled after the war, 'A whole procession of lady majors, lady captains and lady lieutenants came to visit and stare at me, as if I were some particularly rare animal.'[1]

It was an episode which illustrated the high esteem in which the German soldier was held, particularly if he was an SS man or paratrooper; officers of these two formations

*This usage dates back to the time of Goethe, who used the name in this manner in one of his dramas.

German troops break through in the Ardennes and capture American equipment.

very rarely allowed themselves to fall into Allied hands.

For years, the average American and British soldier had believed that the German soldier, the 'Kraut,' 'Heinie' or 'Jerry,' was some kind of superman, the professional *par excellence*. In France he had been shown to be human after all: the German 'Landser', it seemed, *could* be beaten. Yet after the débâcle of France, when the whole German Seventh Army had been destroyed and most Allied soldiers, high and low thought Germany's days were numbered, the Landser had staged a remarkable recovery. Fighting on the borders of his own country at towns such as Aachen and Metz, he had put up a tremendous defence. At Arnhem, as we have seen, he had given the British a very bloody nose indeed. In the 'Green Hell of the Hürtgenwald' inside Germany proper, he had meted out the same treatment to some six American divisions, virtually shattering two of them, the 4th and 28th US Infantry Divisions, and making the going so tough that more than one battalion commander was court-martialled for refusing to go into action and the cases of 'combat fatigue' mounted into their thousands. Indeed, in the Peel Marches on the Dutch-German frontier, the 'beaten' German had gone over to the offensive once more, throwing back the US 7th Armored Division and actually threatening Montgomery's own HQ at Maastricht, so that for the first and last time in the long campaign in Europe, the clerks and cooks of the HQ were forced to grab their weapons and fight for their lives.

According to the divisional history of the British 11th Armoured Division, which fought the Germans on the Maas that winter, the arduous conditions 'would have undermined the morale of any but the staunchest soldiers, but the [German] paratroopers were capable of sustaining their desperate role. Like the SS, they were picked troops, but their reputation rested less on propaganda than that of their rivals … The stubborness of the resistance at Kunsel and Hechtel had given us an impression of these magnificent infantry which was many times to be confirmed during the winter months. But the seasoned paratroopers were now merely the nucleus of the force, and it was from the rest that the prisoners mostly came … Officers were rare birds indeed and to capture one was at this period a considerable feat.'[2]

As Brigadier Essame of the British 43rd Division, a fighting infantryman of both wars, wrote later: 'He who has not fought the German does not know what war is … During the winter battles many of their formations displayed much of the skill, drive, flexibility and endurance which had taken their armies to the gates of Moscow.'[3] Later, after breaking the back of the German paras west of the Rhine, Brigadier Essame would risk considerable press criticism for ordering his staff to stand to attention as a mark of respect as the beaten German paratroopers filed back into the POW cages.

Such was the opinion of the German held by the average Allied fighting soldier – and this at a time when pundits in Ottawa, Washington, London and just behind the front (including Montgomery) were still maintaining that the war would be over by Christmas at the latest.

But what was he *really* like, this 'super soldier' who was soon to give the American High Command its greatest shock of the whole campaign in 'the European Pearl Harbor?' In many ways, he was little different from his British, Canadian and American counterpart. He, too, was primarily concerned with *Futter* (fodder, *i.e.* food), *Thema Eins* (sex), and naturally *Geistige Nährung* (spiritual nourishment, *i.e.* booze), primarily in the form of *Korn,* * *Kognak oder Bier*.

Like the Allied soldier, the Landser lived a short, brutish life at the front, speaking his own special language and observing special values and mores which separated him from those behind the lines – the 'rear échelon stallions' (*Etappenhengste*), as the 'front swine' (*Frontschweine*) contemptuously called the clerks and cooks.

He ate *Alter Mann*, canned meat reputedly made from the dead bodies of old men found in Berlin's workhouses; smoked his *Lungentorpedos* or 'cancer sticks', (*Krebstangen*); drank 'nigger sweat' (*Negerschweiss* – ersatz coffee made of acorns or barley); and referred mockingly to the decorations for bravery handed out at the front by the basket-load as 'tin' (*Blech*).

The Russian campaign medal was christened the *Gefrierfleischordnung* (literally, the 'Order of the Frozen Meat'); Germany's second-highest medal for bravery was the 'Order of the Fried Egg, or Scrambled Eggs'; and the country's highest decoration, the Knight's Cross of the Iron Cross, was simply, in soldiers' parlance, a means of curing 'throatache'.** Naturally, veterans, or 'stubble-hoppers' as the infantrymen called themselves, always accused eager young officers of attempting to gain that coveted award at the cost of their own skin.

These 'super soldiers' could be as ill-disciplined and mutinous at the front as their opposite numbers in the Allied armies, in spite of the fearsome punishments that could be imposed on them by their superiors. There were no rest centres for 'combat fatigue' cases in the German Army. Some 10,000 German soldiers were executed in World War Two, mainly for cowardice and desertion. By contrast, in the whole of the US Army there was only a single such case. In the German Army, wrongdoers could also be sent to one of the three German Army punishment battalions, the 333rd, 555th and 999th Penal Battalions, where their chances of survival were virtually nil,*** and even generals could be shot for disobeying orders at the front or exhibiting cowardice. General Count von Sponeck had been one of the victors of the attack on Holland with his Air-Landing Division. Four years later he was shot by

*A kind of German gin.
**The decoration was worn around the neck.
***In the penal battalions, German soldiers were frequently assigned to *Himmelfahrtskommandos*, *i.e.* missions in which there was no chance of return.

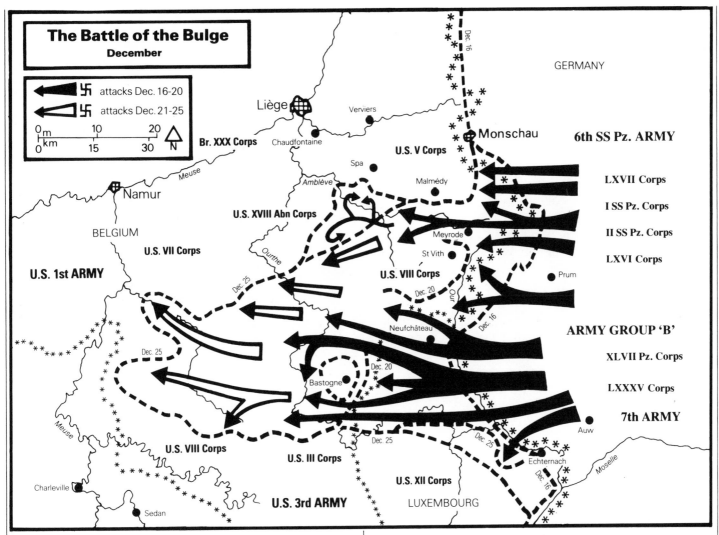

GERMANY

Liège
Verviers
Br. XXX Corps   Chaudfontaine
Meuse
Spa
Amblève   Malmédy
Namur
U.S. XVIII Abn Corps   Meyrode
BELGIUM
U.S. VII Corps   St Vith
Ourthe
U.S. 1st ARMY   Prum
U.S. VIII Corps
Dec. 25   Dec. 20
Our
Dec. 16
Neufchâteau
Dec. 25
Dec. 20
Bastogne
Dec. 25
Meuse
Auw
7th ARMY
U.S. VIII Corps
Echternach
U.S. III Corps   Moselle
Charleville
U.S. XII Corps   Dec. 16
Sedan   LUXEMBOURG
U.S. 3rd ARMY

Monschau   6th SS Pz. ARMY
U.S. V Corps
LXVII Corps
I SS Pz. Corps
II SS Pz. Corps
LXVI Corps

ARMY GROUP 'B'
XLVII Pz. Corps
LXXXV Corps

firing squad for alleged cowardice. That same year, General Count von Schwerin, another highly-decorated hero of the fighting in France and Russia, barely escaped the same fate for alleged cowardice in the face of the enemy at Aachen.

In spite of these penalties, it seemed the Landser still rebelled. In the winter of 1944, for example, discipline was so poor that General Gerhard Franz, commander of the 256th Volksgrenadier Division, was forced to post the following notice to his men stationed in the line in Holland:

Certain events among units have impelled me to point out that discipline and *esprit de corps* among the troops must be raised in the shortest possible time ... It cannot be tolerated that a formation commander should get drunk, then wander around the woods all night shouting and firing his pistol at the sentry ... It shows little discipline in a company when members of the company call each other 'cheats' during a discussion about captured loot ... A unit shows little *esprit de corps* if a soldier can declare that owing to difficulty in walking he can no longer serve with the artillery since he could not escape quickly enough if the Tommy arrived ... During the last eight days no less than eleven desertions have been reported, seven of whom went over into enemy lines ...[4]

That November, Franz's comrade of the 18th Volks-

grenadier Division, General Hoffmann-Schonforn, posted the names of six men who had deserted to the Americans on all unit noticeboards, and added below: 'These bastards have given away important military secrets ... Rest assured the division will see that they never see home and loved ones again. Their families will have to atone for their treason. The destiny of a people has never depended upon traitors and bastards.'[5]

It was a warning that was backed up that month by an edict issued by Himmler, the head of the dreaded secret police. It stated: 'Certain unreliable elements seem to believe that the war will be over for them as soon as they surrender to the enemy. Against this belief it must be pointed out that every deserter will be prosecuted and will find his just punishment. Furthermore, his ignominious behaviour will entail the most severe consequences for his family. Upon examination of the circumstances they will be summarily shot.'[6]

The concept of *Sippenhaft*, the arrest of dependents for the wrong-doings of their menfolk at the front, had been born: yet still the desertions continued.

Naturally, there were differences between the Landser and his Anglo-American opposite number. Surprisingly enough, the officers of the German Army were often more

American troops advance through heavy snow, pulling equipment on sledges.

democratic in their dealings with their men than British and American officers. In spite of all the heel-clicking, barked commands and saluting (in the German Army, even corporals were saluted), no one was forced to use the formula, 'Permission to speak, sir,' as in the British Army. Also, German officers often messed with the men, eating from the same 'goulash-cannon' (as the mobile stove on wheels was nicknamed); this was true even in the élite SS, where all aspiring officers had to come from the ranks and, if possible, do a stint at the front before being commissioned. Many German officers also manged without a batman or servant (generals and colonels excepted), unlike officers in the British and American Armies; even in the supposedly democratic US Army, the batman still survived, although disguised as 'an officer's driver'. The only clear sign of difference between a German officer and his men at the front was that the officer called his men collectively by the familiar '*Ihr*' form normally used with children and intimates; individually, however, the soldier was always addressed by the respectful, more formal, '*Sie*'.

The majority of the Landser came from a more rural background than the average Tommy or GI and tended to be physically harder than their Allied opposite number.

The younger men were particularly tough, for most of them had had years of paramilitary training, first in the Hitler Youth and later in the *Arbeitsdienst*, or Labour Corps, before joining the army. They knew how to live off the land and were used to the hardships of country living, out in the open all day on short rations, and sleeping rough at night. Unlike the Americans, too, they were not dependent on 'wheels'.

The Landser also had the advantage of the German military system, in which cadres of experienced officers and NCOs were periodically withdrawn from 'burnt-out' divisions to rebuild or train other units. This meant that the 'green beaks' (*Grünschnabel*, as they were called contemptuously by older soldiers) had the benefit of the experience of the 'old hares' (*alte Hasen*).

The training of the Landser was long and exhaustive. Unlike the *Tommis* and *Amis*, the Landser learned to dig deep and then place the earth removed from the foxholes to the *rear* of the position so that the fresh soil wouldn't give them away; they were then trained to cover the hole with logs to protect themselves from airbursts, and camouflage the position with branches. Even today, forty years on, one can still find well-preserved German positions in the heart of the Ardennes forests, easily recognisable as German by

152

(1) *Paying a Visit.*
Visiting hours 11.30 – 13.00 hours on Sunday, 17.00 – 18.00 hours on week-days. Never later and never in the afternoon … On entering the room carry hat in left hand. On taking a seat lay the hat down …
Coming and going: Length of visit should be about ten minutes. Do not look at your watch. No reason should be given for the termination of your visit. On leaving do not turn your back on the company when opening the door.

(2) *Entertainments*
Wine: White wine to be drunk from tall glasses, red from short glasses.
Dances: First dance and quadrilles always with the dinner partner. Never dance continually with one and the same lady.
Flowers: In presenting flowers, hold the stalks … *etc.etc.*[7]

This in the middle of total war, four months after Stalingrad!

It was hardly surprising, given this kind of training, that many German officers still seemed to hold a romantic, nineteenth-century view of war, in which gentlemen and officers gallantly surrendered their swords* after a battle, shook hands and departed, heads held high against adversity, but with no hard feelings.

Time and time again, American soldiers were bewildered by this old-fashioned *antebellum* attitude. Yet equally, the Germans were bemused by what they saw as the Americans' lack of finesse. When they surrendered after what they considered a fair fight at cities ranging from Brest to Aachen, the Germans encountered not respect as from one officer to another, but what they considered to be American coarseness, even brutality. Paratroop General McAuliffe's famous one-word reply to the German offer of surrender at Bastogne in December, 1944: 'Nuts!', must have bewildered the aristocratic German commander, General von Lüttwitz, considerably.

The main difference, however, between the German soldier of late 1944 and his Anglo-American opposite number was his bitterness. The Landser had seen great German cities bombed day and night, month after month, for nearly two years now, ever since the great RAF 1,000-bomber raid on Cologne in May, 1942. They had seen what had happened to their cities right across the Reich, and many of them had lost their dear ones in such raids. Obersturmbannführer Jochen Peiper of the 1st SS Panzer Division, who would play a key role in the events of this December, had seen for himself the destruction at the nearby town of Duren that month, where 'the civilians had to be scraped from the walls.' Afterwards, Peiper swore that he would 'personally castrate the men who did that – with a piece of broken glass – blunt at that!'[8] and the twenty-nine-year-old SS tank group commander was only one of many. Directly or indirectly, all of these men who would bring about such a startling change in the course of

*Off-duty, German officers, officer-cadets and certain senior NCOs still carried dirks, or even swords in some cases.

their log roofs. They also learned how to make night patrols in complete silence and *without* leaving a trail of trash behind them, as the Americans often did. They learned how to keep warm and dry in the line under hard physical conditions. Instead of socks, they wrapped their feet in foot-rags and wore their 'dice-beakers,' or jackboots, one size too big, filling the gap with straw or shredded paper to keep their feet dry. 'Trench foot,' which often resulted in the loss of toes and caused more casualties than bullets among the US Army that winter, was hardly known in the German Army. The old hares taught the green beaks well.

In many ways, however, the Germans were much more naive and old-fashioned than their opponents. As late as 1944 officer-cadets were taught the correct way to drink champagne – 'glass parallel with third tunic button, arm extended at a forty-five-degree angle'; how to present flowers to their senior officer's wife – 'the wrapping paper will be removed immediately before presentation and placed behind one's back with the left hand, to be disposed of later'; and how to 'pay a visit'. Here is a sample order on that subject intended for the cadets of an artillery school. The date is April, 1943:

the campaign later that month had suffered in the 'terror raids' carried out by the British and American 'air gangsters' and were itching to pay back the score.

They also felt grotesquely misrepresented by Allied propaganda, which had made out that they had terrorised a half-starved Europe. In their opinion, the contrary had been true – most of them, naturally, dissociated themselves entirely from the kind of terror conducted by the Gestapo. They knew that in every western-European occupied country – France, Holland, Denmark, Belgium, Norway – volunteers had flocked in their thousands to join the German Armed Forces, and in particular, the SS. And hadn't the Germans been the first to introduce to Czechoslovakia the concept of rest homes for workers, sick pay and insurance contributions, bringing the Czechs all the benefits of the world's first attempt at a 'social welfare state' as envisaged by Bismarck back in the 1880s? Hadn't they achieved full employment in France and Belgium after two decades of mass unemployment? Wasn't Denmark a land of milk and honey under their control? Weren't the shops in Luxembourg and Belgium filled with gateaux, clotted cream, silk stockings, perfumes and fine clothes, the like of which the British soldiers who had 'liberated' them hadn't seen these five years? Conquerors they might have been once, but *oppressors*? Surely not!

They resented, too, the Allied claim that they alone treated prisoners at the front brutally. They knew and admitted that in the heat of battle, prisoners were sometimes treated roughly, even shot by young soldiers carried away by the *Blutrausch* of combat. But such incidents, they claimed, weren't confined to the German side. The British, the Canadians and the Americans could be just as cruel.

There was some evidence to support this view. In the summer of 1943, for instance, a British war correspondent, Alexander Clifford, saw men of the 45th US Infantry Division, possibly inflamed by a fighting speech made to them by Patton just before they went into battle, fire into a truckload of German POWs at Comiso Airfield. Only two or three prisoners escaped alive. Later, the same correspondent saw the 45th kill a further 60 Italian prisoners. Another correspondent, American Clark Lee, reported further incidents of the same kind in Sicily, among them the killing carried out by Sergeant Barry West of the 45th. Ordered to take 36 German prisoners of war to the rear near the town of Gela, West shot them at the roadside in cold blood. On the very same day, Captain Jerry Compton, also of the 45th, lined up 43 German snipers against the side of a barn and machine-gunned them to death. Patton, when told of the incidents, told Bradley, then his subordinate commander: 'Tell the officer [i.e. Compton, who faced court-martial] to certify the men were snipers, or had attempted to escape, or something.'*[9]

There had been similar incidents during the early days of the invasion. Major Meyer-Detering of Field Marshal von

*Subsequently, both the captain and the sergeant were convicted, but were returned to their units and later killed in action.

Schimmwagen (amphibious volkswagen) of 2nd Panzer Grenadier Regiment near Recht.

Rundstedt's staff swore on oath after the war that he had twice received reports from reliable units at the front in Normandy that instead of taking prisoners, the Canadians were shooting them out of hand. On another occasion, a Lieutenant Colonel Zeissler of an armoured unit was captured with some of his men. They were then brutally beaten up, and shortly afterwards the shooting began. Zeissler managed to escape and reported what was happening, but nobody believed him until a one-armed German colonel, Oberst Luxenburger, was discovered tied to the turret of a Canadian tank which was subsequently knocked out by a German anti-tank gun. Three days later Luxenburger died of his wounds in hospital.

Nor was it only the Americans and Canadians, the tough guys of the 'New World', who committed atrocities: the British were also to blame. William Douglas Home at his court-martial in Bruges detailed how RAF fighters had shot up German ambulances which had been filled with wounded and clearly marked with a Red Cross. Major Brodie, that ill-fated Highlander of the many wounds, also recorded how 'a much decorated Sergeant from Bromley, once approached him and pointed to one of his prisoners, a newly captured German officer. 'Can't we have him, sir?' asked the sergeant. Brodie asked what the veteran NCO meant, and by way of reply the latter 'pointed out that some of the younger soldiers had not killed a German yet.' The sergeant spoke as if the killing of prisoners were commonplace and widespread. Brodie, however, was suitably shocked and refused.[10]

When responsible officers such as Brodie weren't present, there was nothing to stop subordinate officers and men doing just as they pleased. Captain John Long, a company commander in the black 761st Tank Battalion, records how his men brought in a wounded German sniper who shortly before had killed one of the company medics. 'In one second I knew I wasn't about to ask those men to tend this bastard who had chosen the conspicuous crosses on the medics' helmet as target. I told my sergeant to shoot the sniper. The kid turned ashen, then fumbled for his gun. It was an unfair order so I pulled my revolver and did it myself.'[11]

Corporal Alexander McKee of the British Army came across a similar incident behind the front in Holland, where he found 30 German paratroopers being chased into captivity by two Tommies. One armed with a Sten-gun was 'riding herd' on a bicycle; the other was on foot and wielding an evil-looking whip. McKee asked the one with the whip how long the sweat-drenched, exhausted and very frightened paras had been running. Three or four miles, was the reply. 'And what happens if they can't keep up?' McKee asked. 'If the whip doesn't encourage them,' the Tommy replied easily, 'I leave them to my mate and they stays there for good. We haven't had to leave too many behind so far. These boys like running.' With that they were off again, to hearty cries of 'Schnell!' and much whip-cracking, leaving McKee to wonder how many of them would ever reach the POW cage alive.[12]

(Below) Generals Blolskowitz, Rommel and Field Marshal von Rundstedt. (Right) Gun crew on their way to the Luxembourg front by convoy.

As the date set for the German counter-offensive drew nearer, excitement mounted among the Landser. But although many rejoiced at the prospect of hitting back at the enemy, many also had misgivings about the manner and timing of the attack. Even one of their commanders in chief, ex-sergeant major Sepp Dietrich, now head of the newly-created Sixth SS Panzer Army, had strong reservations. After his capture, he later complained to his interrogators: ' "All I had to do was to cross a river [the Meuse], capture Brussels and then go on and take the port of Antwerp. And all this in December, January and February, the worst three months of the year; through the Ardennes where the snow was waist deep and there wasn't room to deploy four tanks abreast, let alone six armoured divisions; when it didn't get light until eight in the morning and was dark again at four in the afternoon and my tanks can't fight at night; with divisions that had just been reformed and were composed chiefly of raw untrained recruits – and at Christmas time!" The crack in Dietrich's voice when he mentioned this last obstacle made it sound the most heart-breaking one of all.'[13]

His aged chief, Field Marshal von Rundstedt, who

would give the great new attack his name, was even blunter. 'It was a nonsensical operation,' he snorted to his interrogators, 'and the most stupid part of it was the setting of Antwerp as the target. If we reached the Meuse we should have got down on our knees and thanked God – let alone try to reach Antwerp!'[14]

But if the generals were unenthusiastic, their soldiers, raw and untrained as they may have been, felt differently. For them it was a chance to settle old scores. And thanks to the efforts of the club-footed 'poison dwarf', Minister of Propaganda Josef Goebbels, who had always maintained that American soldiers were little better than undisciplined savages, the Landser also felt confident that ultimate victory would be theirs.

The Landsers' poor opinion of the Americans, however, wasn't solely based on propaganda. Goebbels' claims were also backed up by the old hares who had fought the Americans in Normandy. The latter all agreed that American planes were to be feared; these held mastery of the sky and 'behaved so arrogantly', as one combat unit had reported in Normandy the previous summer, 'that the low-flying planes were often shot down by infantry weapons, or caught their wings in tree tops and crashed.' But *Ami* infantry presented no such threat. As another combat report put it: 'American attacks were only successful when preceded by a solid wall of armour. In many cases when it had not sufficient tank support, the infantry was thrown back by us without difficulty. The almost wasteful use of armoured forces was dictated by the American High Command in order to avoid placing an excessive burden on the infantry, which was the weakest factor in the battle and to keep losses to a minimum.'

In the Ardennes counter-offensive, the Germans were to strike at four such infantry divisions, all without immediate armoured support. And they fully intended to pay back their debts in blood.

That winter, Captain Robert E. Merriam of the Ninth US Army painted the following almost pastoral picture of life at the front: 'All was peaceful; farmers in the fields along the road were ploughing their fields for the winter fallow, and some were taking in the last of the summer harvest; cattle were grazing lazily.'[15] Somewhere along the River

Our, Merriam's driver-guide halted and pointed to the West Wall, held by the Germans; it was completely silent, and not a single German bothered to fire at the two exposed Americans. 'Have to be careful at night,' said the driver, 'Krauts like to sneak over patrols, just to make a social call. Ambushed a jeep in daylight the other day, and got a new battalion commander. Hell, he didn't even have a chance to report in! But the only shelling we get is when Jerry goes to the latrine; seems like they have a machine gun and a mortar there and each one fires a burst – hope they don't get diarrhoea!'[16]

This in other words, was a joke front where nothing happened and new divisions could be broken in gently before being transferred to the real shooting war. There were USO shows and Red Cross girls just behind the line, and although the new men did their target practice at ranges overlooked by German artillery, the Germans never fired on the GIs. It was almost as if both sides had a gentleman's agreement not to disturb each other's peace and quiet. For three long months, this sixty-mile stretch between Monschau in the north and Echternach in the south had been so quiet that even the brass had adopted the GIs' own name for it: the 'Ghost Front.' Soon all that was going to change – dramatically.

At 5.30 precisely on the morning of Saturday December 16th, 1944, 2,000 German guns of all calibres crashed into ear-splitting action all along the 'Ghost Front.'

Out on patrol in the border village of Lanzerath, Lieutenant Bouck of the raw 99th US Infantry Division was horrified as the whole horizon erupted in a mass of flame and concentrated artillery fire poured from the snow-covered Eifel hills, swamping the forward American positions. Back at Bouck's battalion headquarters, one executive officer had been told that along the whole 99th

German soldiers in the Ardennes, advancing through American lines.

Infantry front, the Germans possessed only two horse-drawn artillery pieces. Now that officer groaned in disbelief as his HQ vibrated like a live thing under the impact. 'Christ!' he cursed, 'They sure are working those two poor horses to death!'[17]

Further back in the 99th, half a dozen GIs were lazily drinking their morning coffee in the Mess tent, while the cook stirred batter for the breakfast pancakes, a great GI can of thick yellow mix at his feet. Suddenly the shells started to fly. 'Give 'em hell, boys!' a GI cried enthusiastically. Suddenly a shell landed only a hundred yards away, making the walls of the tent flap and billow alarmingly. 'That's incoming mail!' the cook cried, as yet another exploded overhead, ripping great holes in the canvas and filling the tent with choking fumes. In his fright, he planted his right foot up to the knee in the can of batter but continued to stir, regardless.[18]

At the various headquarters up and down the front, reports of exceedingly heavy shelling flooded in, each one more alarming than the last. Meanwhile, outside in the border villages, half-dressed, panic-stricken civilians were already grabbing their pathetic belongings and heading for the cellars. Junior officers and NCOs barked orders; motor vehicles coughed and spluttered in the icy dawn air, while their angry, frightened drivers fought to get them started. MPs ran to the crossroads to take up their posts. It was obvious even to the humblest peasant and doughboy that a major offensive was being launched.

As suddenly as it had started, the artillery barrage ceased, and in the reverberating silence which followed, radios crackled into life and telephones began to jingle alarmingly in the blacked-out regimental and divisional headquarters. The news was bad. From north to south of the 'Ghost Front,' the Germans had hit the green 99th, the 14th Cavalry Group, the 106th Division (the newest allied division on any front in the world that day*), the new 9th Armored and the veteran but battle-weary 28th Infantry Division. Already most of their forward outfits had been swamped by horses of white-clad German infantry or were withdrawing under immense pressure from the enemy.

Crouched with his handful of men at the edge of the little Belgian hamlet of Lanzerath, Lieutenant Bouck observed two companies of white-clad German paras plodding towards their positions in apparent unconcern. In spite of the fact that all the wires had been torn down by the great barrage and the radio wavelengths were jammed by the Germans playing loud marching music, a badly scared Bouck managed to get through to battalion HQ and called for immediate artillery fire on the advancing Germans. The officer at the other end, however, refused to believe that there were already Germans in Lanzerath. 'Dammit!' Bouck cried in exasperation, 'Don't tell me what I don't see! I have twenty-twenty vision. Bring down some artillery – all the artillery you can on the road south of Lanzareth. There's a Kraut column coming up from that direction!'[19]

*It had been in the line exactly five days.

No artillery came. But the enemy did. A little while later, one of Bouck's men on outpost duty reported over the radio in a frightened whisper: 'Lieutenant, the Krauts are already downstairs. What shall I do?' In the end he did what most of Bouck's men would do that day: surrendered.[20]

Linking the 99th Division with the ill-fated 'Golden Lion'* of the 106th US Infantry Division were 1,600-odd dismounted cavalrymen dug in at six border villages, or 'fortified hedgehogs.' Now all six were under heavy attack by elements of the two German divisions. One by one they either surrendered, became swamped by sheer German weight of numbers, or panicked and fled to the rear. Some, however, fought to the bitter end. Captain Stanley E. Porche, holding the hamlet of Roth, one of the most advanced positions of the whole Allied front-line, radioed the following message back to HQ: 'Tiger tank seventy-five yards from CP.** Belting us with direct fire. Out.'[21] It was the last ever heard of Captain Porche and his brave men until the war was over.

Now it was the turn of the 106th to come under pressure, as the 18th Volksgrenadier Division started to swing through a narrow draw from the hamlet of Auw, Germany, towards that of Andler in Belgium, advancing on the American positions under cover of a snowstorm. They were spotted at the very last moment by the artillerymen of the 106th's 589th Artillery Battalion on the heights beyond Andler. Immediately, Lieutenant Eric Wood, Battery A's executive officer and a former Princeton football player, rushed to the nearest gun and ordered the No. 4 piece to open fire. The howitzer erupted with a roar. A German tank leading the attack was hit and burst into flames. White tracer bullets exploded inside it and zig-zagged crazily into the leaden sky. Momentarily the German attack was stalled. However, later that day, 'artillery and mortar fire came down in earnest into Battery A, so hotly that the personnel were withdrawn temporarily to defiladed positions. Battery A lost here and later that night thirty-six officers and men. They went back to the pieces at 6.30 p.m.'[22]

Lieutenant Wood and his men managed to hold firm against the German onslaught. Many didn't. At the headquarters of the 14th Cavalry at the Belgian village of Manderfeld, the staff panicked. In their fear they set fire to the whole village and fled, led by their senior officers, all of whom would later be court-martialled.

The narrow, winding Belgian country roads leading from the front rapidly became impassable as vehicles and hordes of demoralised infantry fought their way through the slush and mud. Trucks and tanks skidded on the icy roads and inclines, often careering into the drainage ditches. Vehicles that ran out of gas were simply abandoned; platoon leaders ordered their soldiers to dump

*So named on account of its 'golden lion' divisional patch.
**Command Post.

American troops on the move again, supported by infantry.

their heavy equipment so that they could move faster. The 'big bug-out,' as the GIs called it, had commenced.

The attacking Landser were understandably euphoric at this rout. A triumphant Leutnant Rockhammer wrote home a letter, later taken from his dead body, which vividly captured their mood:

This time we are a thousand times better off than you at home. You cannot imagine what glorious hours and days we are experiencing now. It looks as if the Amis cannot withstand our important push. Today we overtook a fleeing column and finished it off. We overtook it by taking a backroad through the woods to the retreat lane of the Ami vehicles; then, just like on manoeuvres, we pulled up along the road with sixty Panthers. And then came the endless convoy driving in two columns, side by side, hub by hub, filled to the brim with soldiers. And then a concentrated fire from sixty cannon and one hundred and twenty machine guns. It was a glorious bloodbath, vengeance for our destroyed homeland. Our soldiers still have the old zip … Victory was never so close as it is now![23]

Another German, perhaps not as bloodthirsty as Leutnant Rockhammer, wrote home that same week: 'Even I, as a poor private, can easily tell that it won't take much longer until the Ami will throw away his weapons. For if he sees that everybody is retreating, he runs away and cannot be stopped any more. He is also war-weary, as I myself learned from prisoners.'[24]

Another wrote home to his wife: 'The main thing is that the Americans are on the run … We cleared an enemy supply dump. Everybody took things he wanted most. I took only chocolate. I have all my pockets full of it. I eat chocolate all the time in order to sweeten somewhat this wretched life … Don't worry about me. The worst is behind me. Now this is just a hunt. The Americans hardly get to fire a round and the American prisoners say that they are war-weary, and don't want to hear anything more about the war. Things might move very quickly in the West …'[25]

Ironically, none of the letter-writers survived to see just how wrong they were.

The streets of the little border town of St. Vith, the headquarters of the 106th Infantry Division, were now packed with men of all units 'bugging out' from the front. They were everywhere, wet, dejected and frightened. Private William MacDonald, who had previously served with the veteran 2nd Division and was now with the 106th, had once called the greenhorns, without malice, 'the sick and the hungry'; now he was angered and disgusted by them. Without regard to rank, he pushed his way through a khaki-clad crowd of rookies blocking the Haupstrasse and roared at a full colonel who was bugging out with the rest: 'Why you goddam coward …'. He was too enraged to be able to say any more. It seems the colonel, however, was too frightened to react.[26]

Americans digging in for protection against German artillery fire.

Later that same day, a full general, Brigadier Clarke of the 7th Armored Division had to patrol the streets brandishing his pistol in a bid to stop the fleeing soldiers and restore order. Once he even threatened to shoot a colonel if he didn't get his 'goddam vehicles' out of the way. As Captain Dudley Britton of the 23rd Armored Infantry Battalion said later: '(That day) I saw the highest-ranking traffic cops I have ever seen.'[27]

Still the 'big bug-out' went on. As the historian of the 106th Division wrote afterwards: 'Let's get down to hard facts. Panic, sheer unreasoning panic, flamed that road all day and into the night. Everyone, it seemed, who had any excuse and many who had none, was going west that day – west from Schoenberg, west from St. Vith too.'[28]

Vehicles from half a dozen different formations joined the exodus, some of them taking up three-quarters of the road. Now and again vehicles went weaving into a third line and crashed into ditches or were forced off into the snowy fields by other angry drivers.

It was through this chaos that the US 7th Armored Division had to fight its way as it raced down from Holland to attempt the 'rescue' of the already trapped 106th Division. Leading the 7th's long columns in a jeep was bespectacled Major Don Boyer. He soon bumped into a long line of stalled vehicles. Voices shouted angry imprecations. Horns honked hysterically. Drivers gunned their engines, afraid that they might die on them in the freezing weather. Fuming with rage, the major got out of his jeep and ran to where a group of officers were arguing loudly. 'What's the score?' he asked. 'Two panzer armies – at least six panzer divisions – hit us yesterday!' the scared officer gasped in reply. 'What are you doing about it?' Boyer yelled above the din. '*Me*, I'm leaving!' the officer answered with an air of finality.[29]

The answer was typical of the reaction of many badly rattled GIs that day. Those who could, fled; the remainder had little choice but to accept their fate. Even the veterans were caught off guard. The 110th Infantry Regiment of the 28th Infantry Division, which had fought since the beginning of the campaign, was dug in around the

Luxembourg tourist resort of Clervaux. The men had started to pull back when they were hit by German paras and tanks, and the panic was only stopped when Colonel Hurley Fuller, the craggy-faced regimental commander, took personal charge and tongue-lashed his frightened men back into action. Fuller, a veteran of the Argonne in '18 and the fighting in Brittany, was of such a cantankerous disposition that a reaming from the 'Old Man' was feared almost more than the enemy. But this time even Fuller couldn't stem the tide: soon the veterans were 'bugging out' with the rest.

It was the same with Fuller's old outfit, the US 2nd Division. There, Captain MacDonald led his men into the attack for the first time to support men of the 99th who had already broken and run, only to find that he, too, was soon 'running like hell.'

Over the noise of Lopez's machine-gun firing I could hear Captain Wilson shouting to withdraw into Rocherath. I wanted to obey but I was caught in the crossfire of the heavy machine-gun and the attackers. I gritted my teeth and waited for a lull in the firing. None came. I jumped from the hole and ran blindly toward the rear. Bullets snipped at my heels. The tank saw that we were running again and opened up with renewed vigor, the shells snapping the tops from the trees around us as if they were matchsticks … I felt like we were helpless little bugs scurrying blindly about now that some man-monster had lifted the log under which we had been hiding. I wondered if it would not be better to be killed and perhaps that would be an end to everything.[30]

Even Eric Wood and his men of the 106th Division's artillery were on the run now. But as their truck careered down into the Belgian village of Schoenberg, towing a cannon behind, they came under fire from both sides. Seeing a German tank lumber up from a side street, one of the gunners dropped over the side of the truck and took hasty aim with his bazooka. There was a vicious streak of red flame followed by angry sparks, and suddenly white smoke started to pour from the German tank. The gunner climbed back up and the truck rolled on.

Now machine-guns opened up to the right of them. Kroll, Wood's driver, braked to a squealing halt. Two men, Sergeant Scannapico and Private Campagna, jumped out. There was another German Mark IV tank 75 yards away. Campagna fired and missed, but for some reason the tank didn't return the American fire. Scannapico didn't stop to find out why. He and Campagna raced back to the vehicle. Campagna managed to fling himself over the track. Scannapico wasn't so lucky. Just as Kroll let out the clutch and the heavy towing vehicle started to move forward, the sergeant was hit in the back by a burst of bullets. As the others watched, horrified, he staggered after them a few paces, face contorted with pain, arms held out as if appealing for help. Hit again, he flopped face downwards in the mud of the road.

The towing vehicle cleared a little bridge and was starting to climb out of Schoenberg on the narrow road to St. Vith and safety when a German tank appeared around a bend and immediately opened fire. The shell struck the cab of the truck and Kroll slumped over the shattered wheel, blood streaming down his face. Hastily the rest baled out into a nearby ditch.

Desperately, Wood cast around for some way out of the trap. Ahead of them were the Germans. To their right, a steep wooded embankment. Below and to the left was a marshy field with another wooded hillside beyond it. Before Wood could make a decision, however, a soldier next to him began to raise his hands. 'Get down!' Wood yelled. But already the others, including an officer, were starting to take off their helmets and prepare to surrender.

Wood made a split-second decision. Just as the German infantry started to come forward to receive the surrender of the American artillerymen, he burst loose. Running in a wild zig-zag course across the snow-covered field to his left, head tucked down between his shoulders in true American-football style, he dashed for the woods, the slugs cutting up white spurts of snow at his flying heels.

That was the last the US Army ever saw of Lieutenant Eric Fisher Wood. Six weeks later when the Allies regained the area, the soldiers of the 7th Armored Division found his dead body at a crossroads in the forest. Around it lay dead Germans. In Wood's hand was found an empty Colt.45.

Afterwards, villagers of the nearby hamlet of Meyerode, which had been SS General Sepp Dietrich's HQ during the battle, told US investigators that Wood had lived off looted supplies, carrying out a one-man guerrilla campaign against German convoys as they rolled through the dense woods. Finally he had been trapped by the Germans and had fought it out to the last.

Today a stone cross still marks the spot where Wood died forty years ago in that remote Ardennes wood. Ironically enough, his epitaph is in German.[31]

Now the wounded were streaming back in their hundreds, mingled with the cowards and deserters, the broken men, the combat fatigue cases – the shattered remnants of outfits destroyed in that terrible first day of battle.

Private Lester Atwell, who six weeks before had been at

sea on the *Queen Elisabeth* as a replacement, was now deep in the heart of the snow-bound Ardennes, bringing out the wounded on stretchers and piling them on board a tank, ready to be driven off.

The tank bore a grotesque resemblance to a float in a mardi gras. Figures were strewn over it, some sitting with their bandaged heads bowed. A wounded man, accompanied by a friend, hobbled toward it, white-faced. There were ten or twelve idlers standing about. They relieved us of the litter and lifted it up onto the tank. A jeep raced by. I turned around and started back once more through the woods. It seemed about twenty minutes to four; it had that feeling. In the dense shade, there was something sad – no, more than sad, tragic – the sense of failure.[32]

Trapped in the same woods, the commanders of the ill-fated 106th US Infantry Division felt the same sense of failure. Thirty-five-year-old Colonel Descheneaux, commanding the 422nd Regiment, saw how the wounded were filling up the bunkers next to his command post, and moaned, 'We're sitting like fish in a pond.'[33] Colonel Cavender, an older man commanding the neighbouring 423rd, was of the same opinion. His men were dirty, hungry, confused and worn out from constantly toiling up and down the steep, wooded heights looking for ways of escape, only to find that the Germans held all the roads around the forest. Now both he and Descheneaux, unlike many commanders in similar situations that third week of December, 1944, were preparing to sacrifice their military careers in order to save their men.*

For a while they hung on, hoping against hope that there was some way out of the trap. Once, a German shell scored a direct hit on a group of senior officers, killing a colonel and scattering the men in panic. At one point a lone black GI armed with a Tommy-gun came from nowhere and rallied the panicked white men – but not for long. Soon he, too, disappeared into obscurity, and morale disintegrated again.

Soon afterwards, the two regiments discovered that they had been firing at each other in the confusion, and at that point it seems that Descheneaux, or 'Desch' as he was known to his officers, finally reached his decision. That afternoon, gathering his men, he told them: 'As far as I am concerned, I'm going to save the lives of as many men as I can. And I don't give a damn if I am court-martialled!'[34]

A little later Cavender came to the same conclusion. 'I was a GI in the First World War,' he explained to his staff, 'and I want to try to see things from their [*i.e.* the men's] standpoint. No man in this outfit has eaten all day and we haven't had water since early morning. Now what's your attitude to surrendering?'[35]

*Colonel Descheneaux was a West-Pointer – and West-Pointers do *not* surrender.

Watching the long columns of nearly 10,000 GIs come pouring out of the forests, hands held in the air in surrender, the young German grenadiers went wild with joy. One wrote to his parents later: 'Endless columns of prisoners pass. At first about one hundred, half of them negroes ... American soldiers have little spirit for fighting. Most of them often said, what do we want here? At home we can have everything much better.'[36]

But not all the 'Golden Lions' of the 106th Division surrendered that afternoon. Five hundred or more held out in the forest for another 36 hours, surrounded on all sides by Germans. Of these, a score or more managed to break through the German front to their own lines in twos and threes, dealing savagely with any opposition they happened to meet on the way. Captain Murray, a first sergeant, and a Private Dickens, for example, sneaked through the German positions at night, waded the River Our and were just congratulating themselves on having made it when they bumped into a German sentry in the darkness. Murray stabbed the German with his trench knife, but the blow wasn't fatal, so Dickens and the NCO grabbed the German before he could raise the alarm. While the other two held him, a terror-stricken Murray sawed through his exposed throat. When the butchery was over and the German sank limp and dead to the snow, Murray found he had slashed his own hand to pieces too. Shaking with nerves, the three escapers pushed on to Allied-held St. Vith.[37]

They were the lucky ones. For many, the grim prospect of life as a POW now loomed. That same night, marching across the border with a great crowd of prisoners towards the German railhead at Prum, Colonel Descheneaux was approached by one of the men whose life he had saved at the expense of his career. The GI said cockily: 'I've got a message for you, Colonel.' With that, he stuck out his tongue and gave his former CO the Bronx cheer. Shocked, the colonel marched on, not knowing that he had helped bring about the greatest defeat of American arms in the whole campaign and the second biggest surrender of US troops since the Civil War nearly a century before.

For the 110th Infantry Regiment at Clervaux, too, the end was near. Abandoned by the tanks which had been sent to his aid, the fierce-tongued Colonel Fuller vainly tried to hold his battalions together in the face of a severe attack. Finally he called division and asked to be connected with General Cota of D-Day fame. He wanted permission to withdraw while there was still time. Coldly, Colonel Gibney, Cota's chief of staff, told Fuller, a newcomer to the 28th Division, that the general was at dinner and couldn't be reached. 'All right, Gibney,' Fuller cried, as German tanks rolled ever closer to his hotel HQ, 'You're transmitting the general's orders and I've got to obey them! But I'm telling you it's going to be the Alamo all over again.'[38]

And so it was. At midnight, with twelve survivors and a

blinded officer hanging on to his coat-tails, all that remained of his HQ, Fuller slipped away into the heights that dominated the once-beautiful tourist resort, leaving Clervaux a blazing holocaust behind them. The only place still being defended was the ruined ninth-century castle that overlooked the river. Here, a handful of clerks and cooks held off the German infantry who now swarmed through the narrow, débris-littered cobbled streets. Soon it was all over. The 110th had virtually disappeared. Of its original strength of 3,117, only 500-odd reached their own lines.

By this stage, two and a half American divisions in the centre of the Ardennes line had been effectively wrecked, and a large hole had been made in the Allied line. This hole Churchill would later call the 'Bulge', thus giving the whole, confused battle its lasting name. Now the Germans poured forward in a dash for the River Meuse.

This last German invasion of the West in World War Two caused panic not only at the front, but far back among the rear échelons. Soldiers and civilians, French, Belgian, Luxembourg, Dutch and even German (there was a sizeable German population in US-occupied Aachen) – all were seized by terror at the prospect of the Germans' return.

At the Belgian resort town of Spa, General Hodges' First Army HQ took off in double-quick time when it was reported that Colonel Peiper's 1st SS Battle Group was rapidly approaching. As soon as the last American truck had vanished, the frightened civilians took matters into their own hands. Immediately, the mayor personally released from gaol twenty civilians suspected of having collaborated with the Germans, while other civilians hastily removed the pictures of Churchill and Roosevelt which had decorated the windows. American, British and Belgian flags also disappeared, and US cigarettes and rations were buried in the cellars so that all trace of the town's association with the Americans was erased.

Arriving at the abandoned HQ, which had been located at the same Hotel Britannique where the Kaiser had learnt of Germany's defeat in a previous war, two last officers of the US 7th Armored Division discovered that in their panic-stricken flight the HQ staff had left top-secret maps hanging on the walls. Carefully the two men collected them and reported on their findings when they finally reached their commander, General Clarke, in embattled St. Vith. Grimly Clarke ordered the officers to burn the maps and make no report. 'Hell,' he snarled, 'when this fight's over, there's going to be grief enough court-martialling generals! I'm not in a mood for making any more trouble.'[39]

To the rear, the rumours flew thick and fast: the Germans had agents everywhere who had come to pay off old scores; SS Colonel Otto Skorzeny's killers were roaming freely behind Allied lines, wearing American uniforms. According to widespread reports, they were to meet in Paris and then drive out to Versailles to murder the supreme commander. For three days Eisenhower was confined to the Petit Trianon, and when he did finally venture out, he was escorted by a whole company of heavily armed MPs, complete with armoured cars. Meanwhile, the black market died a quick death. No one wanted to be associated with the liberators now. The men of the Belgian resistance, the so-called 'White Army' which had dominated, sometimes terrorised the rear areas since September, scuttled back to their holes. It had been one thing to shave the heads of local women who had slept with Germans and stick them in the cages of Antwerp's zoo to be mocked and tormented like animals, but it was another thing to tackle the Germans. In France, the frightened new recruits guarding the last German strongholds at Lorient and St. Nazaire were alerted for a German *seaborne* landing. In England, a plan had allegedly been discovered for a mass breakout of all German POWs to coincide with the great new German offensive. For many hundreds of miles behind the front, fear and panic reigned.

Matters were not helped either by the precipitate withdrawal not only of the fighting troops, but also of the men of the supply services. Captain Robert Merriam of the Ninth Army recorded later: 'I shall never forget the looks on the faces of the Belgians in the little town of Chaudfontaine ... as headquarters of the First Army packed up and rolled to the west. Stark fear gripped those dazed peasants as the last trucks vanished in the final gentle curve in the road. "Is there no one who can help us?" one of them asked me. I could only stammer helplessly and vanish into the distance myself.'[40]

BBC correspondent Robert Barr witnessed similar scenes as an American outfit pulled out of a village where they had been stationed for the past three months. 'There was handshaking and many questions. How near were the Germans? Did we think they'd come to their town again? Was it true that German tanks were just over the hill? There were awkward silences. The GIs couldn't answer that question. A truck driver tying a tarpaulin over his loaded truck swore quietly and said, "I never thought this would happen to us."'[41]

But it had. For the first time in the six-month-long campaign in Europe, the Allies, and in particular the Americans, were suffering a major defeat. And it hurt.

As yet the British weren't involved; but already Montgomery was swinging his troops behind the Americans at a stop-line based on the Meuse, and soon some three and a half British divisions would be over that river, fighting side by side with the hard-pressed Yanks. Montgomery himself would take over command of the northern side of the Bulge, with two entire American Armies, the First and Ninth, fighting under his command.

Nonetheless, for a while at least, many British soldiers profited in unexpected ways from the panic behind the lines, as the following episode illustrates. R.W. Cooper was with a group of eighteen-year-old troopers of the Reconnaissance Corps at the Louvain reinforcement

Ninth US Air Force
fighter-bombers in
co-operation with ground
artillery knocked out this
King Tiger tank on the
main road from Bastogne.

holding unit, waiting to be sent up the line. 'First time we reinforcements knew that the balloon had gone up at the front was when we had braised steak for dinner instead of the usual mutton stew muck that had been the standard fare up to then. Next thing we got two free bottles of beer from the NAAFI. We nearly fainted!'[42] There were more surprises to come:

All night long the NAAFI wallahs broke bottle after bottle of the hard stuff against the walls. I suppose they thought that if the Jerries came, the reinforcements might loot the place and get pissed. Soon afterwards the permanent staff under a decrepit old sergeant major who was running a brothel just outside the barracks with his teenage girlfriend on the side, started burning secret documents in the courtyard and packing their loot into the trucks for a swift take-off, as if the Germans were only down the road.

Then they started to post the lot of us. On every landing there were big lists of blokes from every regiment in the British Army being sent to the front or to front-line RHUs.* That morning I rubbed the window closest to me free of frost after we'd taken the blackout down and looked down because there was a lot of commotion going on in the courtyard. One of the blokes who had been posted to the front had got the wind up and had flung himself from the fifth floor of our barracks during the night. Now he lay there frozen stiff in a red star of his own blood in the snow.[43]

Desertions in the US Army increased dramatically. Some of the men who had fled from the line that first terrible Saturday were later found as far back as the French cities of Metz and Verdun, nearly a hundred miles to the rear. The big cities of Belgium and France were flooded with badly frightened men who had gone 'over the hill' and preferred to face the prospect of a court-martial and a possible death sentence than square up to the enemy. The problem had become so great that the brass now realised they would either have to frighten or coerce the doughs into sticking it out in the line. Fortunately, however, just as the Battle of the Bulge reached its height and both sides fought for survival, two celebrated cases came to the rescue of the High Command.

Back in November, Private Eddie Slovik, who had run away after his first night under fire and later surrendered to the MPs, had been brought to trial by General Cota, commander of the 28th Infantry Division. Slovik's trial had been one of the shortest in the annals of US military justice. The court had met at 10.00 on the morning of Armistice Day, November 11th at the little German border town of Roettgen, and by 11.40 the verdict had been reached.

None of the men who tried the deserter were combat officers, though one of them would soon be seriously wounded in the Battle of the Bulge and later die in German custody. The officers were, however, from a division which had suffered severe disciplinary problems in the freezing

*Reinforcement holding units.

mire of the Hürtgenwald, and several of their units had cracked and fled from the enemy. It wasn't altogether surprising, therefore, that they sentenced Eddie Slovik to death According to their verdict, Slovik was to be 'dishonorably discharged the service, to forfeit pay and allowances due or to become due and to be shot to death with musketry.'[44]

Slovik, however, left the court not unduly worried. Unlike his buddy Tankey, who had deserted with him but had then gone up the line, he was still alive. He also knew by now that no one had been shot for desertion since the Civil War. In the stockades and gaols of the COMZ area there were probably hundreds of American soldiers with similar death threats hanging over them, yet not one of them had been shot. Why should he be the exception?*

Sixteen days later, on November 27th, Slovik's case came before General Cota, who was never one to mollycoddle soldiers and often railed against 'trick cyclists' and 'head shrinks' for allowing his soldiers to feign combat fatigue Cota approved the death sentence, and afterwards even went so far as to state that 'a deserter should be shot by the outfit he deserts.'[45]

From that point on, only one person could save Eddie Slovik from the firing squad, and that was Eisenhower himself. However, Ike's legal staff now discovered to their amazement that no American soldier had been shot for desertion since 1865. Confidently Slovik awaited the results of the supreme commander's deliberations. He knew he would get away with it.

But that had been before the Battle of the Bulge, and before Paris and other cities had been invaded by swarms of American deserters. Now, two days before Christmas on December 23rd, 1944, Ike took a decision which had last been undertaken by Abraham Lincoln himself. He confirmed the sentence passed by the 28th Infantry Division. This December, while a great battle was waged at the front, an undersized, frightened ex-jailbird would be executed *pour encourager les autres.*

The trial of Private Slovik was forgotten as soon as it had served its purpose and didn't become a *cause célèbre* until some time after the war. But the notorious 'Malmédy Massacre' which took place in the third week of that December captured the headlines almost immediately, for it, too, had a purpose to serve.

Five days before Eisenhower confirmed Slovik's sentence, a signal reached SHAEF, Eisenhower's headquarters. It ran: 'SS troops vicinity L 8199 captured US soldier, traffic MP, with about two hundred US soldiers. American prisoners searched. When finished, Germans lined up Americans and shot them with machine-pistols and machine-guns. Wounded informant

*In all, 40,000 American soldiers deserted while on active service, although many more went AWOL, which US military law regards as less serious. Of these deserters, 2,864 were tried by courts-martial. Forty-nine were sentenced to death. Only one was executed – Slovik.

Air supplies being dropped.

who escaped and more details follow later.'[46]

It wasn't until January, 1945, that American investigators finally searched the area at the little crossroads settlement of Baugnez, Belgium, above the town of Malmédy and found the bodies of 'approximately 120 POWs' under the snow. Only then could it be confirmed that American prisoners had actually been shot there. But almost immediately after the first report had been received in Paris, the Allied propaganda machine went into action, pulling out all the stops and using the 'Malmédy Massacre' to bolster up the sagging morale of the badly shaken doughs.

Obersturmbannführer Jochen Peiper and his battle group from the 1st Panzer Divison of the Waffen SS were accused of the crime; yet Peiper himself was miles away when the massacre occurred. It was his view that the truth of the matter would never be known, since there were 'too many lies and half-truths' surrounding the episode.[47] Yet in spite of this, news of the event spread like wildfire through the US Army. Three hours after the killings had taken place at noon on December 17th, the inspector general of the US First Army was informed. That evening, the First's chief of staff wrote in his diary: 'There is absolutely no question as to its proof – immediate publicity is being given to the story. General Quesada had told every one of his pilots about it during their briefing.'[48]

The consequences of the massacre for the Germans were unpleasant. At least two regimental orders survive from that day in which American commanders instructed their men to take no further German prisoners, especially if they came from the SS. And Patton, who had often run into trouble in the past for shooting prisoners, was soon being informed that there had been further incidents, this time involving his green 11th Armored Division. 'There were also some unfortunate incidents in the shooting of prisoners,' he wrote, and added in brackets: 'I hope we can conceal it.'[49]

The overall effect of the massacre, therefore, was to bring a new element of bitterness and brutality into this key battle between the Germans and the Allies. Even President Roosevelt himself seems to have taken a fairly cynical view of the matter. On learning of the massacre, he commented to secretary of state for war Stimson: 'Well, it will only serve to make our troops feel toward the Germans as they have already learned to feel about the Japs.'[50]

So the crucial battle in the Ardennes raged back and forth, with both sides giving their utmost. The weather was the worst in Europe for a quarter of a century. Snow fell for days on end, and it was so cold that advancing infantry were able to cross minefields with impunity, since the mechanisms which activated the mines were frozen solid. Many soldiers went into battle in blinding, blanketing snow. Drivers drove without gloves in order to get a better grip on steering wheels which slipped this way and that as the vehicles skidded all over the frozen roads. Windscreens

Victims of the Malmédy Massacre.

German prisoners of war dig graves for members of the 101st US Airborne Division who were killed defending Bastogne against the Germans.

became transformed into solid sheets of ice. Tanks foundered on the steep, icy slopes and more than once had to be physically pushed into the attack. Several times the Shermans of the 2nd US Armored Division, the 'Hell on Wheels,' had to make direct frontal attacks on German-held positions rather than risk flank assaults up steep, icy hills. In the end, the army of the most highly industrialised nation in the world had to go back to using horses and mules to bring up supplies and take out casualties. Indeed, there still exists a picture of the most modern arm of the service, the gliderborne infantry of the US 82nd Airborne Division, going into action at the Belgian village of Herresbach aided by mules, just like their

predecessors of the 'Rainbow Division' a quarter of a century before.

Ironically, the hit of that year was Bing Crosby's 'White Christmas,' but for most of the men at the front it was undoubtedly the blackest Christmas they could remember. Several thousands had already been killed in action since that fateful Saturday when the battle had commenced. Thousands and thousands more were flooding into the hospitals behind the front, wounded, exhausted, suffering from trench foot, pneumonia and combat fatigue; and approximately 20,000 of them were already in German POW cages in the Reich, or on their way there.

Colonel Fuller of Clervaux was one such unfortunate,

leading a column of his men up and down the steep, snow-bound hills towards Germany. More than once the craggy-faced, evil-tempered colonel tried to convince the guards that his GIs were too weak and exhausted to keep up the pace, but they refused to listen. They were in a hurry to get to Germany. Even those who stopped to relieve themselves in the snow were bayoneted in the buttocks as they squatted. Life had become cheap, cruel and heartless.[51]

Major Don Boyer of the 7th Armored Division, also a POW now, was taken before an SS officer who ordered him to take off his galoshes and hand them over. Boyer refused. 'We don't have to treat you as a prisoner until

(Above) At the US First Army Interrogation Centre at Herbesthal in Belgium, German soldiers who had been disguised as US troops were shot. (Left) Soldiers of the 82nd Airborne Division bring in a German SS trooper.

The tankers prepared to escape while they still had a chance. But there was a catch. Not only were they burdened by a number of wounded men and German prisoners, but there were also two very dead German soldiers just off the crossroads, both shot in the back of the head.

Captain Louis Spiegelmann, the battalion surgeon, volunteered to stay behind with the wounded while the tankers hurriedly set out burying the murdered Germans beneath a rosebush. Then came the question of the prisoners. Colonel Hogan in charge, hated to turn them loose, but as he told his officers, 'This is hardly the appropriate time or place to knock them off. Pretty soon we all might be prisoners ourselves.' So they let it go at that.[53]

The fighting had now become so confused and relentless that the Allied ground forces were no longer safe from their own air crews. In Malmédy, the Christmas present to General Hobbs' 30th Infantry Division, which had suffered so badly in Normandy at the hands of Allied bombers, was its third air-raid of the week, again carried out by the US Air Force, now bitterly named by the doughs of the 30th, 'the American Luftwaffe.'

There were similar incidents further back on the Meuse, where British and Americans had finally stopped the German dash for the river. Here the tankers of the US 2nd Armored Division fought desperately against the German 2nd Panzer Division to link up with the British 29th Armored Brigade. That morning, after heavy fighting, they finally succeeded, and the first tanks of the 29th Armoured advanced to meet their American allies of Colonel Merriam's 82nd Reconnaissance Battalion. But this time the Americans were taking no chances: they fired first and asked questions afterwards. The first British tank went up in flames. Standing next to Colonel Merriam, the British CO frowned and said laconically, 'Well, your boys just browned off one of my boys.'[54]

Slowly that black Christmas drew to an end. General Clarke, at last relieved of the job of defending St. Vith, for the town had now fallen to the Germans, snored as his jeep trundled to the rear. Not far away, Lieutenant Eric Fisher Wood shivered in the freezing woods of Meyerode, a hunted man, far away from a home he would never see again. Colonel Descheneaux was now on the second stage of his journey by cattle truck to Oflag 79, where he would contract TB and die in captivity. Meanwhile the battle-weary remnants of his command, the survivors of Wood's 589th Artillery Battalion, were fighting their last battle for the disputed crossroads at Baraque-de-Fraiture. Of the original 116 defenders, only 44 would manage to escape back to their own lines that Christmas night.

Yet here and there in the midst of battle the spirit of Christmas prevailed – faintly. Just behind the front, medic Lester Atwell, armed and wearing a helmet, attended Mass at a civilian church. 'Helmets came off, rifles were stacked against the back wall. All the stained glass windows were blown out and the still air was icy and damp ... Civilians

your Red Cross card is dispatched,' the German threatened. 'Now take them off!' Stubbornly Boyer once more refused. The officer shouted a command. A bayonet was jabbed into the American's back. Then the SS officer struck Boyer in the face. He fell, was picked up and then knocked down again. 'Now will you give me the galoshes!' the officer demanded. Boyer tried to refuse one more time, but no longer had the strength. His overshoes were ripped off his feet and he was helped away by two soldiers.[52]

On Christmas Day the battle reached its climax. Twenty-five miles away from where Boyer faced up to the SS officer, the survivors of a trapped combat team of the US 3rd Armored Division were holding a hotly-contested crossroads at the Belgian village of Marcouray. Solemnly they ate a Christmas dinner of K-rations, heated by a fire made of ration boxes. Most of them had a strong suspicion that this would be the last Christmas dinner they ever ate, for the Germans had nearly surrounded them and would soon come in for the kill.

Suddenly their radio crackled into life and they heard the voice of their divisional commander, General Rose, ordering them to destroy their equipment and make their way out as best they could. The commander finished by wishing them good luck.

sat on one side. We on the other. An organist played unfamiliar hymns … The children sang hymns in French, but when the priest – sickly, middle-aged and dark – ascended the pulpit, the long sermon, surprisingly, was in German!'[55]

In beleaguered Bastogne, which had again been severely bombed, the snow was still falling heavily. There, huddled in the cellars of a local seminary, men and officers of the 'Screaming Eagles' sang, 'Oh, little town of Bethlehem, how still we see thee lie …' while outside, the guns thundered and thundered on as the Germans prepared for their final attack.

Although few British troops were actually under attack, the Tommies in the line fared little better than their American comrades that cold, cheerless Christmas night. That afternoon their poor, stuttering king had given them his traditional three o'clock Christmas Day speech, and three front-line soldiers had been asked by the BBC to introduce him. One of them was an 'old sweat,' Sniper-Corporal Arthur Hare, MM. But when the BBC correspondent Frank Gillard had shown him what he was to read, Hare backed down, for part of the prepared message, read: 'We are looking forward to returning home, but for some of us, this will not be.' Like all snipers, with their good-luck charms and strange ritualistic observances, Hare was very superstitious, and those words seemed to be tempting fate. Another corporal from the same battalion took over the task, and that afternoon his voice was heard all around the far-flung British Empire. Three months later the corporal was dead, shot while attempting to rescue a wounded German.[56]

Lance Corporal Robert Wingfield, now an old sweat himself, was also in the line that Christmas night, though unlike Hare, who survived unscathed, Wingfield had a mere six weeks left before he 'bought it'. For some time he and his comrades crouched in the freezing cold, discussing how in the last war the Tommies and Jerries had fraternised in no-man's land on Christmas Day, 1914. Suddenly they were surprised by the faint sounds of their enemies on the other side singing 'Silent Night.'

'The age-old carol gained in strength,' Wingfield wrote after the war, 'as it floated to us on the frosty air. The war was distant, almost stopped. Over all the earth, the anniversary of Christ's birth was now – tonight. Jerry across the river, the British on this side, all were made in God's image, all were God's children. The river wasn't there. The whole world was one huge, moonlit meadow.

'The first verse ended. After a short silence the second verse began – from *our* side of the river. We listened to the voices, alternating the verses back and forth across the river. At the end faint greetings could be heard intermingled: Happy Christmas … "*Fröhliche Weihnacht*".'[60]

And that was how Christmas Day ended in this Year of Liberation, 1944.

Battle-weary American soldiers in Bastogne.

A la population
de
BASTOGNE

EPILOGUE

For Johnny

Do not despair
For Johnny-head-in-air
He sleeps as sound
As Johnny underground.

Fetch out no shroud
For Johnny-in-the-cloud
And keep your tears
For him in after years.

Better by far
For Johnny-the-bright-star,
To keep your head,
And see his children fed.

John Pudney

So there was no Allied victory in 1944. The high hopes of that glorious summer had vanished, irretrievably lost in the snowy hills of the Ardennes. There had been 76,000 Allied casualties, mostly American, in the course of that bloody December, and now all Allied plans for an offensive into the Reich had to be postponed for another six weeks. It was three months before the Allies crossed the Rhine, and nearly a further two before the campaign was over. In the end, of the 45 percent of Eisenhower's armies who at some time or other were actively engaged in combat, some two million British, Canadian and American soldiers in all, 164,954 were killed in action or died of wounds before the war ended; 538,763 were wounded; and 78,657 were captured or reported missing. A further 700,000 died due to non-battle accidents or illness. The cost was high.

Now there is little visible trace of that terrible expenditure in human life. On the Normandy coast where Allied forces landed that June, full of hopes, the canny French have turned the beaches into profitable tourist attractions. There you will find monuments, plaques, museums aplenty. But who remembers the wounded dough on Utah who warned, 'Watch yourself, fella, there's a mine!' before he died? Or the East Yorks forming a khaki-coloured carpet of dead bodies on Gold?

It is the same when you drive through the villages and towns of Normandy and follow the straight narrow roads they once marched along. It took them two months to do so, at high cost. Yet today you can cover the same distance in an hour and see nothing to mark their passing except for an old cottage with bullet-chipped walls, or a series of gentle depressions in a meadow in the Bocage which when caught at a certain angle reveal themselves to be a foxhole line.

Americans, having consolidated, march off Omaha beach.

The great cities of France, Belgium, Luxembourg and Holland which were once liberated to such scenes of jubilation, these, too, contain little to remind the visitor of those dramatic days of forty years ago. The countryside, too, seems transformed: fields and villages that were once littered with shattered tanks, abandoned equipment, and grotesquely crumpled figures in khaki and grey, now look innocent and peaceful. Could it really have taken a whole regiment a week to fight its way up that gentle slope? Did that heap of concrete rubble that was once a bunker really cost the lives of a hundred young men in a desperate eight-hour battle? Suddenly the mind is unwilling to accept the map you carry. Suddenly you feel awkward to be old, and alive, where young men once laughed and joked and died. Somehow you feel you have broken faith with them; there seems so little to show for all their sacrifice. Time, progress, nature itself have drawn an almost impenetrable cloak over those scenes of desperate action of forty years ago.

It is only when you reach the Ardennes, those tranquil forests that mark the border with the Federal Republic of Germany, that you are once again aware of the scars of battle. At La Gleize, you can find the last panzer of Peiper's last stand, its cannon shattered as it was on that Christmas Day, 1944, when Peiper slipped out of the trap with his 500 survivors. In the woods around St. Vith, where General Clarke held on until he, too, was forced to withdraw that same Christmas, you can discover the water-logged holes of his perimeter line. And if you grub around long enough, you will even find mouldering 75mm shell cases with the date '1944' stamped on their base, or a shattered length of rusty metal attached to a foot-long piece of shaped wood, which falls to pieces as you touch it – the remains of a German 'potato-masher' or stick grenade. Higher up, on the border itself, there are still bunkers with communication wires hanging from the surrounding trees, where Colonel Descheneaux agonised over his wounded men of the 'Golden Lions' and where he finally reached his momentous decision to surrender.

But most poignant of all is a lone grave deep in the forest that stretches between Meyerode, at whose village inn SS General Sepp Dietrich once set up his HQ, and the hamlet of Huem. There, at the side of the forest trail where the villagers found him on January 23rd, 1945, lies the body of twenty-four-year-old Eric Fisher Wood. A simple stone cross marks the grave, and his epitaph reads:

Eric Fisher Wood
fand hier den Heldentod
*nach schweren Einzelkämpfen**

For years it had been graced by a single jamjar containing artificial flowers, but this spring, forty years later, a lone daffodil has appeared, as if by magic.

*'Eric Fisher Wood died a hero's death after unsparing single-handed combat.'

182

An enthusiastic crowd welcomes General de Gaulle in the steets of Bayeux.

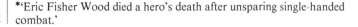

A shattered Tiger tank.

British troops advance
through L'Eveque.

NOTES

Prologue
1 Moorehead, Alan, *Eclipse* (Hamish Hamilton)
2 Ibid.
3 Ibid.

Chapter 1
1 Personal interview
2 Moorehead, op. cit.
3 Wilson, Andrew, *Flame Thrower* (Chatto)
4 Wingfield, Robert, *The Only Way Out* (Hutchinson)
5 Foley, John, *Mailed Fist* (Mayflower)
6 Wingfield, op. cit.
7 Personal interview
8 Personal interview
9 Wilson, op. cit.
10 Fuller, Sam, *The Big Red One* (Corgi)
11 Personal interview
12 Ryan, Cornelius, *The Longest Day* (Gollancz)
13 Giles, J., *The GI Journal of Sergeant Giles* (Houghton Mifflin)
14 Ryan, op. cit.
15 Fuller, op. cit.
16 Thompson, R.W., *D-Day* (Ballantine)
17 Firbank, Thomas, *I Bought A Star* (Gollancz)
18 Codman, Charles, *Drive* (Atlantic Monthly Press)
19 Butcher, H., *My Three Years With Eisenhower* (Cassell)
20 Ibid.
21 Ibid.
22 Saunders, Hilary St George, *The Red Beret* (Michael Joseph)
23 Saunders, Hilary St George, *The Green Beret* (Michael Joseph)
24 Baron, Alexander, *From The City, From The Plough* (Cape)
25 Wingfield, op. cit.
26 Ibid.
27 Moorehead, op. cit.
28 Ryan, op. cit.
29 Wilmot, Chester, *The Struggle For Europe* (Collins)
30 Byrom, James, *The Unfinished Man* (Chatto)
31 Ibid.
32 Ridgway, Gen. Matthew, *Soldier: Memoirs* (Harper)
33 Saunders, *Green Beret*
34 Howarth, David, *Dawn Of D-Day* (Collins)
35 Personal interview

Chapter 2
1 *BBC War Report* (Oxford)
2 Wilmot, Chester, *The Struggle For Europe* (Collins)
3 Ibid.
4 *BBC War Report*
5 Ridgway, Gen. Matthew, *Soldier: Memoirs* (Harper)
6 Critchell, Laurence, *Four Stars of Hell* (Farrar Strauss)
7 Ibid.
8 Ryan, Cornelius, *The Longest Day* (Gollancz)
9 Ibid.
10 Ibid.
11 Howarth, David, *Dawn Of D-Day* (Collins)
12 Byrom, James, *The Unfinished Man* (Chatto)
13 Ryan, op. cit.
14 Howarth, op. cit.
15 Horrocks, Brian, *Corps Commander* (Magnum)
16 Moorehead, Alan *Eclipse* (Hamish Hamilton)
17 Capa, Robert, interviewed in *Life* magazine, summer 1944
18 Baldwin, H., *Battles Lost and Won* (Harper)
19 Quoted in Wilmot, op. cit.
20 *Omaha Beachhead* (US War Dept., Historical Division)
21 Ryan, op. cit.
22 Ibid.
23 Ibid.
24 Ibid.
25 Howarth, op. cit.
26 Ryan, op. cit.
27 Baldwin, op. cit.
28 *BBC War Report*
29 Ryan, op. cit.

30 Ibid.
31 Ibid.
32 Ryan, op. cit.
33 Ibid.
34 Personal interview
35 Ryan, op. cit.
36 Saunders, Hilary St George, *The Green Beret* (Michael Joseph)
37 Ibid.
38 Ryan, op. cit.
39 Grant, Douglas, *The Fuel Of The Fire* (Cresset)
40 Ryan, op. cit.
41 Howarth, op. cit.
42 Reader's Letter, *Purnell's History Of The War*
43 Baldwin, op. cit.
44 Ryan, op. cit.
45 Baldwin, op. cit.
46 Irving, David, *The War Between The Generals* (Allen Lane)
47 Ibid.
48 Ibid.
49 Ibid.
50 Ryan, op. cit.
51 Ibid.

Chapter 3
1 Irving, David, *The War Between The Generals* (Allen Lane)
2 Ibid.
3 Ibid.
4 Ibid.
5 Ibid.
6 Ibid.
7 Moorehead, Alan, *Eclipse* (Hamish Hamilton)
8 Grant, Douglas, *The Fuel Of The Fire* (Cresset)
9 Hewitt, R., *Work Horse Of The Western Front* (privately printed)
10 Irving, op. cit.
11 Grant, R., *The 51st Highland Division* (Ian Allen)
12 Lindsay, Martin, *So Few Got Through* (Collins)
13 *BBC War Report* (Oxford)
14 Huie, E., *The Execution Of Private Slovik* (Panther)
15 Jones, James, *World War Two* (Leo Cooper)
16 Irving, op. cit.
17 Wilson, Andrew, *Flame Thrower* (Chatto)
18 Huie, op. cit.
19 Ibid.
20 The *Stars And Stripes*
21 Ibid.
22 Walsh, Mary, *The Way It Was* (Weidenfeld)
23 Ibid.
24 Ibid.
25 Quoted in *The War 1939-45*, edited by James Flower and Desmond Reeves (Cassell)
26 Scott, Peggy, *They Made Invasion Possible* (Hutchinson)
27 The *Stars And Stripes*
28 Ibid.
29 Wilson, op. cit.
30 Byrom, James, *The Unfinished Man* (Chatto)
31 *BBC War Report*

Chapter 4
1 Moorehead, Alan, *Eclipse* (Hamish Hamilton)
2 Quoted in *The War 1939-45*, edited by James Flower and Desmond Reeves (Cassell)
3 *BBC War Report* (Oxford)
4 Ibid.
5 Ibid.
6 Quoted in *The War 1939-1945*
7 Ibid.
8 Ibid.
9 Irving, David, *The War Between The Generals* (Allen Lane)
10 Interview, *Sunday Times*, April 1982
11 Ibid.
12 Woollcombe, Robert, *Lion Rampant* (Leo Cooper)
13 Personal interview
14 Woollcombe, op. cit.
15 Ibid.

16 Ibid.
17 Ibid.
18 Personal interview
19 Grant, R., *The 51st Highland Division* (Ian Allen)
20 Ibid.
21 Ibid.
22 Ibid.
23 Ibid.
24 Foley, John, *Mailed Fist* (Mayflower)
25 Ibid.
26 Ibid.
27 Carrell, P., *They're Coming* (Dutton)
28 Irving, op. cit.
29 Ibid.
30 Ibid.
31 Ibid.
32 Ibid.
33 Ibid.
34 *BBC War Report*
35 Ibid.
36 Quoted in *The War 1939-1945*
37 Moorehead, op. cit.
38 Wingfield, Robert, *The Only Way Out* (Hutchinson)
39 *BBC War Report*
40 Moorehead, op. cit.
41 *BBC War Report*
42 Shulman, Milton, *Defeat In The West* (Secker)
43 Woollcombe, op. cit.

Chapter 5
1 Quoted in *The War 1939-1945* edited by James Flower and Desmond Reeves (Cassell)
2 Horrocks, Brian, *Corps Commander* (Magnum)
3 Woollcombe, Robert, *Lion Rampant* (Leo Cooper)
4 Horrocks, op. cit.
5 *BBC War Report* (Oxford)
6 Codman, Charles, *Drive* (Atlantic Monthly Press)
7 Essame, Maj.-Gen. Hubert, *The 43rd Wessex Division At War, 1939-45* (William Clowes)
8 Personal interview
9 Personal interview
10 Wilson, Andrew, *Flame Thrower* (Chatto)
11 Ibid.
12 Motley, M., *The Invisible Soldier* (Wayne State University Press)
13 Irving, David, *The War Between The Generals* (Allen Lane)
14 Clostermann, Pierre, *The Big Show* (Chatto)
15 Giles, J., *The GI Journal Of Sergeant Giles* (Houghton Mifflin)
16 Ibid.
17 Ibid.
18 Bailey, R., *Home Front USA* (Time-Life Books)
19 Ibid.
20 Ibid.
21 Longmate, Norman, *GIs* (Scribner)
22 Ibid.
23 Irving, op. cit.
24 Motley, op. cit.
25 Ibid.
26 Ibid.
27 Ibid.
28 The *Stars And Stripes*
29 Ibid.
30 Essame, op. cit.

Chapter 6
1 Ryan, Cornelius, *A Bridge Too Far* (Hamish Hamilton)
2 Ibid.
3 Ibid.
4 Ibid.
5 Ibid.
6 Ibid.
7 Ibid.
8 Ibid.
9 Horrocks, Brian, *Corps Commander* (Magnum)
10 Ryan, op. cit.

11 Ibid.
12 Ibid.
13 Ibid.
14 Ibid.
15 Foley, John, *Mailed fist* (Mayflower)
16 Ryan, op. cit.
17 Moorehead, Alan, *Eclipse* (Hamish Hamilton)
18 Ryan, op. cit.
19 Ibid.
20 Personal interview
21 Urquhart, Maj.-Gen. R.E., *Arnhem* (Cassell)
22 Ryan, op. cit.
23 Hagen, Louis, *Arnhem Lift* (Hammond Hammond)
24 Ibid.
25 Ryan, op. cit.
26 Ibid.
27 Ibid.
28 Hagen, op. cit.
29 Ryan, op. cit.
30 Ibid.
31 Ibid.
32 Ibid.
33 Ibid.
34 Ibid.
35 Whiting, Charles, *Arnhem* (Futura)
36 Ibid.
37 Personal interview
38 Ryan, op. cit.
39 Whiting, *Arhenm.*
40 Ibid.
41 Ryan, op. cit.
42 Ibid.
43 Ibid.
44 Whiting, *Arnhem*
45 Ibid.
46 Ibid.
47 Ryan, op. cit.
48 Ibid.
49 Ibid.
50 Ibid.
51 Ibid.
52 Ibid.
53 Ibid.
54 Ibid.
55 Urquhart, op. cit.
56 Personal interview
57 Ryan, op. cit.
58 Ibid.
59 Personal interview
60 Whiting, *Arnhem*

Chapter 7
1 Ryan, Cornelius, *A Bridge Too Far* (Hamish Hamilton)
2 The *Stars And Stripes*
3 Dominy, John, *Sergeant Escapers* (Corgi)
4 Sims, James, *Arnhem Spearhead* (Imperial War Museum)
5 Wade, David, in *The Listener*, October 1981
6 Ibid.
7 Sims, op. cit.
8 Toland, John, *The Last 100 Days* (Random House)
9 Whiting, Charles, *48 Hours To Hammelberg* (Arrow)
10 The *Stars And Stripes*
11 Ibid.
12 Sims, op. cit.
13 The *Stars And Stripes*
14 Kelly, F., *Private Kelly* (Evans)
15 The *Stars And Stripes*
16 Ibid.
17 Ibid.
18 Toland, op. cit.
19 Ibid.
20 Personal interview
21 Wade, op. cit.
22 Ibid.

23 Whiting, op. cit.
24 Sims, op. cit.
25 Personal interview
26 Personal interview
27 West, Rebecca, *The Meaning Of Treason* (Macmillan)
28 Ibid.
29 Ibid.
30 Personal interview
31 Dominy, op. cit.
32 Toland, op. cit.
33 Ibid.
34 Personal interview

Chapter 8
1 Personal interview
2 *Taurus Pursuant, History of 11th Armoured Division* (privately printed)
3 Essame, Maj.-Gen. Hubert, *The Battle For Germany* (Batsford)
4 Shulman, Milton, *Defeat In the West* (Secker)
5 Ibid.
6 Ibid.
7 Ibid.
8 Personal interview
9 Irving, David, *The War Between The Generals* (Allen Lane)
10 Grant, R., *The 51st Highland Division* (Ian Allen)
11 Motley, M., *The Invisible Soldier* (Wayne State University Press)
12 McKee, Alexander, *Race For The Rhine Bridges* (Collins)
13 Shulman, op. cit.
14 Ibid.
15 Merriam, Robert, *Dark December* (Ziff Davis)
16 Ibid.
17 Toland, John, *Battle: The Story Of The Bulge* (N.A.L.)
18 Ibid.
19 Whiting, Charles, *Massacre At Malmedy* (Leo Cooper)
20 Ibid.
21 Whiting, Charles, *Death Of A Division* (Leo Cooper)
22 Dupuy, Col. R., *Lion In The Way* (Washington Infantry Journal Press)
23 Shulman, op. cit.
24 Ibid.
25 Ibid.
26 Personal interview
27 Personal interview
28 Dupuy, op. cit.
29 Toland, *Battle*
30 MacDonald, Charles, *Company Commander*
31 Whiting, Charles, *Decision At St. Vith* (Ballantine)
32 Atwell, L., *Private* (Popular Books)
33 Toland, *Battle*
34 Ibid.
35 Ibid.
36 Shulman, op. cit.
37 Whiting, *St. Vith*
38 Toland, *Battle*
39 Personal letter
40 Merriam, op. cit.
41 *BBC War Report* (Oxford)
42 Personal interview
43 Ibid.
44 Huie, E., *The Execution Of Private Slovik* (Panther)
45 Ibid.
46 Whiting, *Massacre*
47 Ibid.
48 Ibid.
49 Irving, David, *The War Between The Generals* (Allen Lane)
50 Ibid.
51 Toland, *Battle*
52 Ibid.
53 Ibid.
54 Merriam, op. cit.
55 Atwell, op. cit.
56 Wynne, B., *The Sniper* (N.E.L.)
57 Wingfield, Robert, *The Only Way Out* (Hutchinson)

INDEX

188

A British corporal keeping watch for snipers overlooking the ruins of Caen.

191

ACKNOWLEDGEMENTS

We are most grateful to the Robert Hunt Library (many of whose photographs come courtesy of the US Army) for permission to use the photographs which appear on the jacket and those photographs in the book which are not credited below.

We also thank the Imperial War Museum for permission to use the photographs which appear on pages 6/7, 16/17, 44/45, 50/51, 67, 72/73, 92/93, 100/101, 103, 106, 107, 110/111, 112/113, 117, 118/119, 121, 122/123, 128/129, 131, 176, 189 and Bundesarchiv for permission to use the photographs which appear on pages 27 (bottom), 134/135, 156, 183 (bottom).